T0203315

The Digital Era 1

Series Editor
Fabrice Papy

The Digital Era 1

Big Data Stakes

Edited by

Jean-Pierre Chamoux

WILEY

First published 2018 in Great Britain and the United States by ISTE Ltd and John Wiley & Sons, Inc.

ISTE Ltd
27-37 St George's Road
London SW19 4EU
UK

www.iste.co.uk

John Wiley & Sons, Inc.
111 River Street
Hoboken, NJ 07030
USA

www.wiley.com

Library of Congress Control Number: 2018935038

British Library Cataloguing-in-Publication Data
A CIP record for this book is available from the British Library
ISBN 978-1-84821-736-2

Contents

Note to Reader

Data telecommunications and digital processing are omnipresent in today's society. Administrations, businesses and even leisure activities produce, disseminate and exploit data related to human activity and trade. These data, the raw material of information industries, are vital for our society. This is why our era can rightly be called the "digital era".

Many experts were consulted prior to producing this series. The main idea took three years to prepare. The overall content, which was finished at the beginning of 2016, includes three successive volumes. This collective work is a trilogy that aims to describe and understand the technical, economic and social phenomena that result from widespread use of the Internet, a digital network that has been present everywhere since the end of the 20th Century.

The first volume summarizes the state of play and issues raised by the enormous amount of data that accompanies human activities: demographic, biological, physical, geographical, political, industrial, economic and environmental data. This data feeds into records, inspires people, guides their businesses and even their countries. This first volume sheds light on the practical, technical and methodological advances that are associated with the Internet and big data.

The second volume explores how and why the digital era is transforming commercial trade and interpersonal relations, as well as our living conditions. How are the media, commerce and trade evolving? How is wealth formed and transmitted? What causes the digital wave in economic and social life described in the first volume? According to Adam Smith, *The Wealth of Nations*[1] has been the

1 Smith A., *An Inquiry into the Nature and Causes of the Wealth of Nations*, Campbell R.H and Skinner A.S. ed., Oxford U. Press, 1976.

core of political economy; is it shattered or transformed? This second volume emphasizes that the *new economy* is not stable. Its social dimension is still unclear. But thinking is progressing: didn't it take a good century for the political economy to adapt to industrial society? Why wouldn't it be the same for a knowledge-based society to be delivered, one that even futurists in the 1970s[2] had already announced?

The third volume attempts to summarize the questions that the digital age suggests to our contemporaries: questions about society, interests and politics, which were partly mentioned in the first two volumes, are reformulated and developed in this last volume in order to encourage the reader to reflect and contribute to the debate on the "issues of the century", as Ellul said in 1954[3]. A debate that will hopefully help us understand the digital society that is being built before our very eyes; and perhaps it will help us to get the best and not the worst out of it...

This series is based on competent, attentive and precise specialists. The authors wrote freely, as they should; they inserted their texts within the proposed outline. We owe them a great debt of gratitude. May they be sincerely thanked here for their scholarly assistance. As for the shortcomings, as is customary, only the project coordinator will be accountable[4].

---

2 Kahn H., Wiener A., *The Year 2000*, McMillan, New York, 1967 (introduction by Daniel Bell).
3 Ellul J., *La technique ou l'enjeu du siècle*, Armand Colin, Paris, 1954 (reissued by Economica, Paris, 1970) [English translation: *The Technological Society*, Knopf, New York, 1964].
4 Editor's notes in the book correspond to comments by the coordinator.

Preface

Understanding Digital Society

CONIUGI DILECTISSIMAE

During my childhood, only the local bar, the baker, the grocer, the mayor, the doctor, the notary and the veterinarian of the village had a telephone installed in their homes, mainly to deal with the necessities of their trade. Only a dozen telephone sets existed in our small town in the French countryside. The telephone was rare, expensive, reserved for supposedly important uses, which only a very small minority of users were privileged to have. Less than 20 years later, Fernand Raynaud's memorable sketch, which marks the memory of our generation and even the next one that follows, stigmatized this incredible under-equipment in France: in 1966, while everyone knew *Number 22 at Asnières*[1], our family home still had no automatic telephone, neither did the neighbors, nor did the village cafe. It was not until the government promoted telephone catch-up as an essential and urgent national priority through a huge advertising campaign that the former subscribers of the manual network were finally provided with automatic equipment, which was only established from 1974 onwards in our rural community[2]!

---

1 The French title of Raynaud's short story: *"Le 22 à Asnières"*.

2 Manual network communications were set up by the "telephone ladies", employees of Post Offices who connected the subscriber by hand to the recipient's line; these operators could therefore follow all conversations and especially in rural areas the exchange between correspondents was hardly discreet. However, this was still only the time of the local "small ears"; the process has since then improved considerably with the Internet, taking on a global dimension, the "big ears" that will be mentioned in Volume 3.

Thirteen years on, another telephone revolution took off in France, albeit several years later than in countries such as Sweden: wired telephone equipment having become the norm, a first cellular telephone license, prepared by the team I was coordinating at the French Ministry of Post and Telecommunications, was awarded to a private operator, SFR, at the end of 1987; the first customer of this commercial company was only served in the first quarter of 1989. At the same time, the Post and Telecommunications Administration began the transformation that would split the Post Office and telecoms. After several intermediate stages, France Télécom SA was created thanks to a law in July 1996. In the meantime, the GSM digital cellular service had been put into service by France Télécom in July 1992; it was the first link in a long series of digital communications that gradually equipped the planet and made the telephone what it is today, everywhere in the world: a digital smartphone[3], a multifunctional device that has sold billions worldwide in a just few years!

What a transformation of objects, techniques and modes of interpersonal communication in barely 20 years! But the story does not stop there. At the beginning of the period that is today glorified by history as the one where everything is (supposed to be) possible[4], the students that we were had two traditional instruments for calculations, in addition to our own aptitude for mental arithmetic: a table of logarithms and a slide rule which, just to clarify, is only a personal calculator based on logarithms! These two calculation assistants, which are totally forgotten today, refer not to actual figures, but to analog calculation[5]: add two lengths of a ruler, on a logarithmic scale, for multiplication; or subtract, on the contrary, two lengths of the same ruler to do a division.

Analog calculation has proved its worth for a long time. For the practitioner, it entailed two important consequences: the obligation to remain wary, in any calculation, of the orders of magnitude, and at the same time, to train the calculator, whether he was an engineer, biologist or architect, to remain aware of the error implied by any measurement. In this case, inevitable approximations upon reading

---

3 An equivalent proposed by French *ad hoc* terminology commissions: "ordiphone", a term that use has not endorsed.
4 The years of industrial reconstruction of Western Europe continued after the Second World War; see Fourastié J., *Les Trente Glorieuses*, Hachette, Paris, 1979.
5 Designed and developed in Europe around 1630, this method of calculation was used for over three centuries (mid-17th Century to mid-20th Century) and thus accompanied most of the industrial revolution up to modern times. It remained the only authorized calculation assistant in official examinations and competitions in France until the mid-1980s.

the ruler scale. None of my children knew, during the course of their studies, how to use a slide rule; from high school onwards, they were all allowed to have an electronic pocket calculator; for them, the digital age began with their entry into sixth grade! As for current students in high schools and colleges, my grandchildren's generation, they now take their classroom notes on a tablet, on a smartphone or a laptop. Nobody pays any attention to analog calculation any more: the object, the industries that manufactured them, the logarithm tables printed in the minds of thousands of past high school students have been wiped from existence. In the 1980s, one stroke of a pen drawn by technical progress dissolved the small precise mechanics that manufactured our slide rules. This disappearance heralded, with our lack of taking any serious precautions, the digital disruption that we will find in almost all the chapters of this series, as a consequence of the disruptions that are now largely felt in the economy, trade, education, health and transport.

After my studies at the *Ecole Centrale*, I discovered modern digital calculation when I became a Fullbright scholar at the American university where I was able to program, for the first time, those IBM computers that none of our great schools had yet installed, to make their students discover this new instrument that would, in a few years, flood into companies, transform business management, industrial research, physics, chemistry and biology in less than half a generation. For us, it was a matter of simulating, by digital calculation alone, the physico-chemical phenomena preparing industrial production. When I returned to the Parisian Faculty of Science laboratory, we had to use resources that were occasionally available in Orsay to be able to do calculations that were important at the time, because Parisian universities were generally badly equipped, a bit like the retorts and lab benches used by Pasteur or even Lavoisier!

Over the next 10 years, I then witnessed the birth and growth of a generation of management programmers who trained and oversaw the administrative and commercial management of public services (urban planning, land use planning and social services) and businesses: insurance, banks, pension funds, industries, transport and cities. They were my traveling companions and fellow students, and made the strength of the service, research and IT consulting companies (IT Services) who, for more than a quarter of a century, have branded European computing and software engineering. These businesses, which were competitive and rapidly growing, quickly opened up to the international market, maintaining a competitive advantage for a long time. They converged from the mid-1970s with the transmission of remote computing to produce, around 1980, the famous report to the President of the French Republic, christened with the forged name "*Télématique*" that permanently marked the coupling between telecommunications and information technology: telematics (Nora-Minc Report, 1978). Let us make no mistake, this was the first tangible manifestation of what would then be called "digital convergence", the scope of which we have been constantly expanding since the Internet began to emerge around 1995.

Let us sum up our observations: during a lifetime like mine, a multi-centenary calculation method, the analog calculation, has fallen into oblivion. Only the digital calculator is now used. This changeover, in the time span of just two generations, has two consequences that deserve to be considered:

– a profound change of perspective on measurement and the instruments we use to measure;

– the symbolic overestimation of numbers in our understanding of the world and nature.

By becoming purely digital, our tools now detail each measurement by aligning numbers that are not necessarily significant for our practical needs (temperature, pressure, distance, volume, speed, percentage, etc.): do we really need to know body temperature to two decimal places to diagnose a fever? Is a measurement of land surface per hundredth of a square meter necessary for a real estate agent? Does displaying the result of one-tenth of a percent on a political popularity survey mean anything when you know the level of statistical error associated with the percentages calculated from a survey of 1,600 interviews (approximately +/- 2.5%[6])? The race for display accuracy implicated by the digitization of our tools, to evaluate physical quantities as well as social behaviors is an illusion: accuracy becomes a decoy, a smoke screen that conceals the reality of things, because measurement is only an approximation, an order of magnitude that we seek to evaluate.

We have been going astray for half a century, particularly for those in human sciences. The preliminary thoughts that opened Raymond Aron's 1956–57 lessons titled "*La lutte de classes*"[7] rightly pointed out, with regard to sociological studies: "You can [by survey] determine the proportion of individuals in the community who belong to various classes" (p. 86); and, a little further on: "There will always be a certain difficulty in delimiting (these) groups... the particular of social groups is to be equivocal, to have poorly defined boundaries". So, what is the point of precision, if it is not an illusion? What is important, as I mentioned earlier about the profession of construction engineer, is not to have a precise number, but to identify the order of magnitude of the phenomenon that we observe and describe. I, therefore, insist that

6 See J. L. Boursin, *Les dés et les urnes*, Le Seuil, Paris, 1990, p. 232 ff.
7 Publication titled *Nouvelles leçons sur les sociétés industrielles*, Gallimard, Paris, 1964 (reissued in *Idées*, no. 47, 1972).

with its digital display, this tool is lulling us with illusions, making us believe in a misleading precision to the detriment of what really matters: the appreciation of magnitudes, both in the world of material objects and in the world of living beings with economic and social functions!

Analog calculation required calibration of the measuring tool, in direct relation to empirical knowledge; digital calculation favors a completely different convention that is detached from the sensitive apprehension of our five senses, which are all eminently analogical. By eliminating (or omitting) the doubt and approximation that characterize any measurement, we dissociate the empirical apprehension of an object or phenomenon from its representation by digital measurement; the scientific approach is then more tempted than ever to take off from reality! My point here is not to negate the advent or usefulness of a new time, on the contrary; it is to insist on the fact that the generalization of numbers does indeed induce consequences that have been significant for some time. The more digital calculation is diffused in our society (without us actually looking out for it), the more its effects extend in various forms: changes of reference, of method and reasoning which mark the beginning of the new era. To become aware of this is, without a doubt, a first step towards wisdom!

Why speak any further on this part of life that has nothing exceptional, apart from the fact that it is characteristic of what people of my generation have experienced? To bear witness to the fact that, contrary to certain common thoughts, the diffusion of digital objects, practices and digital uses is neither as brutal nor as recent as many of our contemporaries believe, as they are slaves of novelty at any price. On the contrary, it is a long-running technical, economic and social phenomenon that began in the middle of the 20th Century, in the aftermath of the Second World War. The effects of digital technologies are gradually inducing society as a whole, as the steam engine and electricity[8] did in their time. The transformation of customs, habits and communication between humans is progressing in stages. Change is initially only noticeable in a minority, which is directly affected by emerging technical progress; then it spreads more widely, sometimes under the influence of unforeseen circumstances[9], and the majority of humans become receptive to it because they finally feel the effect of this technical

---

8 Reference is made to the comparative study published by Daniel Sichel under the Brookings Institution stamp: *The Computer Revolution*, Washington DC, 1997; Chapter 5 compares the rise in power of the information, electrical, air transport and rail industries over a long period of time in which each of these industries has matured and taken its place in modern times.

9 Such as those that allowed the extraordinary extension of the Internet to large parts of the world population in recent years!

progress in their daily lives or in their jobs. These ruptures and disruptions will be discussed in the three volumes of this series.

No nostalgia dulls my words; I have no reluctance to adapt to change. On the other hand, I believe that concrete testimonies can, in their diversity and multiple perspectives, usefully illustrate contemporary digital practices and place them in a historical perspective outside of which the observer, even if attentive, risks either losing himself or being blinded by novelty. Moreover, we know this perfectly well, but it is worth repeating: our electronic machines do nothing more than what we have taught them to do: calculate, compare, reproduce, record and transmit the data we entrust to them. Exploiting this data to deduce a better understanding of the world, of social facts and of the entire universe, is at the end of the line because, if the lone data, which is not classified, nor treated, nor interpreted, is worthless, the data which is carefully pursued, put into perspective, can contribute to our knowledge, and enlighten our thinking. It is by observing, for example, the displacements of a population, its uses, its customs and demographic vibrancy that we can begin to understand it.

There is evidence that the digital data collected and made available on a human group supports knowledge and helps prepare for action. However, we must want to act and do so consciously. Let's hope that the work gathered in this series will not only help us to understand the digital age, but also to attain a certain mastery of it!

Jean-Pierre CHAMOUX
February 2018

Introduction

Big Data Challenges

"No man steps in the same river twice...
Nothing endures but change."
Heraclitus

Philosopher, born in Ephesus, Asia Minor, early
5th Century BC. He proclaimed that everything is
perpetual: conflict, movement and becoming!

The youngest of us, our students in particular, who are fortunate enough to live in the pivotal part of this new century, know that novelties follow one another, that one item replaces the other and that commercial propaganda often tries to present an old-fashioned costume by disguising it as new: merchants of illusion never tire of these tricks. Let us learn how to arm ourselves, so that we know what is worth believing! Social behavior is changing, and so are technology and the relationships between people. It is a law of evolution: the beginning of this century has already been marked by the installation of digital tools in our cars, our professions, our homes, in most of the infrastructures of modern life: telephones, entertainment, transport, health and banking, all have been invaded.

What is important to us in the first part of this volume is to appreciate whether or not this omnipresence, depicted in Chapter 1, leads to radical changes or *progressive* evolutions, in every sense of the word: regular transformations and sources of progress. Are its uses and morals affected? What are the underlying domains that facilitate the adoption of digital devices that multiply in our daily lives: television, telephone, electricity meters, games and toys for our children,

Introduction written by Jean-Pierre CHAMOUX.

etc.? We emphasized, a few pages earlier, that digital machines are based on calculation and formal logic. For over a century, part of mathematics has focused on the study of numbers, long before computers and huge databases, which required the use of different computing methods than those implemented in the 1970s or 1980s. A foundation of abstract knowledge feeds the powerful software and algorithms that benefit from the accumulated storage of data from space observation, search engines and particle accelerators. Chapter 2, "Mathematical Culture and Massive Data", written by epistemologist and mathematician Jean Dhombres, explains the important contribution of mathematics in this rapidly growing field.

The figures that accompany our daily lives also come from large-scale enumerations, the traditional and ancient model of which is that of population censuses, a practice that dates back to ancient times[1]. Designed and written by statistician, business leader and leading expert in audience research Philippe Tassi, Chapter 3, "From Sample to Big Data: Competing or Complementary Paradigms", illustrates the growing importance of methods used to extend statistics and take advantage of the vast digital content that characterizes the Internet. Analyzing metadata makes it possible to identify and to benefit from sometimes very heterogeneous information lost within a magma of data. Chapter 4, "Researching Forms and Correlations: the Big Data Approach", edited and written by Gilles Santini, an expert on large numbers, surveys and their interpretation, illustrates how to "play with the devil" so that the network's *deus ex machina* can extract useful elements for action from the apparent disorder, to notably inspire commercial uses.

Chapters 5 and 6 were written and edited by Gérard Dréan, a very experienced practitioner in the IT industry and services, whose analysis and inquisitiveness are flawless. Chapter 5, "*Bitcoin*: an Innovative System", describes a virtual universe consisting of 10,000 nodes where operators establish a register and reproduce thousands of copies around the world in order to keep a faithful and lasting record of the commitments already contracted. It is an original invention, intimately inspired by the principles of the Internet: Bitcoin relies on thousands of programmers who share a common goal that of building this unique electronic register that attests to the authenticity, existence, purpose and amount of commitments contracted on the Net by third parties who trust it. These two chapters, linked to one another, form the hinge between the two parts of this book.

---

1 There is evidence of numerous censuses in Imperial China and Pharaonic Egypt, many centuries before Christ. The history of Christianity begins with "the decree of the Emperor Augustus ordering the census of the whole universe... while Quirinius was governor of Syria", a census that forced Joseph to go to Bethlehem where Christ was born, see *Luke, 2, 1-4.*

In the second part of this volume, we have brought together concrete cases that illustrate tactical or strategic challenges that characterize the contemporary digital world. Chapter 6, *"Bitcoin* and other Cyber-currency", focuses on the financial applications of this cooperative, peer-managed system. Fulfilling both the role of an exchange platform and a financial institution, Bitcoin and its emulators emit cyber money. The operators, paid on assignment, receive the counterpart of their contribution in bitcoins for this cross-border job. Multiple projects of a similar nature follow the same itinerary, and only the future will determine whether or not they will contribute to inventing new monetary mechanisms[2].

Chapters 7 and 8 elaborate on the very significant case of healthcare and social benefits which are all preparing themselves, in no apparent order, for the digital era: benefits, hospitalization, medical diagnoses and treatments, pension schemes and social coverages generate enormous flows of data relating to patients, contributions and the living conditions of the population. This heterogeneous whole produces and absorbs a great deal of information about everyone; the corresponding cash flows exceed, in most modern countries, government spending. Chapter 7, "Health and Care: Digital Challenges", was written and edited by Isabelle Hilali, who has been working on integrating digital technologies into healthcare systems for many years. The author provides a general overview of the applications, present and future, within this vast, disconnected and costly ensemble. Chapter 8, "Access to Health Data: Debates and Controversies in France", focuses on the conditions of access to data in a country like France, and describes the exploitation and potential value of existing metadata, to inform as much as generate new research. Based on the literature review she conducted with Gabriella Salzano and Christian Bourret, Joumana Boustany, in this chapter, points out that access to this data is limited, even though exploiting it could lead to the emergence of knowledge and actively contribute to the economy.

Chapter 9, "Artificial Intelligence: Utopia or Progress?", finally attempts to ask in weighted terms the questions raised for decades with the potential convergence between digital machines, software and human intelligence. For centuries, the construction of robots and machines has fascinated mankind; this passion is once again of topical interest, since the joint progress of biology and cybernetics makes it possible to imagine a hybrid creature that would benefit from the common progress of biology and digital machines. Artificial intelligence inspires fantasies, like the sea serpents from fantastic literature used to, among enthusiasts of the new age. It is never useless to recall implicit theories that inspire today's inventors, just as

---

2 Volume 2 of this series illustrates more broadly the effects of digital disruption on economic paradigms and on notions of value, wealth and growth.

yesterday's; they lend their intelligence to man-made objects: "They are not madmen and their goal is not anarchy, but social stability. It is in order to ensure (this) stability that they carry out, by scientific means, the ultimate revolution... in the meantime, we are in the first phase of what is perhaps the penultimate revolution". The best of all possible worlds[3]?

3 Quote taken from the Foreword to Huxley A., *Brave New World*, Vintage Classics, New York, 2007 [French translation reviewed by the author: *Le meilleur des monde* Presse Pocket no. 1 438, Paris, 1972, p. 12]. Huxley was French-speaking; he dedicated his work to Voltaire's *Candide*, whose famous aphorism justifies the French title: "everything is for the best in *the best of all possible worlds*" (our translation).

PART 1

What's New and Why?

Introduction to Part 1

The information industries have enabled the collection and exploitation of huge data storages that represent the world around us. What used to take months of thankless work to solve a combinatorial problem, sort sources or describe a natural phenomenon in detail is now done in a matter of moments, provided adequate hardware, software and an effective method is used. And, if there is no instrument, if the search engine returns empty handed at our request, nothing prevents us from venturing out, to create what is missing in order to benefit others! The digital wave is transforming the way we act, observe, describe and explain facts, living beings and nature. It favors those who are able to imagine how to gather, process and exploit the resourceful information that hangs around us. Fortunately, digital machines are doing these recurring tasks quickly and well, as we are mentally incapable of managing the abundance and complexity of raw information. The man-machine relationship has been taking advantage of this natural complementarity for the past 50 years, and still retains a great deal of potential for invention.

The Internet broadens and prolongs this trend. Of course, the ubiquity of the network multiplies data, diversifies sources and facilitates its exploration; the web further increases the complexity of the digital world. But, alongside our electronic assistants – phones, tablets and computers that store images, sounds, texts, charts and databases that accumulate on our virtual desktop – the field of exploration and discovery is immense. That's why so many people are rushing to the El Dorado of data that their great predecessors have been ploughing through for the past 15 years: Apple, Amazon, eBay, Google, Leboncoin, Microsoft, Oracle, Symantec and many others, the overwhelming majority of whom were established in North America. In this context, there is still much to be done and much to invent, since change is rapid. The flow of innovation does not dry up: technical discoveries, certainly; but also method or process improvements, transfers of skills and expertise, geographical and sectoral, etc. Creative imagination is expressed everywhere and often finds the human and financial resources needed to attempt the venture.

The five chapters that follow describe the challenges of such ventures, whose impetus comes more often from the mind than from the hand: from mathematics to medical practice and pharmacopoeia, the field of investigation is very broad and the forms of inventive cooperation are very diverse, as demonstrated on a global scale by the extraordinary success of blockchains, a venture which is located in the antipodes of the multinational giants frequently associated with the digital industry and America. The games are afoot: so, let's get to work!

Digital Omnipresence:
Its Causes and Consequences

The objects that connect us to one another are numerous and varied: telephones, computers, tablets, consoles, televisions, etc. Each of them collects, processes and stores digital data. Some focus on specific activities: playing, reading, writing, working and having fun. Many extend their usefulness far beyond their original purpose: computers are designed for versatility; telephones too. Others, such as watches, are trying to be killjoys in this digital world where the number and variety of devices are increasing, each one seeking to replace a part of the others: we play games on a computer, we take photos with a phone, we Skype with a tablet, etc.

Digital storage and transmission facilitates media convergence and merging. The services to which the connected devices give access were unknown in 1990, before the Internet conquered Europe and the rest of the world. Just 25 years have been enough for it to reach billions of children, men and women, on five continents.

The combined faculties of electronics and digital signal have enabled this rapid evolution: in just a few years, digital tools and services have transformed our lives and habits; they are disrupting social relationships and renewing a growing part of the economy. This great upheaval could inspire us to adopt a formula that is analogous to the words of La Rochefoucault addressing King Louis XVI on July 14, 1789: "Sire, it is a revolution!" For it is one; in this introductory chapter, we try to define it and understand its causes before its effects submerge us; this is what the book will be about.

Chapter written by Jean-Pierre CHAMOUX.

Forty years ago, clever minds were already trying to understand and predict the impact of digital technology on man and society[1]. A plethora of industrial, commercial and service innovations aroused our curiosity: the digitization of radio communications, the widespread use of consumer electronics, the nature and role of public policy have changed. We are followers of multiple digital applications, in all circumstances of our lives; and everywhere in the world, it is the same. The technical evolution that seemed to us to only have affected developed countries has extended to everyone, even to the borders of industrial society. The information economy – characterized by activities that Daniel Bell[2] [BEL 76] had foreseen for the future – continues to attract the attention of our contemporaries. It is a truism to underline its importance in our personal life, in our work and in society. The digital era has therefore arrived: practically universal in scope, it concerns all conscious humanity and marks our time by its omnipresence; some of its ambitions could prove to be promising according to the bold prophecies of the few "gurus", to whom the largest companies in this industry give their undivided attention[3]!

From analog to digital

As early as the industrial revolution of the 18th Century, machines were analogue. Locomotives, cars, presses, industrial machines, energy production (turbines, alternators, boilers), airplanes and the telephone were all controlled and assisted by hydraulic or electromechanical devices, transmitting a signal proportional to the pilot's or production agent's gesture; the pedals necessary to

---

1 The first debate on the diffusion of computer science begun in North America, in a pragmatic form [WOL 72]. In Europe, the main encyclopedic study was commissioned to Simon Nora in December 1976 by the French President of the Republic at the time, V. Giscard d'Estaing. This report [NOR 80] covered almost all the issues that could be conceived at that time. This document has been very successful; its massive and international distribution has had little equivalent since then.

2 Dedicated to demonstrating the empirical character of its industrial analysis (already indisputable at the time Bell was writing in 1973, then *a fortiori* for the revised and completed edition referenced here) its sociotechnical description of services and amenities still prevails [BEL 76].

3 I am referring here to the positions of certain "minds" from Google such as Niel Jacobstein, a "Chair" holder in artificial intelligence at the singular university directed by Ray Kurzweil: "We will soon be a hybrid of biological and non-biological thinking" (quoted by: https/singularityhub.com, July 28, 2016). The company's research on "neural networks" (electronic, not biological!) and "artificial intelligence" are, beyond this adventurous leap into the future, mainly of an operational nature, as Greg Corrado, a Google specialist in neural networks at the Brain Forum in Lausanne, pointed out on May 28, 2016 (*Le Temps*, p. 24, May 28, 2016); see Chapter 9.

drive a car still act like this. The more I press the brake, the stronger the deceleration; the more I turn the steering wheel, the more the car turns.

The first industrial computers, around 1960, tried to maintain this analogical mode, as it is natural for a human operator to adapt his act to the importance of the effort he exerts! This period is over, with a few exceptions. All industrial equipment is now digitally controlled: sensors deliver a digital signal (e.g. a thermometer), motors, actuators, sensors and valves only receive or emit digital signals, all industrial processes are controlled by one or more computers, for example, the dispatching system that organizes the production and distribution of electricity in a country such as France is a digital machine that symbolically – or analogically – represents the condition of the electricity network. Likewise, a bank's table of exchange rate and the operation of an airliner have been subject to digital control for some 20 years: the financiers decide on their orders to buy, sell or exchange securities, currencies or raw materials, guided by a computer; the on-board commanders are surrounded by digital instruments. As for countries, companies or households, their daily lives are also regulated by digital tools (telephones, computers, tablets, etc.) connected to interactive web services, a network of international networks, 24/7.

Computerization, prior to the digital revolution

IT services have slipped into the heart of the economic activities they were being absorbed by without actually changing the essentials of careers. For example, the introduction of management computers in banks and insurance companies during the 1970s did create new professional functions (such as analyst programmers); but, in most circumstances, neither essential professional practices nor procedures were really disrupted by the computerization of management tasks. Old habits have been adapted; IT procedures are faster, more detailed and less clumsy, but ultimately unchanged[4]. A large part of the jobs prior to computerization has not disappeared; some new practices have been added to the existing ones. Habits and organizations have changed, more by distorting themselves than by disappearing!

On the other hand, many facts underline that digital objects and services have been easily accepted by the population [TRE 15]: in half a generation (less than 15

---

4 Some forms of employment, however, have been disrupted by computerization, such as secretarial roles: for example, typing practically disappeared between 1985 and 2000, simply because of the disappearance of typewriters and the widespread use of personal computers in the essential services sector (administration, auditing, commerce, accounting, consulting, studies, engineering, logistics, transport etc.).

years), households and consumers have discovered and then adopted without hesitation (for the vast majority of them) these new, mobile and wireless devices that equip the individual and the household in which he or she lives (decoder, telephone, VCR, DVD, HDTV, home computer, tablet, game console, etc.). This acceptance also involves the benefits (that were totally unknown to previous generations), which have been integrated into society in a very short time. This change is spectacular; it proves that in all languages and without any special education, people, especially on an individual basis, have a fantastic capacity to adapt to technical objects, which the most optimistic of foresights have consistently underestimated: the market evaluation of the consumer mobile phone market around 1995 was much lower than the actual sales recorded afterwards, this was very clear with the GSM and also with mobile phones (or "smartphones") for 3G networks (known as "third generation") of which the American company Apple was the main instigator[5]!

The Internet, a real breakthrough factor

The services delivered on the Internet are presented in a different form from the one we have just mentioned for computerization between 1960 and 1990: they are no longer punctual tasks whose execution changes in an overall stable context, but radically new practices that appear broken from their past: search engines, for example, completely change access to knowledge. The inevitable consequence of such a disruption: unable to satisfy, as quickly and as well as Wikipedia, the abundant curiosity of Internet users, printed encyclopedias have practically disappeared from the editorial landscape in less than five years! These practices, which we will henceforth refer to as "disruptive"[6], stimulate the imagination and self-feed the change; people invent new ways of operating, working, thinking and trading. Entire sections of tradition are destabilized by this inventiveness that shakes up the former order, somewhat like the way that the automobile transport and the combustion engine destabilized then made horse-drawn transport disappear at the turn of the 20th Century.

---

5 This observation also proves the inanity of attempts, in France and elsewhere, to devise public policies to combat the "digital divide"; the facts have proved that not only did this "divide" exist mainly in the minds of those who affirmed it, but also that the adoption of new techniques by the population as a whole far exceeded the most optimistic predictions. See our survey for the French Higher Council for Information Technology (CSTI, Ministry of Industry): *Frein à l'usage des NTIC* etc. ["Deterrents to the use of NTIC in the French population"] Paris, 2002 p. 29 (mimeo.).

6 Properly formed neologism, whose use is now widespread.

The list of radical changes brought about by the Internet is already very long: the organization of the industry, relations with the public, the connection between supply and demand, advertising practices, the organization of election campaigns, opinion polls and political propaganda have all been put to the test in a few years. For example: the chain of intermediaries that traditionally linked consumers to producers (import/export; wholesalers, retailers) was traditionally tied to a geographical territory. Such an organization is now an excessive burden compared to e-commerce, which establishes a direct relationship with the ultimate consumer via the Internet; the consumer utopia that promised buyers a "short circuit" in 1960, cutting down the commercial margins of intermediaries in trade and industry, attracts consumers (or some of them). The example comes (as it often does!) from the United States: distribution by Internet is conquering an urban, solvent and trendy clientele that is launching this new mode of distribution with as much force as the baby boomers' generation did for Carrefour or Leclerc in the 1960s. It was then discovered that Amazon's economies of scope and of scale, for example, are widening the market because they ignore borders; combined with liberalization of international trade, automated logistics, rapid multimodal transport, maritime containerization and other innovations that facilitate supply, re-supply and fast, guaranteed delivery, the Internet platform is fulfilling the consumer's desires!

"Disruption" expands its effects

This change in trade is reflected in increasing concentration and a strong tendency to diversify the commercial offer, which is perfectly illustrated by the spectrum of services offered by eBay or Amazon. The effect of size is indeed essential to succeed in these new professions. Only very large companies, integrated on (at least) a continental scale with very large means (automated warehouses, fleets of cargo aircrafts, harbors, specialized trucks, direct courier services, etc.) can breakthrough and last.

The successes of PriceMinister, a company born in France but now integrated into the significant Japanese e-commerce group Rakuten; and Alibaba, a Chinese distributor that has been omnipresent in the world for several years, are icons of this electronic commerce. In addition to general distributors, specialized operators are also responding to the zeitgeist, for example, by combining distribution with an exchange function that extends the fashion of garage sales and street markets, whose success does not dry up.

What has just been summarized for commerce applies, by analogy, to other domains that put through a demand and an offer: dating sites (Meetic), classified ads (Leboncoin), sales or rentals (seloger.com), travel and leisure (lastminute.com), etc.

The wind of change is everywhere. Internet access profoundly disrupts established practices and businesses.

Evolution or revolution?

Beyond multiple concrete cases, it is important to assess the impact of change on behavior, on social balances, on the intensity and duration of the transformations affecting the very large number of companies and professions affected by this wave of change. This is why part of our book describes the innovative but disruptive role of digital intermediation. The list can be endlessly expanded, because the influence of the web and multipurpose devices is constantly expanding. Here are a few examples:

– e-commerce revolutionizes distribution;

– remote banking (ING direct, boursorama) competes with banking networks;

– online brokerage disrupts insurance companies;

– the initiative of Uber or Chauffeurprive.com calls taxis into question;

– eHealth reinvents part of the health and care supply;

– iTunes and peer-to-peer exchange reshape production and broadcasting;

– TV channels are disrupted by the offer of online television, Netflix, etc.

These facts raise many of questions like the following:

– are they favorable or unfavorable to the consumer?

– do they condemn a section of former jobs, a classic argument against the expansion of machinery and technical progress?

– do the activities generated by the disruption create enough wealth to stimulate growth?

Importance of competition

These issues will be addressed frequently in this set of books. They immediately call for a first reflection on the competitive mechanism because it is necessary to distinguish, in this respect, the activities that are genuinely carried out in an open market, such as trade; and others that, like communication, transport, financial activities and energy, are also managed by public policies.

Activities that are naturally delivered on a competitive market (such as manufacturing and entertainment) can be used as benchmarks: the Internet, because it is free of borders, changes the size of the market and significantly disrupts traditionally local or regional operators. Trading and service are essentially competitive: Internet operators already have a very clear influence on classified ads and travel; on automobile distribution and consumer electronics. In insurance, the situation is contrasted, as the switch to the Internet may only be partial, allowing for a more balanced approach between a traditional service and a strong presence on the Internet[7]; food distribution adopts, in part, home delivery or drive-ins that could appeal to customers, etc. As a general rule, Internet distribution can sometimes be integrated into the pre-existing market: it also takes its place, complementary to former distribution. Competition pushes one another to integrate new techniques into their own practices.

Effects on employment

In the wake of "The Glorious Thirties"[8], we remain very sensible to manufacturing employment, but this category of employment is shrinking over the long term, we've known this for a long time with certainty. This reduction is noticeable in terms of total employment; it is also significant in absolute[9] terms. Correspondingly, the labor force employed in today's factories is very different from the industrial employment of the past: this is no longer really a laborer job; it becomes closer to the services sector than to the former manufacturing sector, because the production tools used are complex, often automated machines. The modern factory, therefore, requires technicians for troubleshooting, software, control and automation. In countries such as Germany, Great Britain and France, industrial tasks are concentrated on the design, installation and intelligent operation of machines; clever maintenance and repair take precedence over production. Thus, until the closure of this type of activity in Finland, we could see far lesser workers on a Nokia production line 20 years ago than we could in a Matra factory that

---

7 This phenomenon is also observed in the real estate sector, whose regulations protect, as in the case of insurers, their brokers!

8 Editor's note: Jean Fourastié, a French economist (1907–1990) called the 1946–1975 period "Les Trente Glorieuses", which is also the title of his famous book first published in 1979. This expression is still commonly used.

9 Orders of magnitude for France, in millions of industrial jobs recorded in the 20th Century: in 1906: 5.9m, in 1973: 8.3m, in 2001: 5.4m. In proportion to total employment, the percentage of industrial employment fell deeply between 1980 (about 5.2 m) and 2007 (about 3.5 m) [DEM 10].

manufactured telephones in France at the time! On the other hand, marketing, design and maintenance are the drivers for jobs in these current manufacturing industries; services account for most of the factory jobs. Employment is lower than before, more skilled and better paid.

The communication sector is a good example of this change in employment, qualifications and skills required for the workforce. Communication services are much more important in terms of jobs than manufacturers. For the period from 1995 to 2000, the operators delivering the telephone and data transmission services in France created approximately 9,000 jobs per mobile phone operator, to which were added a significant number of commercial jobs in companies such as Orange, SFR and Bouygues; but also in distributors such as Coriolis, Fnac, Free, Virgin, Carrefour, Darty, Auchan and others. In short, if there was a new economy in telephony during the period following the liberalization of services and networks, it was due to the commercial and competitive nature of these new activities; this joint creation of added value and employment lasted more than 20 years[10].

This evolution is characteristic of what has been called "the new economy"; human labor is becoming different from what we knew until digitization[11]. The change is not very recent, it has accelerated notably under the combined effect of the shift of labor-intensive manufacturing to countries where unskilled employment is much cheaper than in Western Europe or in the United States and the automation of production processes that require very large investments. Since automation allows production of very large numbers, the industry is also moving towards a very large-scale customer base (e.g. automobiles, aircraft or integrated circuits); this large customer base, extended to the international market, in turn requires integrated logistics at all levels of production (stretched flows, integration of subcontracting, upstream and downstream transport, etc.). These phenomena, largely anticipated by industrial economists during the last quarter of the 20th Century, were confirmed and accelerated in the 21st Century; they accompany the international consolidation of major manufacturers (chemical, automotive, aeronautical and consumer

---

10 That is to say, in France, from approximately 1988 to 2008; because from 2008 onwards, this very active market turned around under the influence of many factors, the most visible, if not the most important of which was the financial crisis of 2007. See *Digital Yearbook*, IDATE, Montpellier, pp. 48–51, 2011. The appendix shows that the dot-com bubble from the year 2000 did not have the same devastating effect in America.

11 Blauc G., *Le travail au XXI° siècle*, Dunod, Paris, 1995; notably "the meaning of work will change", conclusive reflections from Gérard Blanc, p. 266.

electronics, etc.), which make full use of the potential for coordination via the Internet, through internal company or group networks (Intranet)[12].

Highly regulated communication infrastructure and services

We are beginning to perceive the positive effects of these activities, which have developed in a much less competitive framework, because the means of communication have always directly involved governments. Doctrine and practice consider communication as an activity of public interest, even when the management of services is delegated to private companies[13].

Traditional monopolies

To link one private property to another, to cover a territory properly, a network of infrastructures is needed that occupies part of the public domain: it follows roads, crosses streets and rivers. Therefore, the establishment of infrastructures is a kind of public work. This implies some political authority in the organization of telecommunications, radio broadcasting and cable television. The right of way for cables along the paths and radio transmitters is subject to licensing. All policed countries are thus involved in setting up infrastructures, whether they are the prime contractors or not. For this reason alone, these activities are always and everywhere regulated. However, the control of technical installations and equipment is not a public control. The operation of "private correspondence" on the telephone and telegraph has also been described as a public service. The same has been true of broadcasting and television since their appearance in the 20th Century.

The European colonies in Africa and Asia inherited this regime, which they retained well beyond their independence. Associated with the exploitation of public service, public appropriation of infrastructure was therefore widespread throughout the world, with a few exceptions, mainly located in America: Canada, the United States and several Latin American countries had conceded telephone and broadcasting rights to private companies, the best known of which were AT&T

---

12 "The core of the industry (manufacturing) will evolve towards the intellectual functions on which production depends" [NAI 82, p. 31]. Another perfectly predicted observation for France: "there is a strong growth for white collar jobs, employed as much in the tertiary sector as in the secondary sector" [MIS 81, p. 222].

13 Like the manufacture and distribution of weapons systems, we are far removed from economic activity applied in a free and autonomous market. Public authority is always present, visible or not. For details, see [CHA 93, pp. 32–55].

(American Telephone and Telegraph), which operated for a very long time in the United States and was the world's largest company, and ITT (International Telephone and Telegraph, now extinct in this form) which was a phone operator in many countries, notably Spanish-speaking countries. In simple terms, it can therefore be said that telephone, telegraph, radio and television were national monopolies for almost a century. In order to ensure international trade, which has long since extended national links, a minimum of coordination between countries was necessary. It is an international institution that has been in charge since 1865, the ITU (see Box 1.1).

The International Telecommunication Union (ITU), which had its headquarters in Paris for a long time before emigrating to Geneva, celebrated its 150th anniversary in 2015. It is a specialized organization attached to the United Nations, like the Universal Postal Union or the International Labor Office, ITU coordinated the telegraph and telephone infrastructures, as well as radio communications after their first industrial applications around 1920. With the space era and the proliferation of communication satellites, ITU has also become involved in the coordination of frequency bands, their distribution between various uses (TSF, civil and military radiotelephone, radars, remote sensing, etc.) and the allocation of orbital positions, particularly in geostationary orbit, which enables satellites to maintain a practically fixed position over the earth, which greatly facilitates the reception of signals by a satellite dish.

ITU is an assembly of sovereign countries. Private operators participate only as observers. For more than a century, this was not of practical importance because the means of communication were managed by public authorities or public service distributors. For over 20 years (from 1975 to 1995) this scheme has fallen into disuse, as communications are now delegated to companies in most countries[14]. The fall of the Soviet Union at the end of 1989 contributed to this great change and digital technology is radically changing the approach to telephones, data transmission and broadcasting. This liberalization is a challenge for an institution composed of countries, because digital innovations are pushed by powerful and ubiquitous multinational corporations. With digital services, is there still a credible mandate for ITU? "Disruption" also troubles such an international institution.

Box 1.1. *An international specialized organization, ITU*

---

14 In huge and densely populated countries such as China or India, access to telephone and data transmission is still a state privilege, of strategic and political value. For a long time, this sovereign privilege slowed down the change of telecommunications companies in European countries, whose transformation was delayed until the promulgation of binding European directives.

New rules in Europe[15]

In 1934[16], a regulation of broadcasting and telecommunications, independent of the executive branch, was installed in the United States. In the wake of Roosevelt's New Deal, the main task was to delegate radio media management to a committee of experts: the executive branch no longer wanted to be involved in the allocation of frequencies or in branch responsibilities. By entrusting the FCC with the supervision of broadcasters and telephone companies, the President of the United States was freeing himself from a political risk that was difficult to undertake in the American democracy, whose institutions very effectively protect freedom of speech and expression, especially those of the press[17]! This institutional framework was set in motion in Europe around 1985, in the wake of what was called the 'deregulation of telecommunications". The first "independent regulator" of Europe was established in Great Britain after 1982[18].

Inspired to a great extent by British and American consultants who have always been very active in Brussels, the numerous European directives on telecoms and communications have partly demarcated the British scheme and American regulation which, in the eyes of European civil servants, constitute a federal model that many of them would appreciate for Europe[19].

---

15 Describing and commenting on this profound reconfiguration of the regulatory context is not the subject of this book. For Europe, reference can be made to monographs, sometimes written on the spot, which retain good testimonial value [DAR 85, LIB 94, BES 89, PIC 06, CHA 93].

16 1934 Communication Act: this federal law created the Federal Communications Commission (FCC), still in operation today, which allocates radio frequencies and regulates audiovisual media and communications at a federal level (inter-state and international); see [WIE 88].

17 See the "First Amendment" of the U. S. Constitution (1791): "Congress shall make no law respecting an establishment of religion, or prohibiting the free exercise thereof; or abridging the freedom of speech, or of the press; or the right of the people peaceably to assemble, and to petition the government for a redress of grievances". These constitutional guarantees, with their very broad jurisprudential interpretation, have little equivalent in European democracies, with the exception of the Federal Republic of Germany, whose law was inspired in part by American constitutionalists in the aftermath of the Second World War.

18 Oftel (Office of Telecommunications) was charged with duopoly between British Telecom (now BT) and an operator created in the circumstances, in cooperation with the imperial company Cable and Wireless (which had, until the 1980s, a telephone monopoly in the colonies of the British Crown, notably in the West Indies). This inspired other projects, for example: "Mercure de France", *Le Communicateur*, pp. 185–202, July 1987.

19 Many Europeans have dissected US regulation in detail in previous years; see Garnham N. (eds.), CPR 88, *European Telecommunications Policy Research*, IOS, Amsterdam, pp. 5–39, 93–111, 175–201,1988.

In the long term, and without interfering with economic freedoms, it is practically impossible for a regulator to monitor competition as smoothly as a competitive market does; at best, a dissymmetry of information places the regulator in a position of strategic inferiority compared to competitors. The regulator therefore needs their cooperation to stay informed; at worst, this may lead the regulator to more or less take the side of the regulated operators to whom his/her fate is, in a way, linked.

Any disruption of the regulated market therefore has an impact on the regulator, whose mandate is to sustain this market with some serenity. This mechanism has been very well documented in America for a long time; it induces, almost mechanically, a bias that has been described as the capture of the regulator by regulated companies[20]; the risk of capture is increased by the fact that, under cover of their professional competence, the political authorities tend to entrust the regulatory body to personalities familiar with the regulated sector, a common practice for postings in the CSA and ARCEP in France, like the American FCC[21].

The steering of the industry by a supervising authority, even in oligopolistic competition (currently the case of radio, private television and cellular telephony) does, therefore place a real political risk on the regulator: that of being accused of all the evils when one or even several of the regulated operators encounter serious difficulties[22]. Over the long term, this leads the regulator (like CSA or ARCEP in France, or OFCOM in the UK) to multiply the number of precautions prior to each decision, in short, to be more conservative than innovative, a behavior rather supportive of the established companies. Such a conservative policy may eventually produce quasi-rents, which were supposed to vanish in light of the competitive regime.

Box 1.2. *Boundaries and drawbacks of independent regulation*

Despite this, however, politics has not given up on telecommunications and broadcasting: classified as state services in Germany, France and Great Britain for more than a century[23], these services have not yet escaped national control. Since the

---

20 See George Stigler's article: "The theory of economic regulation" in *Bell J. Eco. and Mangt. Sc.* at 3-21, 1971. Beyond the risk of capture, the risks of corruption are not negligible. Multiple examples are cited in literature, concerning the approval of medicines in the United States, or the monitoring of nuclear power plants in Japan, a question raised at the event of the land disaster which the Fukushima region fell victim to in 2011.

21 The five members of this Federal Communications Commission are chosen by the President of the United States, but their appointment must be confirmed by the Senate. In France, the commissioners of ARCEP and CSA are appointed by the Presidents of the Republic, the Senate and the National Assembly.

22 Let us not forget, in order to set these ideas, the period before the disappearance of the fifth French television channel in 1992; an almost unique case of license abandonment, as the operator closed up shop!

23 Even concessions such as the AT&T American telephone and the Western Union telegraph were public services in practice, if not by law, for more than a century.

disappearance of the public monopoly, each operator has received a license (similar to that of cafés in France); the public authority sets the conditions for their practice and the private operator owes them accounts.

Whether they are commercial companies or public corporations such as France Télécom, France Télévision or the BBC (British Broadcasting Corporation), all are administered: no event in their social life escapes the watchful eye of a public authority. The texts are clear in this regard[24].

Changes in European markets

A large number of European telecommunication directives were promulgated in Brussels during the period of 1986–2002, shaping the regulatory framework of each member country[25]. Two French laws, passed in June 1996, introduced a regime conforming with community principles requiring all services to be opened up to competition by the beginning of 1998. This target was actually achieved in the European Union, with the exception of Greece, although this date was somewhat delayed. The notorious privileges of national public services were abolished. This transformation took place without major drama in our countries (Spain, France, Italy, Germany, Holland, etc.). Part of the credit must be attributed to political management (in France, during the pivotal period from 1986 to 1998) and the climate of optimism that marked this period (see above). This significant turnaround benefited from an extremely demanding market. Two factors facilitated the transition:

– the very rapid expansion of the mobile phone: between the publication of the first French cellular license in December 1986 and mid-1996, this market was calm, prices were high and competition between France Télécom and SFR was fairly comfortable; the advent of the third operator, Bouygues Télécom, changed the situation from May 1996 onwards; in a few months, competition between three typical operators stimulated commercial conditions, territorial coverage and performance. In the autumn of 2001, mobile phone subscribers outnumbered fixed-

---

24 In France: The Electronic Communications and Postal Regulatory Authority (ARCEP, previously ART) and the Higher Council of Audiovisual (CSA). For a summary of the doctrine, see Cohen E. and Henry C. (ed.), *Rapport No. 3* of the French Council of Economic Analysis, La Documentation française, Paris, p. 16 ff, 1997.

25 About 25 texts; in this area, as in others (electricity, transport, gas, etc.), the European situation is characterized by a division of competence between the European Commission and the member states. Reinforced since 1992 by the Treaties which established the European Union, the Commission's powers are important; however, political realities limit certain Commission initiatives.

line subscribers; (48 million cellular customers in 2005 compared to around 33 million fixed-line customers[26]);

– the rise of Internet services: around 1995, our countries became aware of the challenge posed by these new communication services. The French population, initiated to electronic services by the interactive telematics of Minitel, showed less immediate interest in the Internet than their neighbors in Northern Europe (Germany, Holland, Scandinavia, Great Britain, etc.): e-mail, information and entertainment services became widespread two or three years later than our neighbors and by the year 2000 demand for new e-services had increased. This push was a blessing for incumbent operators such as France Télécom, owner of a national network largely adapted to data transmission, who took advantage of the Internet to enter the residential market.

The above elements were thus nurturing optimism, both among old and new operators alike. This optimism was fueled by a favorable international context: the boom in the US net economy heralded a new economy. Investors rushed into microelectronics, software and telecommunications. This interest in "new start-ups" has nourished American wealth since 1990; a wealth that the crisis of 1999/2000 did not really break[27].

In short: European public policies aimed at accelerating the spread of 3G telephones have accentuated the impact of the dotcoms crisis. The high tax levies on licenses, which were unrealistic in terms of the investments that had to be financed, sustained the economic crisis. These levies, inspired by a community scheme, accentuated the impact of the American Internet bubble; European operators were trapped in a policy which, hoping to repeat the success of the GSM[28], increased the disruption in the period preceding the digital convergence. The difficulties of several European operators (at least half of which were still public companies) spread to their traditional suppliers who, for their part, had underestimated the drying up of public contracts, without which their development could not continue. So many errors, misunderstandings and cumulative difficulties at the very time when the US

---

26 See the telecommunications services market in 2005, ART Observatory (mimeo), pp. 12–20. Growth rate of the mobile customer base: +24.8% for the year and stability of the fixed customer base (+ 0%).

27 The subprime crisis in 2007 was much deeper than that of dot-com, see *Lettres de Présaje*, no. 4–5, December 2008–February 2009, available at: www.presaje.com/media (see the Appendix at the end of this chapter).

28 The development of this standard was long and laborious, something that has often been forgotten *ex-post*!

economy was experiencing its first digital growth crisis. This requires a mixed assessment of the European regulators – still without experience – who had recently been entrusted with the regulation of telecommunications in Europe.

From crisis to American rebound

In America, the years following the year 2000 erased the traces of the big sweep described in the Appendix of this chapter. After curettage, the sustainable companies restarted. Computers, telecommunications and the Internet (ignoring audio-visual media) regained their colors and so did growth. The crisis of the year 2000 has therefore only interrupted the impetus of American start-ups for a few months. Less than three years after the dot-com bubble exploded, Internet-oriented businesses (smart devices such as the iPhone, network equipment such as Cisco, security software such as McAfee, technical and commercial innovations preparing digital platforms, etc.) blossomed again in the United States. These pivotal years were those in which the transition from computer intelligence to digital, mobile and interactive devices (such as tablets and laptops) took shape; they are also the years that announced social networks and intermediate platforms that would transform the web into a series of very large marketplaces such as eBay or Amazon; an interactive bookstore quickly converted into a remote distribution chain. Apple would find a new growth engine with its high-end phones, audio players and tablets, all combined with "proprietary" services that opened up new perspectives in music (iTunes) and interpersonal communications (iChat). Facebook became accessible to everyone in 2006; Google, whose services are at the forefront of search engines, would soon associate its Android access software with the new digital phones in 2007.

These novelties combined devices (the Apple iPhone), new software and services that were quickly and internationally successful (instant messaging and music, for example) and were the result of close cooperation with Asian manufacturers subcontracting to American corporations. Most western industries did not gain momentum in time and were overwhelmed by the surge of new services and mass-produced smartphones in Asia; to respond, various alliances such as Nokia's with Siemens (June 2006) or Alcatel's with Lucent (April 2006) were formed. But the technological mastery of the new Internet corporations retained the advantage, in a context of entrusting manufacturing to the Far East; engineering, commercial inventiveness and large legions of investors to America (and soon to Korea).

Information and communication services, now referred to as digital, flourished very quickly. Despite bankruptcies, plant or design office closures, business continued to grow (mobile telephone, fixed-line telephone, Internet, audiovisual services, interactive games, etc.). Fixed and cellular operators remained healthy despite (or thanks to) competition. Asset devaluation has stabilized most of the industrial market segments (devices, fiber optics, network equipment, etc.). Although the crisis left its mark, activity resumed despite the heavy losses that had plagued this industry (see the Appendix of this chapter for comments).

Changing manufacturing industries

At the end of the 20th Century, European telephone companies no longer had a genuine interest in developing their own products, as had been the practice in the past. They stopped financing their usual suppliers such as Siemens in the FRG (funded by DT) and Alcatel in France (funded by FT). The equipment manufacturers were therefore forced to support their finance by their own means[29]; the challenge proved difficult. The equipment manufacturers also sought to acquire new technologies to improve their Internet proficiency and prepare for the rapid migration of GSM networks to the new 3G standard that licensing imposed in order to multiply mobile multimedia services.

Basically, the former European public services still endured, managing their residential clientele as much as their professional clients: those who didn't want to venture out remained loyal to the historical operator, at least for telephone and data transmission. As for the needs of companies, it was reliability that concerned them first and foremost; France Telecom understood this issue. Its approach has improved over the years. For voice services, the heart of the market until around 2004, the new entrants (in France: Télé 2, a subsidiary of a Swedish multinational group, later acquired by Cegetel in 2006) scored few points. On the contrary, mobile operators confirmed their position year after year, resulting in a gradual shift from fixed telephone lines to new mobiles. In this respect, we had two very different situations in Europe: that of France and Italy, countries where the main mobile operator and market leader was a branch of the former public service (TIM in Italy, Orange in France), and that of England and Germany, where mobile services were conquered by new companies, in this case by Vodafone in Great Britain and Mannesmann in Germany, the latter having been absorbed by its British counterpart, becoming the leader of this branch in Europe and perhaps one of the world's leading operators!

---

29 This explains their bulimia in taking control of the Internet's start-ups, sometimes at high prices. Nokia, driven by global demand until recently, was a temporary exception (see footnote 38).

Telephone and Internet companies

Since the year 2000, the digital world has relied on existing infrastructures, but the plan of purely digital corporations was completely different from that of telephone operators who transported data: operators are attached to their territory, whereas major Internet companies are merchants combining, as the case may be:

– services (search engines, algorithms and software);

– the sale of electronic equipment and services associated with such equipment (such as the case for Apple or Samsung and video games for Sony or Nintendo);

– the singular sale of equipment (cameras);

– a combination of distribution (Amazon), assorted services of equipment (Amazon, Apple, Google) and media where the web is the only access mode (social networks and cloud services in particular).

Driven by an international ambition, such companies certainly mobilize significant capital; for them, movement is essential in order to keep their place in the sun, because in this ecosystem, whoever does not progress gets left behind[30]. Web corporations that attract attention form a small competitive circle, united by their common ability to offer complementary services on an Internet platform to two distinct customer segments:

– a useful service for the general public (or a category of the public) that is funded by advertising, such as outdoor, radio, press and television;

– and, for those who have something to sell, a targeted access to the market that web mechanisms facilitate through sorting or algorithms, which are agglomerated under a catch-all system. This is "big data", which we will mention throughout this book[31].

Two conditions are necessary for such a project to succeed: access to a very wide public in order to establish its advertising network on a large and diverse market, and finely pinpointing what makes it possible to combine an offer with a solvent demand. Operators like Google have become masters in this practice thanks to the search engine and the data they permanently record on Internet users in most of the

---

30 As many examples have shown: the search engine Alta Vista could not compete with Yahoo! or Google; for years, Yahoo! has been losing its momentum, etc. Successful companies rapidly reach multinational size, but few of them are able to sustain themselves for good; a more detailed analysis of these phenomena can be found in Volume 2.
31 For methods, see chapters 2 to 4 of this volume.

countries where this service is accessible (which is no longer the case in China, for example!); on a different model, the Facebook social network is also very efficient.

Size is therefore of great importance. In order to attract advertisers, the Internet operator must assemble a customer base in line with the advertiser's target audience[32]. When it comes to products or services that are directly aimed at a global market, which is what the Internet does by nature, the conjunction of interest between advertisers and the media is obvious: soft drinks, cinema films, video games, cars, telephones, cosmetics and air travel are all beneficiaries. At the same time, however, the investment required to maintain international access is very high, especially since it must be diversified to maintain the main assets of a platform: its audience, well defined in terms of purchasing power, food habits (and therefore religion, for example), language, geographical location, socio-professional category, education, etc.

The two categories of enterprises that we have just discussed (telephone companies and Internet platforms) have certain converging interests: to perpetuate their business, extend their reach and profitability. However, their ambitions are at odds with each other, as they compete for the loyalty of the final customers that pay infrastructure operators for access to the network, and who benefit, most often free of charge, from the platforms financed by advertising. Two heavily opposing ambitions, as infrastructure operators connect Internet platforms to their respective subscribers, which they do not want to lose.

Since interactive services also allow video exchanges, platforms requiring a large digital bandwidth. Traffic flows generated by the Internet[33] are hence considerable; these traffic flows overload the networks of telephone companies or cable companies. However, the customary rules established from the beginning of the Internet stipulated that network access should be provided on an "au pair" basis, assuming that over the long term, these exchanges would be broadly "peer-to-peer"; this old rule is no longer in line with the reality of exchanges; in practice, it is occasionally bypassed.

Summary

The majority of the products and services that characterize today's information and digital economy were born in the United States. The restructuring that followed the year 2000 led to a major reconfiguration of large operators. During this period of consolidation, the highlights were as follows:

---

32 See Chapter 4 for a concrete illustration of the commercial sector.
33 The professional jargon commonly used: *over the top* operators (initials: OTT) to signify they are adding their services on an access network that does not belong to them.

– the United States federal regulators took note, after some hesitation, of the concentration of telephone operators, for both fixed-line and mobile networks, which incidentally had taken a little longer to establish themselves widely in America, no doubt because of the regulatory terms imposed by the FCC on mobile operators. In 2006, the regional division of the gigantic company AT&T which was dismantled in 1984, was abandoned and replaced by a quasi-duopoly between Verizon and AT&T, two powerful companies operating on mobile, Internet access and fixed lines (which has been on the decline since the year 2000, as well as in Europe)[34];

– cable operators have played an essential role in the United States; strongly supported by their local presence and political relays in the federated states, they have made a significant contribution to the spread of Internet access in American households[35];

– the post-2000 years were turbulent for audiovisual production and broadcasting: a sharp drop in advertising resources, stagnation of pay television channels, etc.[36] Only the video game industry performed well, with strong growth for game consoles (Microsoft's Xbox in particular) and game publishers (e.g. Electronic Arts). Music production and distribution finally discovered new sales methods thanks to multimedia subscriptions, the breakthrough of which was confirmed in the general public, who had shunned disc media;

– the visibility of access and Internet service providers had, at the same time, become clearer: 2002 was Amazon's first profit-making year. Google, which had barely reached the age of reason, confirmed its mastery of advertising resources; its competitor Yahoo! disappointed the stock exchange and rejected takeover bids that may have prevented its degradation, which has since confirmed itself[37];

---

34 AT&T's long saga is extraordinary: dismantled since 1984 into 22 regional companies, complex groupings rebounded off the judicial constructivism imposed by the US Department of Justice; this process led to the current duopoly. The essence of this story was well summarized by [WEI 88]. The current AT&T company retains the name of the former monopoly, but only has an indirect relationship with it.

35 Outside Germany, Belgium and the Netherlands, Internet access in Europe was mainly based on the telephone network; in North America, cable television was substantial.

36 Reflecting the uncertainty of investors, the Dow Jones – Euro Stoxx stock market index, relative to the media compartment, dropped by half in 2002 (cited by *Digiworld* 2003, IDATE, Montpellier, 2003).

37 Google's revenues for 2006 exceeded US10.6 billion, 90% of which were advertising resources, market capitalization in January 2007: US150 billion, purchase of YouTube in October 2006 for US1.65 billion (in shares) (*Digiworld 2007*, IDATE, Montpellier, pp. 9–11,

– the consequences of the downfall of dot-coms for European and American manufacturers beyond 2001–2002 cannot be overlooked: order cancellations disrupted a large number of equipment manufacturers. The relation between supply and demand for equipment was reversed; it is very likely that Chinese manufacturers thus found the opportunity to infiltrate two key markets for which they have become the main supplier[38].

Personal and portable telephones have become firmly established, even beyond the former iron curtain, where telephone service was destitute. This mode of communication is very well suited to new generations, it has also broken through to the older classes of our populations; it covers our territories very well, and meets the demands of the professional, personal and family mobility that fills our time. The telephone of the 21st Century is therefore digital, cellular and multi-faceted. If it can still be improved, it is at the margin of price, for international travel for example, which is still a deterrent for an ordinary consumer. The structures of this activity appear to be stable, but without a significant integration of European markets[39].

Paradoxically, the crisis in the year 2000 did not shake the European oligopoly. The consolidation that brought the American networks together in a very powerful duopoly has therefore no equivalent in Europe. This is a fundamental difference between North America and Western Europe. Moreover, the vast federation of American states is united by a single language (an important condition to take advantage of scale economies for communication); whereas linguistic and cultural diversities, beyond nation states, strongly constrain the economy of scale in Europe.

In addition to the principles of free movement and freedom of establishment, the European Union remains a kaleidoscope of distinct markets between which trade is marginal. There is little or no cross-border synergy for media, telephone or aboriginal social networks. Accordingly, the European Union remains a mosaic of sovereign countries, of diverse economic level and political traditions, divided by its multiple languages, its political fractures and by tensions that the forced march

---

2007). Absorbed by Verizon-AOL in March 2017, Yahoo! is no longer an Internet operator (*Le Temps*, April 10, 2017).

38 Lucent, the former industrial arm of AT&T, was directly affected by the Internet bubble. Nokia, the world leader in mobile telephones and cellular network equipment between 1999 and 2010, invested heavily in dot-com devices. After its merger with Microsoft (which still uses the Nokia brand to sell phones), Nokia abandoned all ambition in telephony, a market it had dominated for some 20 years.

39 Vodafone is a counter-example: it is the only one of the European operators to have an international diversification without being given an unreasonable advantage by its territory of origin (the United Kingdom).

towards the Union has not eradicated, on the contrary: British exit decisions have revealed it in the open[40].

Through dynamic multinational corporations, digital services and information services on the web have profoundly transformed interpersonal communication and part of the social relations within the member countries of the European Union. But it has to be admitted: the main agents of these huge markets are mostly American and sometimes Chinese, like Ali Baba. We have pointed out that the digital world is based on technologies that were born in America and are operated by American companies, although many of the equipment is manufactured outside the United States; this equipment is designed primarily for the American market, it is financed by capital raised in America. Driven by a global ambition, as was already the case for computers from the 1960s to 2000, the corporations driving the global network had (and continue to have) the initiative and creative strength to stay one step ahead.

For infrastructure and data transmission, the multipolar organization inherited from the 20th Century continues to function: very often, it is public service companies from before 1990 that still provide access to the network and collect the fees corresponding to this service [FOS 03]. Those highly capitalized companies (investments of around 10% to 25% of annual turnover) hold a significant share of their national market; they depend (with a few exceptions) on projects and the doctrine of their authority, rather than on their own strategy and on private investors who hold a share of their capital. Supervised by both national governments and the European Union, this context nonetheless ensures that telephone operators will continue to operate under national licenses. Innovation is not the dominant concern of these companies, and market sharing between operators in the same country is a guarantee of their survival.

In summary, we could say: data transmission operators are attached to the field while OTTs are attached to advertisers. Both have the same need: to access the general public in a sustainable and faithful manner. That requires very different conditions in both cases because, while the terrain is compartmentalized by traditions and political boundaries[41], it remains open to trade, cash, trade-in goods and services. So, things are far from simple. All the more so because of the additional fiscal, industrial, social and political considerations that add to the elements we have just reviewed, which complicate the questions raised by the

---

40 This observation is confirmed by the impact of Brexit, to which specialist analysts pay great attention: see, on this subject, the political economy notes of CEPS-Brussels, https://www.ceps.eu/publications/which-model-brexit.

41 As regards, for example, the number and nature of constraints imposed on networks by their license.

impact of the Internet on our lives, habits and customs. These and many other issues are discussed in the following chapters. Several other consequences of the disruptive mechanisms linked to digital technology will also be discussed in volumes 2 and 3 of this book.

Bibliography

[BEL 76] BELL D., *The Coming of Post-Industrial Society, A Venture in Social Forecasting*, Basic Books, New York, 1976.

[CHA 93] CHAMOUX J.-P., *Telecoms, la fin des privilèges*, PUF, Paris, 1993.

[DAR 85] DARMON J., *Le grand dérangement*, J. C. Lattès, Paris, 1985.

[DEM 10] DEMMOU L., "The decline of industrial work in France...", *Economie & Statistiques*, vol. 438, no. 1, pp. 273–296, 2010.

[FOS 03] FOSSIER M., "Back to some basic principles", in EYMERY G., GARCIA ALVES I., TRIBOT LA SPIÈRE L. (eds), *Le paradoxe des télécoms*, A. D. Little-Publisud, Paris, 2003.

[LIB 94] LIBOIS L.J., *Télécommunications: technologies, réseaux, services*, Eyrolles-CNET, Paris, 1994.

[MEU 94] MEURLING J., JEANS R., "The Mobile Phone Book", *Com. Week Int'l*, London, 1994.

[MIS 81] MISSIKA J.L. *et al.*, *Information & Emploi*, La Documentation française, Paris, 1981.

[NAI 82] NAISBITT J., *Megatrends*, Warner Books, New York, 1982–1984.

[NOR 78] NORA S., MINC A., *L'informatisation de la société*, La Documentation française, Paris, 1978.

[PIC 06] PICOT A. (ed.), *The Future of Telecommunications Industries*, Springer-Münchner Kreis, Berlin, 2006.

[TRE 15] TREILLE J.M., *La révolution numérique*, Ovadia, Nice, 2015.

[WAL 95] WALRAVE M. (ed.), *Les réseaux de services publics dans le monde*, Eska, Paris, 1995.

[WEI 88] WEINHAUSS C., OETTINGER A., *Behind the Telephone Debate*, Ablex Pub, Norwood, 1988.

[WOL 72] WOLF C., ENNS J.H., *Computers and Economics*, Rand Paper No. P-4724, 1972.

Appendix. The 2000 crisis: lessons and industrial consequences

Taking over from the public and military investments that had previously stimulated American electronics, the growth of the late 20th Century marked a major turning point: it was no longer the traditional corporations, nor those of the "military-industrial complex" that lead the way; the traditional values lost their splendor, going so far as fearing for their survival in an environment that seemed to be their exclusive domain[42]. The interest of financiers turned to entrepreneurs with exceptional growth prospects: Apple, Compaq, Sun, Dell, Microsoft, Cisco and many other companies whose products, hardware, software and services cleared the explosive market of communications services. Young corporations, bright and optimistic leaders; the financiers placed their trust in them before they even achieved a positive result.

The rise and crisis of dot-coms

This extraordinary, forward-looking climate has nurtured the digital industry and transformed relations between American and foreign industries, for, boosted by their explosive domestic market, start-ups set out to conquer the world: to find new customers on other continents and to outsource the manufacturing they need in a favorable context, thanks to the openness of China and the Asian tigers with whom they established themselves. The 1990s profoundly changed the mindset and outlook of analysts and investors: after a long period of capital investment in established values[43], this period of rapid innovation and fierce competition generated a progressive but massive interest in fast-growing companies. Some of them were disappearing, certainly; but in a very active market, the rescue of smaller companies by stronger ones was not uncommon. Failure is no longer a problem, especially in California where the redevelopment of entrepreneurs is constant; the sense of risk is shared and opportunities to bounce back are frequent.

Industry and stock market climates were intimately intertwined. Success sparked new vocations and investment opportunities; financial intermediaries played a pivotal role in this process, bringing together supply and demand for capital. Driven

---

42 Like the Blue Chips, these well-established companies like IBM, are a very good example. Also, worth mentioning: AT&T, most of the aircraft manufacturers and companies close to the defense, such as Motorola, whose brilliant industrial venture sadly ended in 2011.
43 Dividend values such as those from AT&T and allegedly dominant companies such as General Motors.

by growth, the intermediaries also attracted investors from Europe and Asia, generating in London, Frankfurt and Paris the imitation of American markets. This sustained the rise in the electronics, telecommunications and, to a lesser extent, audiovisual industries such as Viacom[44]. The United States Federal Commission – the FCC – had been in place for a long time, and was inspired by an almost rustic vision of the competitive marketplace. Through these years of unbridled growth, it continued its plans to expand networks in America, Europe and Asia. For with the strong growth of the Internet, demand for infrastructure grew faster than voice traffic. There were two reasons for this:

– digital connections were faster than telephone connections. The organization of traffic on the "net" made it difficult to communicate messages on the network, leading servers and access providers to oversize the infrastructure to avoid disruptions and blockages of traffic;

– in a few years, the spread of fiber optics on land and underwater increased the output rate of cables enormously; Internet operators invested in order to reduce their transport costs between Europe, Korea, Japan and America. A real collapse in the unit price of these links followed, for example on the transatlantic canals or the Pacific Arc[45].

Optimistic expectations led to the development of new infrastructures around 1997–1998. Several large companies made similar investments, but by 2002 some specialized operators had closed down shop or benefited from the US bankruptcy law, which allowed them to continue to operate under conditions. Only the old telephone and cable renters (such as Time Warner, whose fiber investment was devalued by 80%, let alone telephone companies such as SBC, AT&T and Verizon) fared well[46].

Consequences for Europe

The financial crisis of the year 2000 had less of an impact in Europe than the collapse of the Nasdaq in America. However, we have suffered the fallout: most of the American cable distributors have left Europe; Internet operators who had begun

---

44 However, part of this sector was devalued compared to its brilliant past, proof of the selective nature of ratings during this period (IBM for example, already cited).

45 Several major operators with international ambitions fell victim to the dot-com crisis, such as Global Crossing, Level 3 and Worldcom (see Box 1.4); this exacerbated the fall in prices.

46 The cumulative market value of these investors in 1999 was estimated at EUR 500 billion (or US).

to build long-distance relationships in Europe dropped out. Alternative technologies[47] were practically abandoned, because American operators such as Firstmark or Winstar, without whom this technology was not mastered in Europe, closed down or abandoned the part in the wake of the financial crisis. Shaken by the disruptions in the winter of 2000–2001, American operators did not see fit to continue their license application in Europe in the early 2000s: none of them took part in the consortia that installed the third-generation European networks. After having regained their financial strength, they devoted the available financial resources to consolidating American networks. Without this unfortunate accumulation of difficulties, would they have contributed to the installation of digital networks in Europe as they proclaimed? Other phenomena have destabilized the beautiful enthusiasm of the late 20th Century and enabled the overthrow of the European manufacturing industry:

– for nearly two years, the anguish of the millennium[48] mobilized a significant part of the workforce of the IT companies, raised the price of services and led to a vacuum in early 2000, when this millenarian anxiety proved to clearly have been overestimated!

– traditional industries rushed to acquire Internet companies (dot-coms) at high prices, just before the collapse of this segment of the stock market (Alcatel, Lucent and Siemens took part).

Resolution of the American crisis

The dot-com implosion occurred without prior notice; it can be considered retrospectively as an adjustment crisis. It was sorted in a few weeks through natural selection, by bankruptcy deposits; it could have passed off as a simple health operation that would not have been extended, if only other causes had not been added, contributing to a deeper and more lasting economic shock. This did not immediately come to light, but accelerated the collapse of confidence, which as we know takes a long time to build up, but is quick to lose.

---

47 Like the "wireless local loops", for which French ART granted 27 licenses in 2000.

48 It was the fear of transition to the year 2000: for several months, a "major breakdown" of computers, whose internal clocks were not always designed to span the millennium, was feared. In fact, the transition to the new millennium went rather well!

Founded in 1963, MCI created a wireless communications network to compete with the long-distance monopoly of Mamma Bell, the familiar name of AT&T. After many court cases, she obtained long-distance operator licenses and began providing commercial services in 1969. This network was essentially made up of wireless signals (hence its name) and became international in 1982. In 1990, MCI was the second largest U.S. telecommunications company. It laid fiber optic cables to expand its offer of data transmission and became involved in intercontinental and Internet services. The UK operator BT acquired 20% of MCI in 1991. At the end of 1997, MCI merged with Worldcom.

Technology benchmarks in MCI

MCI has contributed to the emergence of satellite communications since 1971, in association with Lockeed and Comsat. This project resulted in an IBM-Comsat-Aetna co-enterprise venture that launched Satellite Business Systems in 1974, supported by IBM and the insurance company Aetna.

By the end of 1982, the MCI Mail packet transmission network was already operating under the X25 standard (like Transpac in France); Vint Serf, who attached his name to the launch of the Internet, was working on this project. MCI, together with Corning Glass and Siemens, commissioned the first operational underwater fiber optic cable between New York and Washington DC, the process of which was standardized. MCI, a partner of the Murdoch Group (News Corp), prepared the launch of direct-to-home satellites in the 1990s, thus creating Direct TV service, which is still operational today.

Box 1.3. *Microwave Communication Inc (MCI): from innovation to merger*

Financial difficulties revealed ambiguous and even fraudulent behavior:

– the mixing of genres multiplied, without anyone really taking any notice of it, especially regarding professional orders and "market authorities": combining the tasks of advising, revising and expert with the same, supposedly independent advice (of which Andersen was a victim);

– the greed of leaders, with their heavy influences, tarnished the image of new digital corporations; some of them degraded the profile of the American entrepreneur. Their collusion with analysts, journalists and intermediaries (e.g. with headhunters who opened up new fields of practice) has sometimes been proven (see Box 1.4);

– the personal interest of business owners: while financial engineering is by no means negligible in today's economy, the multiplication of mergers and acquisitions has led to pernicious practices such as the constant increase in transactions[49].

---

49 Just because, for example, the intermediary is paid proportionally to the amount of the transactions, not pro rata temporis, as are the main professional services.

Founded in Jackson, Mississippi in 1983, Worldcom was dedicated to long distance services such as MCI. After seven successive acquisitions, organized by its president since 1985, Bernard Ebbers, in a few years it became concurrent but rather complementary to MCI. His offer to merge with MCI was completed in a few weeks with the agreement of both the managements, for nearly $37 billion. This mega merger became operational in September 1998. Worlcom-MCI tried to absorb its competitor Sprint in July 2000, in the midst of the dot-com crisis. This attempt was blocked by the US Department of Justice (with grievance from the European Commission).

It was later discovered that B. Ebbers had committed serious abuse of corporate assets and that he maintained fake accounting, imputing significant operating expenses to the corporate assets in order to support his stock market price, which was badly affected by the stock market crisis. MCI-Worldcom went bankrupt and was liquidated in 2004. Leaving a very large social and financial debt, its president and senior executives were convicted of fraud, price manipulation and breach of trust for an approved $400 million loan to Ebbers by his own company to cover purely personal commitments. Ebbers has been serving a 25-year prison sentence since 2006.

Microsoft took over some of MCI's brands and services to expand its instant messaging services. Worldcom also acquired one of the main Internet backbone providers, UUNET.

Box 1.4. *Worldcom: from innovation to bankruptcy*

Links with European public policies

These shortcomings obviously tainted the financial market; a small number of criminal cases marked those dark years (such as the bankruptcy of Worldcom).

The 2000 crisis also combined unfortunate public policies. Two causes can be distinguished here:

– the appetite of Western European governments, around the year 2000, for discovering untapped budgetary resources, following the brilliant but unexpected success of cell phones;

– the race for infrastructure sparked by the popular success of the Internet, a race encouraged by the regulatory authorities who saw the rush as an opportunity to assert their commitment to an industrial policy and thereby strengthen their influence and political visibility.

This bulimia of governments focused itself onto the allocation of third-generation frequencies (known as 3G/UMTS). The European Community imposed the same industrial standard on future 3G operators. This industrial policy was an opportunity for the Commission in Brussels to take up the initiative it was losing after having promulgated some 20 directives on telecommunications since 1986. The main stages of this race for 3G licenses were as follows:

– auctioning: the British government levied more than 30 billion euros from the auctions that were taken away by Vodafone, British Telecom, Orange, Hutchison and Deutsche Telecom for the operation of new networks, for which, at that time, neither the technical conditions nor the business plans were really fixed;

– one quarter later, in the summer of 2000, the German Government similarly awarded six licenses (by public auction) to each of the six applicants, each of whom had to pay significant sums of almost EUR 8 billion, none of which were able to invest three years later and two of which definitively pulled the plug[50];

– coming after Holland, Switzerland, Sweden and Norway, France hesitated for weeks before deciding what to do and how to do it; after a waltz of hesitation from the government authorities, the established operators and the ART, the French government awarded two licenses per competition, without auction, because most of the candidates declined their participation; France Télécom, presumably under the constraint of its supervision, and the Vivendi group, under the influence of a still optimistic management, were each taxed EUR 5 billion, a sum subsequently revised downwards under pressure from beneficiaries and the circumstances that followed.

Between the British auctions and the summer of 2001, there was widespread doubt as to the profitability of these licenses and their economic equilibrium: the Chinese group Hutchison withdrew without prior notice from the German consortium that had just won a license, claiming an unacceptable risk; the winners of these contests saw their shares mishandled on the stock exchange as soon as they were announced as successful[51] (BT, Vodaphone, DT, later Vivendi and France Télécom). The holders of these licenses (mostly European) were unable to immediately initiate the investment, due to the fees owed to the Treasuries of the countries where they had obtained a 3G-UMTS license. Manufacturers obviously suffered and so did the 3G programs to which they had committed themselves. The liquidity crisis had an indirect effect on manufacturing industries such as Alcatel, Ericsson, Lucent, Nokia, Siemens, etc. Several of these industries were also involved in large and costly acquisitions of new economy businesses in America.

---

50 In particular Mobilkom, an operator into which France Télécom unfortunately sunk more than EUR 6 billion, an irrecoverable commitment that contributed to the difficulties of the French operator in 2002.

51 Bringing a formal contradiction to the declarations of the leaders who announced, before the competitions, that the loss of these licenses would cause them great harm.

The pressure imposed on them by the telecom operators, who were caught in the licensing trap themselves, increased the difficulties of the industry. Lastly, the UMTS mobile phone standards that promised to take advantage of the convergence between voice, data, images and entertainment applications were unachieved or incomplete, while the deadline for their implementation was approaching.

Mathematical Culture and Massive Data

It took two centuries for differential calculus to permeate economic theory, thanks to the concept of marginal rates co-created by Walras, Jevons and Menger around 1870. Modern economics has built itself on this mathematical knowledge. Similarly, the computerization of contemporary society is based on discrete mathematics and mathematical logic, which are two domains that really began in the 1930s, but are not part of high school education. This knowledge is now helping to exploit big data, for which hardware development has been driven by computer electronics since the Second World War. If, however, we must investigate the mathematical background that accompanies computer science, calculation and formal algorithms, it is to put to rest an idea that is circulating on the web, that the exploitation of metadata would definitively eliminate the human sciences, linguistics, sociology and even the economy. On the contrary, the already sophisticated processing of massive data still lacks applications.

It is in any case ill-advised to separate, in relation to mathematics, what is theoretical knowledge and applied knowledge and to consider utility independently of theory, even if utility can be considered from non-mathematical points of view. There are two misleading temptations: to claim that a particular application requires a specific mathematical approach, independent of the rest of mathematics or even any other science and to assert that useful knowledge comes only from experience, that it is necessarily the result of trial and error. If it has aimed universally, the universe of mathematics has always been interested in the real world and the other sciences by which it can be used without distorting or subjugating them: the calculation is magnified today by the increasing use of numbers which attempt to represent the world in very different ways, coming from all knowledge.

Chapter written by Jean DHOMBRES.

Since it is probably cheaper to learn a little mathematics than to fumble around without a guide in a world of numbers, some insights will be useful to master the massive data that invade our daily lives and to consider what is still missing. That is the purpose of this chapter.

Differential and integral calculus, which together are just called Calculus, emerged neither before nor after the celestial mechanics which owes so much to Newton: it was established simultaneously with the idea of expressing laws in mathematical form from celestial observations that were sufficiently precise to derive general principles[1] from. Doesn't it seem today that the algorithm has become an unconditional imperative, as if its presence is to be expected? Because mathematical expression does not leave any room for ambiguity, it can give the feeling of crushing all forms of knowledge, including that of human sciences. This is because not enough care has been taken to rightly replace the various mathematical methods in history; those of big data in particular. In order to learn scientific knowledge, we must have an epistemological interest in separating the elaboration of mathematization from its concrete origins; this is what has been done for celestial mechanics, for example. This separation (or analysis), which makes quality education worthwhile, is hardly possible today because of the novelty of massive data processing, which is a mere 10 years old. However, these applications are based on known procedures, their implementation is not random: choices are possible if one agrees not to let oneself be dominated by the customary propaganda of electronic and communication environments. These choices depend on available mathematics, but also on the pursuit of objectives.

As I cannot delve into all the mathematics that is useful to big data here, nor mention the various places in which big data was conceived, I must adopt a presentation strategy. The simplest, somewhat mystifying way, would be to start from an example such as the Louvain algorithm, which extracts, after a few hours of calculation, significant data clusters from a very large set of data, close to a billion units of elementary data[2]. This algorithm and its use are part of a mathematical culture: it is associated with questions that tap into our societies such as determinism, human freedom in the physical world, but also the desire to dominate the vagaries of time in order to predict everything, an old astrological dream. History helps us here. Long after Newton's mechanics appeared, the mathematical notion of potential, governed by a partial differential equation that Newton had not considered, which made "force" lose its concrete meaning, prepared a new physics: that of the field. Laplace installed this equation in his treaty on celestial mechanics whose first volume, published in 1799, would confirm determinism. The discovery

---

1 Distinguishing between the theoretical (what the calculation would be) and the applied (what the celestial mechanics would be) has historically no relevance. On the other hand, astrological pathways, including numerology, which were common at the time of Newton, in no way prepared the appearance of calculation.
2 Readers mainly interested in "massive data" and its exploitation can refer directly to the section on this algorithm below; they can be satisfied if they are familiar with the words algorithms, graphs, computational matrix and probabilities.

of chaos at the end of the 19th Century and Poincaré's work called into question Laplace's way of thinking: not only were new instruments required, but also new theoretical interpretations, still elaborated on the basis of mathematics. As well as that, massive data processing was subject to adjustments. It was not possible to predict them; but they could be prepared for.

To situate massive data in terms of culture and the history of science is not only a rhetorical way of approaching a technical object but also allows the offer of a critical look. My first objective is, therefore, to explain how we have come to interpret what is calculable, in order to really address the question of algorithms, and therefore massive data. In fact, one of the minds who contributed the most to our understanding was Alan Turing, who discussed the *state of mind of somebody while he is computing*[3] in his research; he transcribed it on his "machine". Metaphorically, at least, it is this state of mind that I have to make practically clear. Another way of doing this would be to analyze a sentence found in a good book on these facts[4]. I would have taken the side of programming and the handling of machines, something obviously essential for a practitioner, and I would have censored the mathematical aspect and the functioning of the scientific mind that makes it possible to doubt both an absolute predictability and an optimal approximation.

I start with what needs to be understood from Turing's machine. This will allow me to introduce three general questions: that which is natural in mathematics, that of style and, finally, that of the constraints of any mathematical process. To talk about a mathematical style, there is nothing better than to approach Turing's use of the diagonal process, which is essential for demonstrating a negative result, as a demystification. I will then present positive results, with well-known algorithms still used today, such as gcd. If I conclude with the Louvain algorithm, it is to discuss the representations specific to massive data, to introduce the question of their uses, to see what is possible and what is perhaps missing. My program alternates examples of mathematical use and epistemological reflections; it is not meant to be deductive, in the manner of mathematical demonstrations, but rather enveloping, in the manner

---

3 Many books on Turing and his works are available online. In French, [GIR 95] comments usefully and translates some of Turing's major texts. See also [LEV 15]. It would be fair to also mention Alonzo Church or Kurt Gödel, contemporaries of Turing.

4 "A bolt receives tuples from one or more streams, performs a particular processing and then returns the result as tuples in another stream. In some cases, such as for the spout, it is possible that the bolt emits tuples on several streams. In other cases, the bolt returns no results. This is particularly the case for terminating bolts, whose role is to get the results out of Storm, for example, to save them in a database", reported in [LEM 16]. See also [MOH 15]. And for more historical aspects: [MAH 01]; [WUY 01].

of Gaston Bachelard who evoked the creation of philosophy by science itself. But whoever mentions philosophy also imposes a critical condition.

The Turing machine, the inspiration for massive data?

A description in plain language can be found in Turing's works and in the previously mentioned popular works. A Turing machine consists of the following elements:

1) a ribbon divided into consecutive boxes. Each square contains a symbol from a finite alphabet. The alphabet contains in particular a "blank" symbol (recorded as 0). The ribbon is assumed to be infinitely long, to the left and to the right. The unwritten boxes on the ribbon are considered to contain the "blank" symbol;

2) a head that can read and write symbols on the ribbon and move left or right;

3) a register which memorizes the current state of the machine, what Turing also calls "state of mind", that of a calculator which works with a pen and paper. The number of possible states is finite; the starting state is the initial state of the machine before any execution;

4) a table that tells the machine what symbol to write, as to move the head that reads (L for a box moved to the left, R for a box to the right), and the new state based on the symbol read on the ribbon and the current state of the machine. The machine stops if there is no planned action for a specific combination of a symbol being read and a state.

At each step of the calculation, the machine evolves according to the state in which it finds itself and the symbol written in the box of the ribbon that its head reads; these two pieces of information update the state of the machine thanks to a transition function that makes the head move from a box on the left to a box on the right of the ribbon, or vice versa.

In the initial state, the ribbon box carries the entry of the program. The machine stops, and this is the fundamental point, when it reads a box specifying the terminal state. The result of the calculation is then written on the ribbon.

This description can be written in a short form in formal language (Box 2.1)[5]. Even if it is not necessary to understand it well, especially for those who are

---

5 This definition can be tamed by a comment that links the machine to the formal. The arrows in the definition of δ represent the two possible movements of the reading head, that is to say the left-hand movement and the right-hand movement. The meaning of this transitional

discouraged by mathematical writing, it is at least essential to see that all operations are comprehensively included. I'll leave it to the imagination on how to do a numerical operation on points or bars in binary writing like in computers, and particularly how to perform a subtraction. It is because this machine does operations and obeys a procedural form that it will be possible to define that which is calculable and that which is not. This will be further discussed later. However, at this stage, it is important to reflect on what we know about the electronic machines that we are familiar with. They did not exist in Turing's time and yet, in theory, they depend on Turing's machine.

A Turing machine is a sevenfold $(Q, \Gamma, B, \Sigma, q_0, \delta, F)$ where:

– Q is a finite set of states;

– Γ is the working alphabet of the symbols of the band;

– $B \in \Gamma$ is a special symbol (known as white);

– Σ is the alphabet of the input symbols $(\Sigma \subseteq \Gamma \setminus \{B\})$;

– $q_0 \in Q$ is the initial state;

– $\delta : Q \times \Gamma \to Q \times \Gamma \times \{\leftarrow, \rightarrow\}$ is the transition function;

– $F \subseteq Q$ is the set of accepting (or final, terminal states).

Box 2.1. *Formal mathematical description of a Turing machine*

Distinguishing the pure from the applied does not define the calculable[6]

The definition of the volume that makes up the massive, and consequently the non-massive, only intervenes at the level of the performance of algorithms, of their good convergence (as they are described), and not of the very structure of these algorithms, which work as well on "small" data as on the others. Their implementation is measured however (always from a cost perspective, meant in terms of electronic machine time, or even in terms of space occupied in the machine). We talk about a constant cost when each step of an algorithm is the same, a linear cost when it is 0 (t)[7], a near-linear cost when it is 0 $(tlnt)$, a polynomial cost

---

function can be explained in the following example: $\delta(q_1, x) = (q_2, y, \leftarrow)$ means that if the Turing machine is in the q_1 state and reads the symbol x, it writes y instead of x, goes to the q_2 state, and moves its reading head to the left.

6 Or, think in terms of volume and cost!

7 Where t is the size of the data often referred to as volume.

when it is $0\ (t^k)$, and even exponential or factorials costs, which are exorbitant and must serve as a fail. It is with this expression of cost that the presence of the massive is best seen, since the 0 used measures an infinite behavior.

Among the tasks assigned to the IT tool, which does not seem to make use of numbers, it has an ability to select and under-select in lists and bring data entry in line, with the possibility of cross-checks between them. This gives rise to many programming techniques (mentioned in footnote 4) in which spouts, bolts and joins play a role without any further explanation. There is an abundance of sorting algorithms, each having its own "natural" way of operating to sort a list of integers in ascending order; or to sort a list of names in alphabetical order. Of course, it is natural to consider an optimal strategy when the mass of data exceeds a thousand, especially if one wants to put it into play in a machine, in the form of what is called an algorithm. Of course, we need to clarify what the optimization is about. For example, we need to measure the number of comparisons and exchanges of numbers needed to obtain the desired result. If N is the number of objects to be classified, large or small, it is clear that in order to compare two by two of each other element, $N\ (N\text{-}1)$ operations will have to be carried out; for N large, a work of the same order as N^2 operations[8]. The performance of this comparison algorithm is called polynomial (because it is to the power of two of N, here). In this calculation, it is obviously not possible to take into account any known peculiarity of the N numbers, nor how they form a list in the machine. Still without any specificity of this list, we can improve the strategy by sorting by packages. In the 1960s, Sir Charles Antony Richard Hoare invented the fast sorting, also called quicksort, which still remains widely used. This is then in $0(NlnN)$. Any mathematical culture assures that there is an advantage here over sorting two to two, since the ratio limit of $NlnN$ to N^2 is zero. It is the comparison of the power and logarithm functions that is at stake. A new question arises: would we have an optimum in $0(NlnN)$ when we don't know anything about the list of N numbers? Turing's major contribution is to show that such questions are generally insoluble. This does not block the search for sensible ways to improve performance.

Theoretically, with massive data, we risk making the same error as Aristotle did separating the "heavy" from the "light" as absolutes when discussing the falling of bodies. The "fire", symptom of the light, could only go up! It is without a doubt to avoid such an error that the advocates of such a blissful position on mass data assert that only the ones involved with applied mathematics could really calculate. This applied mathematics would differ radically from general mathematics, because in

---

8 It is the mathematical notion of infinite equivalents, rated $0\ (N^2)$, which makes sure that the limit of the ratio of $N\ (N\text{-}1)$ to N^2 is equal to 1.

this case, their application would be due to the manipulation of massive data alone[9]. Thus, for example, because of an interest in results alone, an economist working with massive data might find the distinction between the two types of mathematics valid, whereas otherwise it is necessary to enter into the performance of a calculation, beyond the volume processed, the speed of processing (which is linked to the cost) and the variety of data. The latter governs the reliability of the results. Rather than the verb "enter", it would be better to use "integrate", a term familiar to mathematicians and that brings much more. Because it is obvious that the result, whatever it may be, is not a calculation.

What does "calculable" mean?

What, then, is calculation when it has to deal with something other than what we usually call numbers, on which the four elementary operations are based? With massive data, if we are talking about calculable data, we would still have to agree on what we are calculating and include the question of the reliability of the result.

The notion of what is calculable was not defined until the 1930s because we thought it was self-evident. The paradoxes of the early 20th Century, in set theory, did not seem to touch this notion. Today, what we call calculable is all that an electronic machine, like the ones that we possess, can supply from data supplied to it in a certain language. That being said, the machine is reduced to a black box whose operation is useless without questioning the conditions of data entry in the said machine. This first response corresponds to what many big data lobbyists suggest. This response can still be validated, provided that it describes what is meant by machine. The operations that the machine performs must be explained in order to achieve a result. I set out to clarify the validity of these operations on data in a mathematical manner that, thanks to the Turing machine, I did not need to validate as achievable.

As we know from Turing and a few others, the notion of what is calculable is related to mathematical logic, we cannot dissociate it from calculability and we cannot omit the questions that concern data, their preparation prior to machine entry, the language that shapes them and an ordered collection. We are talking about input, which is due to the ease of the English language in trivializing the theoretical; but at

---

9 Paradoxically, this was at a time when there was a tendency to no longer differentiate between applied mathematics and pure mathematics, in research at least. The difference would only be due to the temporality of action: immediate, for applications with a view to decision-making; more distant in pure research, after certain mechanisms or structures had finally been elucidated.

least for the sake of comprehension, we would do better to think about the integration of data into the machine itself. Strange as it may seem to anyone who believes that machines do whatever you want if you feed them correctly, the output that has to correspond to the expected stakes should also be discussed.

If my cultural topic is to show, and not to demonstrate the game of mathematics in the processing of massive data and its collection, it is also important to understand how epistemological change implies that the applied and theoretical have more in common today than was thought before 1930. This is as much due to the tools of experimentation as to thought experiences, an expression from the scholarly biologist and epistemologist Ludwik Fleck[10]. These imaginary experiments in the air, which have always existed, are now taking on a form that can be said to be real, thanks to machines. The Turing machine, first conceived as a thought machine, formats what can be calculated. With the undeniable dominance of digital technology, which can reduce the variety of data, we seem to have lost another traditional form of scientific work: the analog which is said to maintain a much closer contact with reality[11].

The relationship of virtual to reality

Let's start by discussing this relationship to reality before we even see what the Turing machine can theoretically do, because there is perhaps a fundamental difficulty: would the use of digital machines introduce a kind of indifference between what is virtual and what is real? This old problem, posed by an automaton which would think like man and would therefore be subject, like him, to passions[12], is transmuted into a new type of confusion: confusion between the objects made by man or found in nature, and the calculated objects which would appear according to their own mode, to the point of building a new world: would it be that of massive data? In another form, I also find the previous discussion on the autonomy of

10 Ludwik Fleck's work in Polish on styles of thought and collective thinking from 1927 onwards was translated into English in 1979 by Chicago University Press, under the title "Genesis and Development of a Scientific Fact", presented by epistemologist Thomas Kuhn, author in 1962 of The Structure of Scientific Revolutions; this work attempted to give a unique form to all profound changes in science. Fleck was translated into French at Les Belles Lettres by Nathalie Jas in 2005, with a foreword by Bruno Latour, himself an anthropologist in the sciences. He published in 1979 a work with Steve Woolgar, remarkable for its descriptive nature of the means used to "pass" a scientific innovation. *The Production of Scientific Facts.*

11 Editor's Note: on this subject, see Chapter 1.

12 See the theme of 2001: A Space Odyssey that echoes the myth of the Golem, as well as Frankenstein.

massive data. We will see the mathematical process that we must put this data through, so that it is computable or calculable; and deduce what we must do to make the output of the machine representative, an objective too often ignored. A first return to reality takes place because it is ultimately a question of finding realistic effects, seeing images of the mathematical structures that allow us to think about the algorithms to be implemented below.

This difficulty, relative to the virtual, remains no less; it is well perceived by economists who know that they can confuse reality with certain theoretical schemes which would become more real than reality (on growth, for example, or unemployment, or competition, etc.). The question about algorithms is whether their game works without reference to anything other than the virtual world in which they are designed. In other words, does the algorithm lose its modeling status? Does it not construct another reality that no longer needs to connect to anything other than itself?

Put more materially: apart from the issue of bugs and breakdowns, would there be a way to question data processing, whether massive or not, when we do not understand the operations or why we are putting them into play? How can I be precise if I don't know the criteria for classifying opinions or who expresses them? The facility would be to read only the first names provided and to choose among these names alone; therefore, to undergo the imposition of machine sorting. Moreover, the long lists promised by a web search engine are a sham, because only a few hundred are really available, as Eric Guichard rightly pointed out[13].

Falsifiability is an important criteria for science, as Karl Popper has sufficiently explained[14]. Meteorologists now know this, and it adds a confidence rate to their forecasts. What would be the equivalent of this confidence rate in the results of massive data processing, when one assumes that "the machine cannot be mistaken"? This sentence is not binding since the bug can come from the program, especially if it contains millions of instructions! Does verifying programs relieve massive data? Asking the question is not a good idea for those who would like to reduce massive data in marketing. Ludwik Fleck asserted that all scientific creation is the result of a "collective style of thought". Can this be the case with massive data and its

---

13 Guichard E. (ed.), *Regards croisés sur l'Internet*, Presses de l'ENSSIB, Villeurbanne, 2011.

14 Karl Popper published *Logik der Forschung*, translated into English as The Logic of Scientific Discovery; Editor's Note: Popper's logic, first published in German, then in English after his exile in 1937, underlined the strong logical asymmetry between verifying a scientific proposal and seeing and refuting the same proposal. His use of the English term falsifiable has given rise to controversies, which are illuminating for the scientific method: see Magee B., *Popper*, Fontana/Collins, London, pp. 18–28, 1973.

processing? What could this new "style" be? The question conforms to the cultural approach to mathematics that I undertake, provided, of course, that I do not have blinders.

A thinking style: the digital image of the world

In the 1950s, digital specialists such as Hermann H. Goldstine [GOL 77] (close to the famous Hungarian John von Neumann, who became an American after the war), explained that with the machines of the time, which were still very moderate, digital technology finally triumphed over analog[15]. It is doubtful today because a recent work on "black holes" shows how much analogical reasoning subsists in scientific thought, at least when it is impossible to observe or experiment directly[16]. In condensed matter physics, a phonon refers to a quantum of vibration energy. It is considered to be a near-particle, a fictitious particle; a particle that becomes real, from the point of view of calculation and experimentation, only in extreme circumstances. As such, the phonon concept allows an analogy with light, which has similar properties: it is sometimes manifested as a wave, sometimes as a packet of energy corresponding to the elementary photon particle, one of Einstein's contributions. Thus, if the thermal radiation of the astrophysical black hole, as predicted by Stephen Hacking's generally accepted theory, cannot be observed because of its small size in the face of the massive black hole data, at least the analogy with the phonon can suggest its observation in a suitable tube, placed near absolute zero. In these extreme conditions, the phenomenon of sound vibrations takes on the appearance of a particle. This analogy, proposed more than 30 years ago by William Unruh, was recently observed by the physicist Jeff Steinhauer ad hoc on the tube, when one desperately hoped to put it into evidence by the numerical exploration of the sky[17].

---

15 Von Neumann J., Goldstine H., "On the Principle of Large Scale Computing Machines" (1946) in A. H. Taub (ed.), *Collected Works of John von Neumann*, Pergamon Press, New York, pp. 1–33,1961. See also [GOL 72].

16 Without massive data intervening because what is scientifically released is only due to the mass of data in exceptional cases.

17 Hawking's claim of thermal radiation, predicted by the black hole theory that was published in *Nature* in 1974 (no. 248, p. 30). W.G. Unruh envisaged the analogy with phonons in 1981 (*Physical Review Letters*, no. 46, p. 1351). Steinhauer published his experimental results in *Physical Review Letters* in 2011 (no. 106). See experimental black hole evaporation in *Physics Today*, 2016. It is important to specify the meaning of the adjective "analog" which is not that of ancient scholastics (see Robert's (or *Harrap's*) dictionary to this word): the analogy is formal here, in the mathematical sense. It is because the partial differential equations that govern black holes (in the dominant theory) are the same as those that govern phonons; these theories

The analogy mentioned here is mathematical; it can also work for massive data. This will be seen at the end of this chapter in relation to the Louvain algorithm. The example of the black hole and thermal radiation indicates that this is the exception to be measured, a method patiently carried out at CERN concerning the boson, theoretically indicated by Higgs, Englert and Brout in the 1960s. It was revealed by extracting, among billions of others, some collisions caused between particles: this is the typical example of massive data processing where only an exceptional phenomenon is sought [COH 13].

We will object that it is still not necessary to enter into the genesis of these machine-related mathematics; neither into the mathematical logic revolutionized in the 20th Century with Turing and Church, just before the Second World War, nor into the very idea of John von Neumann's programming during the war and the immediate post-war period, before the revolution that led to the electronic chip. The application that would limit the massive certainly does not require work on logic, in the same way that you do not require an automobile driver to know how a diesel engine works. But, if we want to understand the processing of massive data and the cost of operating algorithms, can we ignore its mathematical organization? It would be like seeking energy savings by ignoring the second principle of thermodynamics, which prohibits certain configurations without a double-source (hot and cold). Mathematical logic has discovered that there are impossible questions, at least if we want to solve them with reliable calculable calculations in a sense that can be defined by Turing[18].

From natural to mathematics

I have to make one last general point, and that is to discuss the natural, starting from the word "denomination": that of natural integers. It should not be inferred, however, that the theories about these integers are ipso facto "natural"! Obviously, data processing requires theory, that is to say reasoning as well as calculation[19].

---

are physics. Experimental evidence, too, is proof for which big data plays a role. But, once equations have been set, the analogy is purely mathematical. It is indisputably true, within the framework of theories enlightened by experimentation.

18 Mathematical logic calls for a negative response on anything that could be gullible, on massive data as well as on other subjects. To show that a negative result is, altogether, natural, implies a mathematical culture. For what is said to be natural, in this field stemming from Euclid, is a matter of standardized, rather than natural.

19 Which also means to foresee by thinking in sight of an advantage: Richelieu calculated his encounters with the difficult ruler Louis XIII, and it was the legendary day of the dupes!

Only a magical notion could affirm that "numbers speak for themselves". If that were true, there would be no need for any data processing to sell ad hoc tools. To assert the numerical evidence would be to consider the probabilists and statisticians of large numbers as clowns because they did not have our computers that would work, without having to think[20]. It is not as if the theoretical machine, conceived by Turing in 1936 to solve the logical problems left by Hilbert a few years earlier, had been nothing more than the frivolous pastime of an eccentric young Englishman! Hilbert's "problem of decision" (*Entscheidungsproblem*) challenges the economist, at least metaphorically. And, above all, it reveals a constant of mathematical culture: it was solved by the negative.

I have only quoted two outstanding mathematical interventions in recent centuries here, without going into the corresponding techniques or theories. These mathematical techniques, which have been tamed by several generations, have taken on a natural look: to us, they seem to be evidence of what Fleck called a "style of thought" (*Denkstil*), a common form that schools and universities make even more common, in a standardized form[21].

A theory such as the probability theory preserves something that is specific to mathematics: it does not proceed by accumulation and rejection of theories. The physics of Aristotle has become useless, but the Elements of Euclid, however incomplete they may be, are not wrong; they are still in use. So, I can assume that big data operators are betting on this cultural appropriation of mathematics. It is inevitably long-term. The example cited above about differential calculus and marginal rate confirms this extrapolation. To measure the analogy, it just needs to be recalled that Euclid's Elements, dating from the 3rd Century BC, gave the elementary geometry that made generations of students suffer. These results appeared natural in the 1960s, but only because they were contrasted with other strange expressions called modern mathematics, which had dated from the last third of the 19th Century! The teaching of mathematics was often aimed at naturalizing, if I may say so, new ways of doing things. It is therefore worth considering how mathematicians have been working with algorithms for a very long time, without authenticating them. This will be my next example.

---

20 See Pascal and Fermat in the 17th Century, Bernoulli and Laplace in the 18th Century, and up to Kolmogorov in the 20th Century.
21 An uncommon conception of the natural leads to major errors, both in teaching and in the dissemination of practices. Gaston Bachelard was certainly wrong to say that "good science" is the one we should have thought of first if we were not blinded by epistemological obstacles. What should we reply to Bachelard, is necessarily "first"? [BAC 49]. For Fleck: see footnote 10.

An ancient algorithm and its programming: gcd

Without defining it much until now, I have used the word "algorithm", which some people have never related to mathematics, seeing it as a programming or digital analysis game specific to applied mathematics. However, it is important to understand what an algorithm is, both for processing massive data and for implementing the machines that are inseparable from it. I did say that calculable functions, with the power series (and also the Fourier integral), are not algorithms in the sense that computer scientists give to this word ever since Donald Knuth, to whom we owe an extraordinarily, remarkable stable universal language, known as the TeX, which all mathematicians who want to be published nowadays work with[22]!

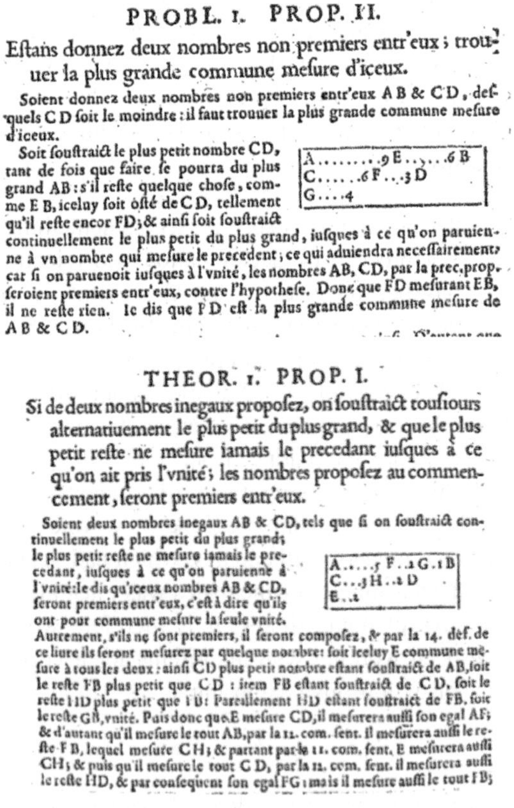

PROBL. I. PROP. II.

Eſtans donnez deux nombres non premiers entr'eux ; trouuer la plus grande commune meſure d'iceux.

Soient donnez deux nombres non premiers entr'eux A B & C D, deſquels C D ſoit le moindre : il faut trouuer la plus grande commune meſure d'iceux.

Soit ſouſtraict le plus petit nombre C D, tant de fois que faire ſe pourra du plus grand AB : s'il reſte quelque choſe, comme E B, iceluy ſoit oſté de C D, tellement qu'il reſte encor FD ; & ainſi ſoit ſouſtraict continuellement le plus petit du plus grand, iuſques à ce qu'on paruienne à vn nombre qui meſure le precedent ; ce qui aduiendra neceſſairement, car ſi on paruenoit iuſques à l'vnité, les nombres AB, CD, par la prec. prop. ſeroient premiers entr'eux, contre l'hypotheſe. Donc que FD meſurant EB, il ne reſte rien. Ie dis que F D eſt la plus grande commune meſure de A B & C D.

A . . . . 9 E . . . . . 6 B
C . . . . . 6 F . . . 3 D
G . . . 4

THEOR. I. PROP. I.

Si de deux nombres inegaux propoſez, on ſouſtraict touſiours alternatiuement le plus petit du plus grand, & que le plus petit reſte ne meſure iamais le precedant iuſques à ce qu'on ait pris l'vnité ; les nombres propoſez au commencement, ſeront premiers entr'eux.

Soient deux nombres inegaux AB & CD, tels que ſi on ſouſtraict continuellement le plus petit du plus grand ; le plus petit reſte ne meſure iamais le precedant, iuſques à ce qu'on paruienne à l'vnité : Ie dis qu'iceux nombres AB & CD, ſeront premiers entr'eux, c'eſt à dire qu'ils ont pour commune meſure la ſeule vnité. Autrement, s'ils ne ſont premiers, il ſeront compoſez, & par la 14. déf. de ce liure ils ſeront meſurez par quelque nombre : ſoit iceluy E commune meſure à tous les deux : ainſi CD plus petit nombre eſtant ſouſtraict de AB, ſoit le reſte FB plus petit que C D : item FB eſtant ſouſtraict de C D, ſoit le reſte HD plus petit que FB : Pareillement HD eſtant ſouſtraict de FB, ſoit le reſte GB, vnité. Puis donc que E meſure CD, il meſurera auſſi ſon egal AF ; & d'autant qu'il meſure le tout AB, par la 12. com. ſent. il meſurera auſſi le reſte F B, lequel meſure C H ; & partant par la 11. com. ſent. E meſurera auſſi CH ; & puis qu'il meſure le tout C D, par la 12. com. ſent. il meſurera auſſi le reſte HD, & par conſequent ſon egal FG ; mais il meſure auſſi le tout FB ;

A . . . . 5 F . . 2 G . 1 B
C . . . 3 H . . 2 D
E . . 2

Figure 2.1. *Calculation of the gcd of two integers [HEN 34]*

22 TeX is a language that most intellectuals, especially economists, do not know. Teaching TeX, easy for a mathematician who is used to writing mathematically, does not guarantee that the person using it will acquire a style of mathematical logic or solve incalculable problems.

This is how Didier Henrion, a professor of mathematics (but not a university professor), translated into French what is called the calculation of the gcd (the greater common divisor, what Euclid called the greatest common measure) of two integers[23]. The interest of this ancient text is to understand how the author represents numbers: by aggregates of points aligned, almost like the Turing machine! To help the mind that demonstrates, it represents the numbers by dots: the number AB by 15 dots and CD by 9 dots. The first result AE, division of 15 by 9 leaves a 6, less than CD; the division of CD by this remainder leaves the rest 3, readable as FD. Since 6 measures two by three, 3 is the gcd of 15 and 9. The author relies on the fact that the algorithm is only blocked if the rest is equal to zero or one. If it's zero, there is the so-called measure. In the previous proposal, which dealt with two prime numbers between them, by the same procedure the rest could only be one. Henrion, repeating Euclid, does not just give an algorithm: he gives a demonstration at the same time[24]. The algorithm of the gcd bears proof of its validity and cannot be defective (or falsified, as defined by Popper).

This Euclidean procedure can be manifested better in successive steps of the same type. Let's note x^1 and x^2 the two integers, assuming only that the former is larger than the latter. The remainder of the division of x^1 by x^2 is called x^3. If this is not zero, the division of x^2 by x^3, necessarily smaller than x^2, is repeated. So on and so forth, until we arrive at a zero balance if the two starting numbers are not first between them: their gcd is the number obtained before the zero balance. If the rest is equal to one, the numbers x^1 and x^2 are first between them: their gcd is one. This procedure, from which any absurd reasoning has disappeared, can be programmed on a computer[25]. In this sense, Euclid had prepared the programming.

Other numerical procedures allow us to find the gcd: all proceed by iteration, a characteristic of the algorithm[26]. A precise definition involves the repetition of

---

23 Henrion is the author of textbooks, notably on logarithms invented in the great digital movement of the early 17th Century: *The 15 books of Euclid's Geometric Elements*, Livre VII, Veuve Henrion, Paris, pp. 255–256, 1632.

24 The number 4, in the third line of the table, is part of the reasoning behind Henrion's absurdity: if he could not find a number that "measures" his predecessor (for example 4), he would be in contradiction with the assumption made at the beginning: the two numbers AB and CD are not relative prime numbers!

25 If we want to be satisfied with the subtraction which is available in the machine, without making play on the Euclidean division, we can proceed as follows: we start from two integers. If one of the two integers is zero, the other is the gcd. Otherwise, subtract the smallest from the largest and leave the smallest unchanged. Then, start again with the new pair until one of the two numbers in the pair is zero and the other number is the gcd. This can be programmed.

26 Comes from the name of the Persian mathematician Al-Khwarizmi, who lived in the 9th Century.

operations that result in a finite number of iterations [KNU 11]. But this definition is no longer respected by those who practice big data; many people mistakenly see the algorithm as a user manual, as a recipe whose reasoning does not have to be understood. The mathematical perspective must shed light on the advantages and limitations of such processes.

I will continue with the example of gcd. At the beginning of computer science, many people wanted to give a recursive version in which the function to be found (the gcd) was involved in its own operation, but at a lower bar on the scale. It was about expressing the gcd functionality (a, b) in this way:

if a = 0, then b; otherwise if b = 0 then a; otherwise if b≤ a then gcd (a-b, b);
otherwise gcd (a, b-a).

This recursive formulation corresponds to what Euclid had undertaken with his first proposal by alternative entrenchments; it shows the descent that takes place, insofar as one speaks of integers. Naturally, its reiteration actually gives the greatest common divisor of the two numbers. It's an algorithmic style that gets rid of the unique thought and the recipe! There is another procedure that involves the Euclidean division and, through inventive writing, visualizes what was recursive: the concept of a fraction extends into a continuous fraction[27]. Taking into account the strict inequality between the rest and Y, for a positive X integer greater than or equal to Y, one can write:

$$\frac{X}{Y} = k + \frac{1}{\dfrac{l}{Y}}$$

where k is an integer. This spatialized arrangement reveals what fraction strictly inferior to the unit the denominator must give and visualizes the repetition of the algorithm by adapting to the Euclidean division of Y by l. This is not all: we can, by writing in indices that allow the steps to be numbered, organize a calculation. One can write p_0 for X, p_1 for Y $(X>Y)$; and, more generally with strictly positive integers, as long as q_i and p_i as integers are not zero, and n is the largest integer such that p_{n+1} is not zero:

$$p_{i-1} = q_{i-1}p_i + p_{i+1}$$

with the inequality $0 \leq p_{i+1} < p_i$. I am not going to get into these easy calculations and I am content to say that successive fractions are constructed, $\dfrac{h_i}{k_i}$, which result, in

_____

27 In French, the bad habit of saying: "*fraction continue*".

a finite number of n steps, in expressing the ratio of X to Y; the advantage is to make recurrence relationships emerge on the h and k, rich in formal properties. Like:

$$h_{i-1}k_i - h_i k_{i-1} = (-1)^i$$

which proves that the fractions are irreducible at each step, also giving an approximation of the X/Y ratio, which is always the best possible one; there is a precise meaning to this optimization.

This study of gcd algorithms – the plural of which is important because it suggests the diversity of mathematical styles – shows that in addition to a repetition and a finite number of steps, various calculations are added to try to understand and thus quantify the success of the procedure indicated by Euclid. These different deepenings show, until they exceed a finite number of stages as we will see later on, that a mathematical theorem is only an intermediate moment, not a final term.

Styles of mathematization

A style is a process of habits, techniques, reasoning, and know-how, both in the theory and practice of a group. Mathematicians have been accustomed to it for a long time: geometric style, arithmetic style and, since the 19th Century, algebraic style. I have just illustrated different styles in the case of gcd, ranging from absurd reasoning to digital procedures. Hybridizations are required, like analytical geometry, hybrid since Descartes, between geometry and algebraic reasoning[28]. This will be the case for massive data. Historical epistemologists such as Alistair Crombie have taken up Fleck's ideas on the *Denkstil kollektiv* and classified scientific thought into distinct styles, partly overlapping and simplifying them [CRO 94]. This classification is useful to us: one of the styles recognized by Crombie is the analogical reasoning mentioned about black holes. Another is the probabilistic and statistical style that has something to do with the natural philosophy of the 18th Century, an expression rarely used today because it is replaced only by the word "science"[29]. These epistemological considerations do not deviate from the path to help us understand the mathematization of big data, because we speak of a probabilistic style only to the extent that probabilities describe broad phenomena of reality and, therefore, support action. I mentioned the confidence rate added to the weather forecasts, which are based on probabilistic methods. That's why I link

---

28 There are of course some purists, especially in teaching, who require that we only use one style! This purity of methods requirement will also be found in the practice of big data.

29 This was a semantic loss, when the father of positivism spoke of different states for the various sciences [COM 07].

probabilities to natural philosophy, because probabilities work on chance or fortune, the effects of which manifest themselves in a less natural way than a rainbow or heat! Therefore, I will have to underline the intervention of probabilities where we least expect it: in graph theory, an important tool for big data[30]. It is impossible, therefore, to claim an autonomy of big data.

Crombie favored the axiomatic style that he perceived as specific to mathematics, for which it was enough to have definitions, sequences and presuppositions like the Euclidean geometry postulates. Economists are familiar with Debreu and Arrow's work on general equilibrium; they know that economic constraints do not always provide an axiomatic in which equilibrium can be demonstrated. This axiomatic style plays a fundamental role in big data. Thus, an axiomatic definition of calculability leads to difficult problems, a euphemism to ensure that they are not treatable by a Turing machine. It is therefore not enough to form a list of axioms to have the key to the mathematical processing of data: mathematical literacy helps to understand the interest of such results.

Beyond axiomatic reasoning whose scholarly advantage is to "naturalize" (which the proponents of modern mathematics were convinced of and which is still lacking for big data), there is room for a constructive mathematical style, distinct from the inductive style: to go towards new definitions from which digital procedures can be deduced. What is calculable is one of those new ideas[31]. The fact that the Turing machine is in thought, and not an actual machine, can be immediately seen by the assumption that the result of the operations can be read on a ribbon of infinite length. Let's be aware of the fact that Turing defines and writes any real number as an unlimited decimal, whereas no one knows all the decimals of a number like Π, not even our machines. Turing's machine applied mathematics well [GIR 95]; it was an extraordinary novelty when it was expressed in a mathematical journal in 1936. However, it took a long time for it to intervene in mathematics and it cannot be said that it has become innate yet.

---

30 This hybridization of probability and graph theory is an illustration of the increasing role of probability in the mathematical field since the 20th Century. See the last section of this chapter below.

31 Turing had mathematically expressed what was calculable: a number or a function. He showed that there are incalculable calculations and that algorithms do not do everything, even for what is mathematically thinkable. Would there have been a vicious cycle in him, since he only envisaged a calculable number if it resulted from his machine? It would be to neglect that his machine is imaginary, that it executes only certain types of operations: Turing's calculable results from the only operations that his machine can perform, without distinguishing between a deterministic machine and one that is not!

Turing contradicts the evidence that would be shown by numbers; his approach is indeed that of mathematics. What he does with what can be calculated is epistemologically analogous to what was achieved in the 4th Century BC when irrational numbers were highlighted, such as the square root of two. The Greeks had a clever play on words which corresponds to an undeniable mathematical proof: the irrational is defined as what is not rational (i.e. what is not a ratio of two integers); a completely rational definition, as well as the operations carried out on it! Likewise, Turing shows that rigorously defined calculability includes that which can be written in the form of procedures (known as algorithms); but it also includes power series with calculable coefficients and for a calculable value of the variable, even if this transition to power series is not an algorithmic procedure, insofar as infinity intervenes. This calculable aspect, which I insist on emphasizing because it cannot be mentioned without its precise meaning, does not extend to everything.

The incalculable, an absurd reasoning by Turing

Turing organizes absurd reasoning rather extraordinarily because he was wrong. But he's correcting it. Two wrongs make a right: it follows the logic of Georg Cantor's absurd reasoning that the set of real numbers, those written by an unlimited decimal development, do not constitute an enumerable set [CAN 90]. It was a question of proving that not all real numbers can be listed in one sequence; X_1, X_2, X_n...for example, all those between 0 and 1. The matter is made by contradiction: one can write each X according to an infinite decimal expression; to avoid any double representation, we prohibit an expression where there would only be 9 from a certain rank. Let's build the real number $Y = 0, y_1y_2y_3...$ so that, for integer i, y_i is worth 1 if the x_{ii} of X_i is not equal to one and is worth two, otherwise; Y is a real number between 0 and 1, its writing respects the restriction on the 9. It is not equal to any of the numbers in the sequence of X numbers; although Y is, by construction, a real number between zero and one, it does not belong to the sequence of X numbers[32].

Georg Cantor is obviously quoted by Turing for his article in late 1891. But there was a geometrical way to obtain the same result that is still common in French presentations: it is Dedekind's method of included segments. It involves, with possible enumeration in X_i of $[0.1]$, choosing for each row i a segment I_i, that is not reduced to one point and included in I_{i-1} (with $I_0 = [0.1]$) such that X_i does not belong to I_i. The intersection of all these I_i is not empty. This is the geometrically visual rule of included segments; by design, any number in this intersection does not

---

32 This is called the diagonal process because we have chosen to work on the figures that make up the diagonal of table x_{ii}.

correspond to any point in the I_i sequence. In terms of geometric visualization, this elegant way does not have the calculating virtues of the other way, the diagonal process. There are two styles, but one is not suitable for what can be calculated.

One might think, by following the diagonal track indicated by Cantor, that all the calculable numbers are as rich as the real ones, so that they are countable. But Turing points out the error: "The error in this argument is due to the hypothesis made about the calculability of Y. The argument would be correct, if we could count the calculable sequences by finite means; but counting the calculable sequences is equivalent to finding the descriptive number of a machine without a cycle; we have no general means to do so in a finite number of steps. In fact, by correctly applying the diagonal procedure, we can show that such a procedure is impossible". Turing adds that the well-executed diagonal process demonstrates the impossibility of calculating an enumerable sequence that would take into account all the proceedings. The evidence, thus returned, provides the proof that incalculability exists. This style by contradiction, stemming from the set theory initiated by Cantor, caused a sensation more than a century ago. It established the existence of the incalculable, which seems incompatible with the very idea of calculation. Empiricists say that this is a pointless question that prevents action but, on the contrary, it must be deduced that it is necessary to control the impossibilities other than by calculation, without prohibiting what is incalculable.

The trick, or *métis* as they say in Greek, is a constant of mathematical culture. That is why this culture is learned by solving problems rather than applying recipes. And it must be used, even for big data: it is not because a problem is judged incalculable that it should be eliminated; we must hope to solve it differently than by means of calculable methods. In the same way that we classify irrationals into algebraic and transcendental irrationals, we can treat that which is incalculable, provided we admit that certain problems (which we would like to solve by a general algorithm) cannot be solved, not because of a lack of memory or an operative technique, but because they are ontologically so. That being said, I would like to point out that since these operations are inconceivable, there can be no automation to execute them, even on a machine of thought!

Incalculable problems are, in particular, due to the search for optimization. The concern is obviously economic because performance is an issue. The best performance is rarely available. It is already clear that the machine imposes compromises: the size of such an algorithm makes it impracticable. It is, therefore, necessary to adopt an alternative, and to trick with the architecture of the machine as much as with the available data. Indeed, since selective sorting algorithms have a cost in O (*NlogN*), instead of O (N²), it is necessary to partition the very large amounts of data, to carry out on these parts parallel calculations on a cluster (a grouping) of several hundreds or thousands of machines. Described in 2004 by engineers working for Google, this method of dividing the data into compartments before reassembling it, known as MapReduce, has the disadvantage of imposing a complex codification (in two distinct operations: Map and Reduce)[33]; it requires a good habit and expertise. It supports the complexity of parallelism, deals with possible breakdowns, etc. This is what the Hadoop framework does[34].

Mathematics, algorithms and measures of complexity

After this incursion into the architecture of systems, it is useful to see another trick valid only for integers, that which mathematicians using the algorithm of gcd have used in order to calculate with irrational numbers; and understand how they play their role. I'll start with a fairly well-known notion, the golden number. The terminology was coined in the 19th Century: in Euclid's time, it was said that the division into extreme and average reason which corresponds to that of a segment of length a, containing a segment of length b so that the ratio of *a* to *b* is equal to the ratio of *a* + *b* to *a*, or again: that the largest (*a* + *b)* is what the *a* is to the smallest (*b*). Posing a/b = x, we find that x is the positive root of the second-degree equation:

$$x^2 = x + 1$$

Add that the expression is indeed:

$$\frac{1+\sqrt{5}}{2} \ (= \phi \text{ according to an ancient usage})$$

which provides little more information, except being between 1 and 2, unless a numerical table is consulted and a certain number of decimal places are available, depending on the quality of the table consulted. The result can be improved by calculation procedures linked to the square root; if one has a certain mathematical culture, this comes back to generalizing the Euclidean division. We can also play on algebraic combinations that allow us to understand the intervention of what looks

---

33 Dean J., Ghemawat S., "Simplified Data Processing on Large Clusters", 2004, article online.
34 Refer to footnote 4 for references.

like an algorithm, but generalizes the notion seriously. Effectively, we have the equation as well:

$$x = 1 + \frac{1}{x}$$

which has the advantage of presenting x in both members. You can therefore repeat the operation and alternatively have[35]:

$$x = 1 + \cfrac{1}{1 + \cfrac{1}{x}}$$

or from:

$$x = 1 + \cfrac{1}{1 + \cfrac{1}{1 + \cfrac{1}{x}}}, \text{ etc.}$$

Making $x = 1$ in the members on the left, we can see that they alternately give below and above: 3/2, 5/3, 8/5, etc. The consistency immediately suggests a rule of calculation for these integers that manifests itself simply by adopting the indexed, symbolic writing, which visualizes and gives meaning to the very idea of steps that is part of the algorithm. Let's call it in:

$$x_n = \frac{f_{n+1}}{f_n}$$

the ratio of two integers is called from the outset an "approximation" of x. This has not yet been proven, but the purpose of this calculation is to do so. The following approximation is calculated by:

$$x_{n+1} = 1 + \frac{1}{x_n}$$

---

35 See above for a discussion of this continuous fraction process.

it'll take the form of:

$$\frac{f_{n+1} + f_n}{f_{n+1}}$$

and therefore:

$$f_{n+2} = f_{n+1} + f_n \tag{A}$$

This recurring formula where the first two terms can be used in f equals 1 (so also $f_0 = 1$) then gives 3, 5, 8, etc., is also well known as illustrating rabbit reproduction, a phenomenon of exponential growth. To be precise: under the assumption that a couple of rabbits reproduce by giving another couple each month. It is not known how this relationship (A) really came into play in history, but it was attested by Fibonacci in the 13th Century and comes from earlier Arab and Indian sources. The link with successive approximations of the square root of 5, or rather the golden number, which is not given by Fibonacci, appears as evidence of sort by Kepler at the beginning of the 17th Century and in some other authors. They seem to know another recurring relationship between the numbers in the sequence. For example:

$$f_n^2 + f_n f_{n+1} - f_{n+1}^2 = (-1)^{n+1} \tag{B}$$

From these relations (B) and (A), we deduce a third relation (C), which proves (this is Bézout's identity) that two successive numbers of type f are relative primes, so that the approximation of x by the quotients of integers $x_n = \dfrac{f_{n+1}}{f_n}$ is an irreducible fraction:

$$f_n f_{n+2} - f_{n+1}^2 = (-1)^{n+1} \tag{C}$$

A little linear algebra, the b.a.-ba of mathematics, makes it possible to give an explicit expression to each row n of f_n, making use of the n-th power of the golden number and thus showing that the quotient:

$$x_n = \frac{f_{n+1}}{f_n}$$

has a limit which is precisely the golden number that legitimizes the approximate designation.

If the simplicity of calculating the golden number from Fibonacci's recurring relation and the quality of the result is appreciated, one notices once again that the spatialization of the writing (the continuous fraction) and the play of the algebra, which are not related to the algorithm itself, allows it to be seen in a much more efficient way. That's what doing mathematics in algorithmic form is. This partially leads, in theoretical computing, to an intrinsic study of the complexity of an algorithmic problem[36] which depends primarily on the means of calculation; and, if necessary, to invent alternative solutions. This brings us to the distant example of what was done with the golden number.

Representations of communities and massive data

I am no longer talking about the Turing machine, but about actual machines whose memory is measured in terabytes, where the computers available in the 1980s only offered a hundred kilobits. This does not change the horizon of what can be calculated, but radically changes the data itself. The gain of memory is certainly unequalled in human history: 10 to the power of six, over about 30 years. This places us in an unexpected situation: we have more resources at our disposal than effective proposals for the use of these resources! Hence the inflation of perspectives ranging from the functioning of the brain (e.g. a possible cure of Alzheimer's disease) to the prediction of climate and its changes, depending on whether human behavior is virtuous or rational according to classical economic theory, or even thoughtless!

It's all there: ecological risk management, security, crime prevention, and so on. Any idea of calculability seems to have been forgotten because the tendency is to consider that the decision of an industrialist, manager or policymaker would be determined by suitably chosen and processed massive data. However, in the cases mentioned above, as for many other subjects, the question is not where and how to collect the data, because the data is simply not available in most cases, even if it is considered as an emanation of reality.

If specialists recognize the inflation of digitized data, they give it the surprising name "universe" and talk about distinguishing communities, cliques, etc. within the data. Something specific appears: massive data bends well to a pictorial representation that is in line with our old habit of thinking geometrically, logically or spatially. The image creates an obviously expected impression of reality, that we integrate with a glance. The use of the term real, ordinary for numbers, is an old habit, but it is not innocent: it hides mathematization. In concrete terms, Figure 2.2

---

36 [ARO 09].

is really a performance. It emanates from an algorithm, that of Louvain, which is not optimal and does not seek to be so: this algorithm, described below, produces a symbolic map[37] [CAM 14]. Figure 2.2 could be a metro map. The multiple points, distinguished in part by their color, clearly show three communities and segments that link some points to others. In our eyes, a community hierarchy is revealed, while the underlying data is digital; for example, links symbolize communication between subscribers of the telephone network, without the arrangement of colored dots being geographically significant. The act of representing communications by segments of straight lines between points is familiar, accentuated by the trick of bringing together certain points that make up the mass, of spatially separating these groupings when the links they maintain are particular. This graph, that represents communities, is based on reality, but the organization of the image is conventional: it is entirely calculated.

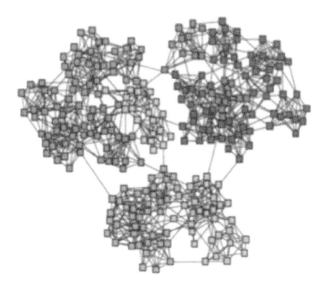

Figure 2.2. *Graph extracted from [BLO 08]. For a color version of the figure, see www.iste.co.uk/chamoux/digital1.zip*

For observing the numerous galaxies in the sky, astronomers use photographs (Figure 2.3, worked out according to the frequencies and radiations used): it is also calculated visually, such as the symbolic representation of the telephone network in Figure 2.2.

---

37 For the original method, see [BLO 08].

Figure 2.3. *Visualization of a galaxy (UGC 1382), according to three views: standard visual spectrum on the left (the elliptical type galaxy, according to Hubble's classification); ultra-violet rays in the center (the galaxy is spiral and this can only be observed by being positioned outside the Earth); and by the radiation of hydrogen gas with low density on the right, which makes it appear gigantic and one of the biggest ever observed. Astronomers then deduced, according to these different images, that this huge galaxy was of the Frankenstein kind, to emphasize its monstrous appearance (NASA/JPL/Caltech/SDSS/NRAO/L. Hagen and M. Seibert). For a color version of the figure, see www.iste.co.uk/chamoux/digital1.zip*

Figure 2.3 also originates from digital data: the photographs translate, according to a precise power of resolution, the photons received by the recording device. The algorithm transcribes them in pixels; it places luminous points in a two-dimensional space (the image), without integrating the distance between these points and performs a conical projection (a perspective). The processing erases everything beyond the galaxy, in relation to us. The algorithm works like our eye: it eliminates what is not in the studied galaxy. It is not an image of reality, but a projected image. Representation here is algorithmic computation's challenge.

Figure 2.4. is a projected map of Mercator. It is not geographical, since the countries are not represented at their usual size, but the area is in proportion to a single value of digital data: the population of each country. The image illustrates distorted digital data without unduly disrupting the geography of the world, particularly preserving the topological relations between the countries represented on this plane. Thus, the vicinity of Canada and the United States is respected, even though Canada is reduced to a single band! Similarly, China remains a neighbor of Russia, although this map causes it to completely cut off its neighbor.

Figures 2.2 to 2.4 are not only the result of big data processing. The first (links between telephone sets) does not need to be geo-located; the links transcribe traffic data and relationships[38]. According to a precise algorithm (whose value is to be efficient), it is possible to both identify communities and arrange them to underline and analyze their links. These calculations are carried out and represented in a mathematical theory (graph theory), developed especially after the Second World War, which has been extraordinarily diffused among computer scientists. The essential intervention of probabilities in this theory is discussed below.

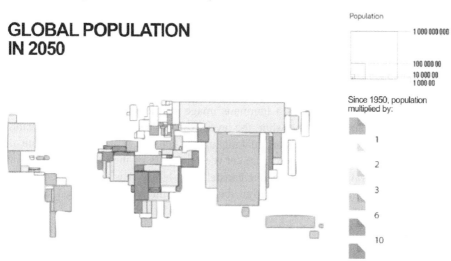

Population

**GLOBAL POPULATION
IN 2050**

1 000 000 000

100 000 00
10 000 00
1 000 00

Since 1950, population
multiplied by:

1

2

3

6

10

Figure 2.4. *Map of the world carried out by anamorphosis, respecting in bulk the geography of countries, in proportion to the population. For a color version of the figure, see www.iste.co.uk/chamoux/digital1.zip*

Figure 2.4 plays with our familiarity with the map of the world. It allows us to understand the distortions introduced by the parameter chosen to compare countries (here, the size of their population), but respects geographical balances: China does not neighbor Mexico! This map only makes sense by comparing it with the usual, implicitly underlying map; the deformations speak for themselves, but the topological relations of the vicinity are left invariant.

---

38 Editor's Note: it has always been observed that telephone subscribers concentrate their calls on a relatively small number of correspondents; the arcs of this graph highlight these privileged relations. A large network is therefore not traversed by a homogeneous flow of calls distributed more or less randomly, but by flows that translate particular social relations, here and now; this is revealed, among other things, in Figure 2.2.

There is no geography underlying the image of communities; the astronomer's visual habit is respected in the images of the sky, given our observation capabilities and telescopes that provide terabytes of data that have to be classified and interpreted as massive data[39]. The representation of communities is a convention without perspective, non-visual, but visualized. It is in fact analogous to the ancient tradition of representation of constellations, zoological forms and geometrical figures such as the Big Dipper, which does not take into account the distance between the stars and our Earth. It is this habit that only makes sense to us, the inhabitants of planet Earth; it allows us to situate ourselves in the system of stars with the naked eye. An astronomer, with telescopic means, computerized by a large amount of data, does not need to recreate the space of the galaxy; he sees it under the convention of projection. It has much more data in infrared radiation, X-rays and visible light that our eye perceives. The astronomer has therefore not abandoned his "natural" use of big data, at least with the representation he gives of it. In Figure 2.3, it can be said that he makes a luminous image supplemented by data from other radiations; it imposes only what the eye expects, namely a three-dimensional geometric shape of all the stars making up the galaxy. It would complicate the algorithmic resources to create links between the stars of the galaxy he is dealing with and situating according to our constellation habits. His only convention has been to erase what separates us from this galaxy: the stars that are on the visual trajectory (of the telescope), the clouds of dust and the radiation that comes from beyond the galaxy. It erases ancestral habits of tracking in the sky.

Constraints of mathematization

As soon as its usefulness is recognized or understood, a mathematical conquest is constrained, whether in physics, economics, or biology. Physical, economic or biological concepts take on a new dimension under the pressure of mathematics, which expresses them and sometimes modifies their meaning. For example, when it became clear that directed quantities such as velocities, which we call vectors since the 19th Century, were composed according to parallelograms (the diagonal gives the addition of two sides from the same summit), the idea that force is a vector was inevitable; the representation of force no longer depends on the will of the physicist:

---

39 A mathematician will say that the conical projection has invariants such as the bi-ratio of any four angular directions of these points to our observation point, the recording device. I discuss bi-ratio, conical projection, a mathematical invariant and its role in image making later on (Figure 2.8).

it is determined. Figure 2.5 shows this[40]. Vectors are not only a useful generalization, but the almost ontological acknowledgment that mechanics is governed by vectors. In other words: mechanics is not an application of mathematics, but a reduction from physics of the idea of the vector. Mathematics, for example, has accustomed mechanics to no longer feel bound by the vertical alone. The introduction of vectors in mechanics is still not accepted in some teachings. And mechanics no longer play any role in the teachings of mathematicians who've established the theory of vectors, which they call linear algebra.

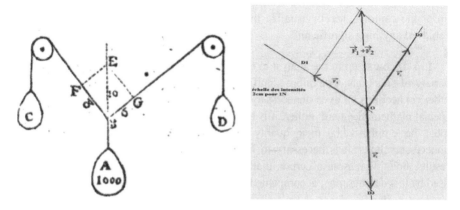

Figure 2.5. *Two examples of force composition: on the left, from a mathematician of the 16th Century, which is a first; on the right, from a physics teacher of the 20th Century, drawing in vectors. For a color version of the figure, see www.iste.co.uk/chamoux/digital1.zip*

Exploiting existing data

Mathematical constraints relate to three aspects: one is obviously the algorithm and how it is installed in the machine that is calculating; the other is the way the results are presented, by maps or images; and the last is the input of data available for processing. Yet, coercion does not always play a role. Thus, the national statistics made by INSEE are an immense source of "data", compiled from the files of investigative teams. However, a book entitled *The Social Anatomy of France* [LE 16] asks the question: what does Big Data say about us? Now that is a question.

---

40 Roberval's figurative experience with his weights and pulleys did not fully prove that forces are vectors since the over-represented vertical is not a geometric notion, but a physical one (see next section).

After estimating the variety of fertility among women and concluding that the criterion determining this fertility was the professional activity of mothers, he questions the consequence of this common sense. Because, thanks to the massive data collected by the general statistical survey for which there was no new work perform, it was possible to cross-reference the fertility of women with other criteria: their social class, their education, etc. This reveals other logic and is enriched by new distinctions: affiliation to rural cantons, for example. The analyst then goes down to the geography of the French departments and observes that fertility varies greatly among the group of working women born in France; this variation does not affect immigrants and inactive women in the same way. Departmental maps, drawn up at the cantonal level, visualize things. A question then arises: have we really achieved anything significant?

It is of course up to the analyst to think about the parameters that can illustrate the variety of situations; to explore significant crossovers, to measure the uselessness of other connections, or even unnecessary crossovers. In my opinion, there is no need for special mathematics here; rather, it is better to stimulate the researcher's sense (which must be emphasized), their quality in valuing data, their capacity to exclude unnecessary links. It is necessary to find meaningful iconographic means to present results. For this reason, a certain mathematical culture is useful: I use some graphs used by this demography, accompanied by essential explanations.

Some people do not want to admit that there is anything that affects big data in these because there is no invention involved in its exploitation [LEM 16]. It is true that INSEE data was expensive to collect, whereas Big Data cost almost nothing[41]. This ecologically-natured argument, which would undoubtedly seduce Pierre Bourdieu, allows us to create a scientific field among others, by putting epistemological barriers at its entrance [BOU 01]. These barriers would be based on the expertise of a group of experts, whose training should be tri-disciplinary: mathematics on the one side and expertise in complex software and an "understanding of the company's business and strategic stakes" on the other. The third discipline (Business/Strategy acumen) is of interest to authors: doesn't it ensure that data scientists, whose names would only take off with an article in the *Harvard Business Review* from October 2012, will become as indispensable as Wall Street financial analysts from the 1980s?

---

41 Editor's Note: access to INSEE census data and other public data is a widely debated issue [BOU 13]; the data collected on commercial sites by operators over the top are indeed very voluminous, but they are not free of charge. See in particular Volume 2, Chapter 3.

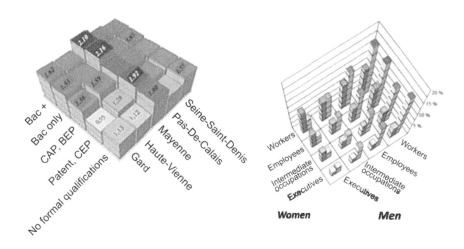

Figure 2.6. *The representation on the left shows, for some French departments indicated on the oblique axis on the right, the average number of children according to the education level identified on the oblique axis on the left. The representation on the right shows the unemployment rate of men and women on two adjacent piles, according to the social category of men and women, on a system of axes analogous to the representation on the right, but with a graduation of the vertical axis [LE 16, pp. 138, 176]. For a color version of the figure, see www.iste.co.uk/chamoux/digital1.zip*

The example of Hervé Le Bras gave rise to an initial response by questioning the relevance of certain configurations. Some authors already cited also speak of a particular quality they attribute to massive data: those data are not "structured". They describe the use of probabilities in these terms: "One of the differences between a statistician and a modern data scientist is that the latter gives less importance to the 'statistical purity' of an indicator or algorithm, than to its 'business utility'" [LAM 16, p. 75]. This notion of purity finds fault, as old as the mathematics described in ancient Greece, attributed to mathematical reasoning (abstract, that is to say cut off from reality). A cultural constant, the "fear of mathematics", has been mentioned above: would we only like to keep the applied aspect of mathematics? It would be an error of a similar nature to that which caused Galileo's invention to be considered a mistake in the 17th Century, the movement of the Earth having no implication for the behavior of earthly events!

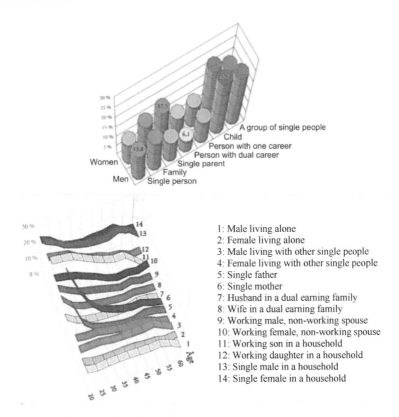

Figure 2.7. *The top representation uses a system similar to the two previous ones, that of the unemployment rate according to sex (identified on the left axis for 2011) and the family situation identified on the right axis. The bottom representation is singularly different: if, like the previous ones, it crosses three different sets of data, their variety forces the establishment of ribbon surfaces. It gives the unemployment rate by sex, family status and age in 2011. Numbers and a copious legend are needed to identify these situations, while numbering by age brackets does not cause any difficulty on the other oblique axis [LE 16]. For a color version of the figure, see www.iste.co.uk/chamoux/digital1.zip*

The notion of the invariant: perspective, vectorial, linear algebra and matrix representation

On the right in Figure 2.8, the conical projection is flat, starting from four coplanar lines. If we make the quotient CA/CB per DA/DB, A, B, C, and D being four points on the same line, we can show that the actual number obtained remains the same if we take the same quotient with projections A', B', C' and D'. This is called invariance from the conical projection of the bi-ratio (also known as the anharmonic ratio). A quantity is available, a number that remains constant when making a conical projection on a figured configuration. This invariance underlies the idea of projective geometry. A visual experience makes the meaning of this geometry understandable. If the two planes in space, represented by two parallelograms in black in the figure on the left, are not sketched, one has a property of plane geometry according to which when the homologous sides of two triangles intersect on the same straight line, the three lines joining the homologous vertices are concurrent. This property is visually evident when drawing the planes and point 0, at the center of the conical projection in space. The double interpretation, plane and space, suggests that there is a single projective geometry. It could also be said to be analytic, because there is indeed a calculation at stake (we can see it in the bi-ratio); but on the one hand the qualification is already taken by the invention of Descartes and, on the other hand, this projective geometry treats concurrent lines and parallel lines in the same way as if point 0 were infinitely present, something that analytical geometry does quite differently with asymptotical curves.

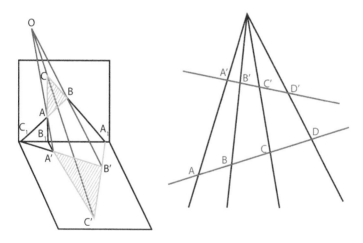

Figure 2.8. *Left: conical projection of a triangle, a plane on another plane. Right: two straight intersections with four other coplanar lines. For a color version of the figure, see www.iste.co.uk/chamoux/digital1.zip*

This ductility of mathematics to realize figurative situations is very general; it can be used to avoid being satisfied with too simple ideas, by associating geometric data with numbers. Therefore, it is common to say that the data of two numbers (its coordinates) is enough to make a vector in a plane. I represented Figure 2.5 as a common experiment with pulleys and weights (it dates back to Roberval in the 17th Century), so that we understand that the equilibrium achieved by force (formed as vectors) requires it to be more than a dipole of numbers. Figure 2.5 on the right shows that vector addition is a geometric operation according to the diagonal of a parallelogram. The sum of two vectors V and V', each represented by a doublet, (x, y) and (x', y') is indeed the resulting vector represented by the doublet $(x + x', y + y')$. This property applies to any two-axis marking, not just the vertical and horizontal markings that ordinary physics adopts with sound judgement. The vector is a geometrical being; the characteristic doubling of its coordinates (in the case of plane vectors) follows precise rules when changing its reference. To put it another way: if we rotate around the origin of the plane, followed by a homothety, this corresponds not only to a change of reference frame, but also to a change in the unit of length; the analytical geometry makes it possible to calculate that vector V is transformed into vector $S(V)$, so that the new coordinates (x', y'), functions of the x and y coordinates of V, will be:

$$x' = ax + by \qquad y' = cx + dy$$

where a, b, c and d are real constants which depend on the angle of rotation and ratio of the homothety. The resulting shape gives that of a linear transformation, when the four constants can then be any of the said four constants. In the second third of the 19th Century, it became customary to represent such a linear transformation by means of a chart, or "matrix". Of course, when you change the reference frame, that is to say the x and y coordinates, the matrix representing the linear transformation also changes. In the same way as vectors, the four new expressions of a', b', c' and d' can be written explicitly from $a, b, c,$ and d.

The important thing is that there remains something of the linear transformation S on the new matrix. This is what is given by the notion of invariant. Therefore, are the roots of x of the characteristic polynomial $(a-x)(d-x)-bc$ the same, if we give primes to the four letters $a, b, c,$ and d? The reason for this is simple: a geometric property, invariant by way of a change of reference, is at stake: the possible x gives a non-zero vector V such that $S(V) = xV$. It is the proper vector of transformation.

Everything I have just outlined can be transposed to a vector space (a space composed of vectors) of finite dimension, beyond the two dimensions of the plane that served as my base. So that a matrix, a table of n^2 numbers arranged in rows and columns, can represent a linear transformation at a certain reference point; there will also be invariants, including the characteristic polynomial. We will then write an order matrix n as (a_{ij}), integers i and j running from 1 to n. The mathematical discipline created in this respect is linear algebra.

To those who doubt its benefit, it suffices to say that it is possible to settle the question of the recurring relation (relation A) at once. Just consider as an object an infinite sequence $X = (x_1, x_2,...x_n,...)$ where the indexed x's are real numbers, and consider the vectorial space E of the X sequences which satisfy this relation (A). Considering that the determination of a sequence X satisfying this recurrence depends only on the knowledge of the first two terms, we can see that the vector space E is dimension 2. It is also obvious that if we are looking for a sequence X of the form xn, x must satisfy the polynomial $x^2 = x + 1$. Things could be presented to make the sequences appear as the proper vectors of a linear transformation and the preceding polynomial as the characteristic polynomial of a 2×2 matrix. In short: x is either the golden number contemplated above, or the opposite of its inverse. Since the two sequences of the n-th power of these two numbers are independent, they form a base for the vector space E; an explicit expression of the Fibonacci sequence is therefore automatically available. This does not mean that the mathematical work on the algorithm would be finished because, for example, relations refered to above as (C) and (B) are still to be considered.

Graphs, their calculations and some algorithms

For this last example, as a sort of synthesis of what has just been said, I'm going to open directly from a typical situation for big data; for example, one where telephone numbers and connections from one number to another are available. We can see that with a small set of numbers, we can have representations as distinct as the five shown in Figure 2.9. These are graphs: the dots (or nodes) represent telephone numbers; and the lines, known as edges, are the links. The first four are called the homogeneous graph, hierarchical graph, cyclic graph and centralized graph. And we will acknowledge the last graph as an amourphous graph.

Similarly, a graph can be broken down into sub-units (or poles) as shown in Figure 2.10: three poles, two of which can be considered, independent of the rest, as centralized graphs.

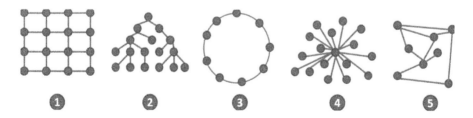

Figure 2.9. *Five types of graphs containing knots (blue dots) and edges (in red). For a color version of the figure, see www.iste.co.uk/chamoux/digital1.zip*

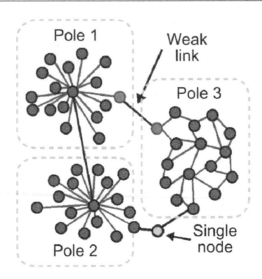

Figure 2.10. *Graph broken down into three poles. For a color version of the figure, see www.iste.co.uk/chamoux/digital1.zip*

We can guess that if there are billions of units of data, we can have all kinds of situations, but also possible subdivisions. The notion of an amorphous situation, vaguely shown in Figure 2.9's graph 5, can take on a precise probabilistic meaning when there is a very large amount of data. This would precisely be the normal situation of a random graph, that of the normal distribution of random values of independent events around the average. As a result, we can use this concept that I've only been outlining to calculate whether it is possible to find communities in a graph. Figure 2.2 is obviously expressive: this representation results from the Louvain algorithm that I will conclude with. But this does not in any way exhaust the questions posed by the mathematical theory of graphs, namely: do cycles exist in a graph? How about Eulerian paths (thought from the problem of the seven bridges of Königsberg, that ordinary mathematical culture presents most often)?

The implementation of the Louvain algorithm requires the consideration of the matrix (a_{ij}), composed of only 0 and 1, taking the value 1 only if there is a link between Pi (that is to say on my example the i-th telephone number) and P_j. This digital matrix obviously depends on the numbering assigned to the different telephone numbers, in order to remain in the example chosen for this graph. But if you exchange two points i and j, you only exchange the two corresponding columns of the matrix. From the vectorial or linear algebra point of view, the intrinsic properties of the corresponding linear transformation remain unchanged. It is therefore possible to work with such a matrix when graph properties are involved.

That is a first point. A second is to know how to measure the size of a community, that is to say to establish a coefficient between -1 and +1, the ratio between the relative density of the edges (characteristics of the graph) within a community and the edges outside that community. It is then necessary to know these communities, and by calling Ci the one to which Pi belongs, one introduces something more than usual graph theory: to give the edge a weight proportional to the number of telephone calls made between the two extremities of the edge and to introduce this number (the weight of the edge) into the coefficients of the matrix (a_{ij}) to obtain A_{ij}. Lastly, we call k_i the sum of the weights of the edges linked to the point P_i, and since it is a question of relative density, we use m, sum of the weights of all the edges of the graph. We then define the modularity by an algebraic expression, the last term in δ taking only two values, 0 and 1, depending on whether i is different from j, or i is equal to j:

$$Q = \frac{1}{2m} \sum_{i,j} \left[a_{ij} - \frac{k_i k_j}{2m} \right] \delta(c_i, c_j)$$

Communities needing to be addressed are to be determined, whereas modularity depends on them. As a result, we proceed heuristically by first asking small communities, then calculating (a sort of differential on whole numbers) that which is brought to modularity with the changing placement of P_i to the community of each of P_i's neighbors. P_i is therefore placed in the community that causes the greatest increase in modularity; otherwise, it is kept in its original community. When this is done, a new graph represents the new communities that are considered as points. Except that the edges going from one point to itself must be used: these are the loops in the graph. The edges of each community must be grouped together, which means that the weight of each community must be better defined. The optimization of the modularity can be repeated on the new graph. Inventors are happy to say that a laptop (PC) takes two minutes to process a network of two million nodes and three hours for graphs of more than a billion peaks and edges!

Optimizing *a priori* the modularity of a community partition of a graph (i.e. a network) is considered an NP-difficult problem, according to the terminology introduced above. The Louvain method does not solve this difficulty and does not calculate the complexity of the algorithm at stake, since it only plays the know-how role by, for example, choosing small communities to start the optimization algorithm. There is, however, a presumption that its cost is expected to be almost linear: O *(NlogN)* as the usual sorting algorithm. The heuristic way of calculating does not favor large communities and can even result in good quality partitions... in graphs that do not have a community. However, we have seen earlier that the search for small, exceptional communities can be the subject of research. This was, of course, the primary object of intelligence services on terrorism. For the Leuven method, improvements that involve not only size, but also "quality", are sought; the reliability of the method is taken into account. This state of research must be reported, especially since the algorithm is available to everyone. So, we are absolutely not in the setting of Big Science, nor are we in context of military research on the atomic bomb.

Conclusion

The reason I started by referring to Turing's machine is that big data practitioners seem to be more and more in favor of a return to Turing's origins and thinking, preceding that of von Neumann. It is nevertheless frightening because it would be too focused on mathematics. The fear of mathematics is in fact due to the fear of the artifact, which would only be a metaphysical rigor. I wanted to show concretely that a learning of linear algebra, which would amount to matrix computation, would immediately omit the analogical game which also intervenes in mathematics. It allows precisely for what is *a priori* only a numerical matrix for graphs, to think in terms of linear transformation, eigenvector, etc.; so, to envisage that a notion of distance carried by this matrix (the modularity of the Louvain algorithm) intervenes, without magical effect, to correctly estimate the communities, as we have just seen in the previous section (with telephone networks) which was the aim of this presentation. It is also rightly true to say that, like any mathematization, this implies constraints. They may well be misidentified if we do not dominate what we put mathematically. This recognition is the fruit of what I call a mathematical culture. Obviously, treating a vector only by its coordinates, forgetting its behavior in changes of reference, or considering that these changes are a simple computational technique, is to avoid understanding the contribution of linear algebra to mechanics, since this science gives a vectorial definition of its fundamental concepts such as strength, speed, etc.

This example completely renews the question by which I began: checking whether machine processing of big data would play a role analogous to the one linear algebra assumed for mechanics, a linguistic foundation without which nothing would be possible. I didn't answer such a question head-on; I preferred raising different styles, including the one resulting from the set theory of the Turing machine, but also the approximation of algorithms of continuous fractions, emphasizing as much writing problems (that the electronic machines of course find) as the calculation of frames or statistical estimation; the mass of massive data is not a mass of information. Like inventors, I used the word "heuristic" for Louvain's algorithm.

From a mathematical understanding point of view, nothing is gained by making a distinction of principle between, on the one hand, calculation, meaning the automatic work on data that can be called algorithms, and, on the other hand, the storage of data, the making of this data for availability to the machine, without forgetting the image formatting of results. It is the historical specificity of massive data that has been recognized, and that it is most often latent, in one form or another. We are talking about web mining, text mining, image mining. It is a question of inventing, on the basis of what has already been collected, mathematical organizations that can produce results; but also of recognizing what hope is not justified. There is always a cost to be paid and approximations to be made (maybe it would be better to say: compromises to be made!). Of course, massive data is affected by its origin (accumulation by intelligence services) and the questioning caused by the accumulation itself. Indeed, since some algorithms can be effective, we must not neglect the alerts issued in 2013 by E. Snowden and simply think that crushing data will suffice[42]. A good mathematical literacy is necessary to understand these types of invention; that is what I tried to suggest. This culture also makes it possible to judge claims of obtaining miraculous results as inadequate, without any work.

Perhaps the old word used in ancient techniques should be used: the processing of massive data is an art from which one component, and only one component, highlights mathematics; inventive and varied mathematics, as we have seen. I have insisted on the representation of images which, governed by algorithms, are nonetheless linked to our aesthetic sense and can therefore allow various choices (see Figure 2.11). One can smile at the propagandistic title of an article published in November 2016, but at least the term 'visualization' sounds accurate [BOL 16].

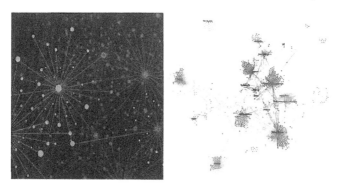

Figure 2.11. *Decomposed cloud graphs of illustrative points. For a color version of the figure, see www.iste.co.uk/chamoux/digital1.zip*

---

42 Regarding this, see Chapter 3 of this volume; and the chapters on "Raison d'Etat" in Volume 3.

Bibliography

[ARO 09] ARORA S., BOAZ B., *Computational Complexity: a Modern Approach*, Cambridge University Press, Cambridge, 2009.

[BAC 38] BACHELARD G., *La formation de l'esprit scientifique. Contribution à une psychanalyse de la connaissance*, Vrin, Paris, 1938.

[BAC 49] BACHELARD G., *Le rationalisme appliqué*, PUF, Paris, 1949.

[BLO 08] BLONDEL V.D., GUILLAUME J.-L., LAMBIOTT R. *et al.*, "Fast unfolding of communities in large networks", *Journal of Statistical Mechanics: Theory and Experiment*, no. 10, 2008.

[BOL 16] BOLA R.I., RAHUL C.B., "Visualization to Understand Ecosystems. Mapping Relationship between stakeholders in an ecosystem to increase understanding and make better-informed strategic decisions", *Communications of the ACM*, vol. 59, no. 11, November 2016.

[BOU 01] BOURDIEU P., *Science de la science et réflexivité: cours du Collège de France*, Raisons d'agir, Paris, 2001.

[BRE 92] BREZINSKI C., *History of Continued Fractions and Padé Approximants*, Springer Verlag, Berlin, 1992.

[CAM 14] CAMPIGOTTO P., CONDE-CESPEDES P., GUILLAUME J-L., "La méthode de Louvain générique: un algorithme adaptatif pour la détection de communautés sur de très grands graphes", *15th Congrès SFRO*, Bordeaux, 2014.

[CAN 90] CANTOR G., "Über eine elementare Frage der Mannigfaltigkeitslehre", *Jahresbericht der deutschen Vereinigung*, I, pp. 75–78, 1890–91.

[COH 13] COHEN-TANNOUDJI G., SPIRO M., *Le boson et le chapeau mexicain*, Gallimard, Paris, 2013.

[COM 07] COMTE A., *Premiers cours de philosophie positive*, Quadrige PUF, Paris, 2007.

[CRO 94] CROMBIE A., *Styles of Scientific Thinking in the European Tradition*, Duckworth, London, 1994.

[GIR 95] GIRARD J.Y., *La machine de Turing*, Editions du Seuil, Paris, 1995.

[GOL 72] GOLDSTINE H., *The Computer from Pascal to Von Neumann*, Princeton University Press, Princeton, 1972.

[GOL 77] GOLDSTINE H., *A History of Numerical Analysis from the 16th through the 19th Century*, Springer Verlag, Berlin, 1977.

[HEN 34] HENRION D., *Cours mathématique, Cursus mathematicus*, vol. 1, Paris, 1634.

[KNU 11] KNUTH D., *The Art of Computer Programming*, Addison Wesley, Reading, 2011.

[LE 16] LE BRAS H., *Anatomie sociale de la France. Ce que des Big Data disent de nous*, Robert Laffont, Paris, 2016.

[LEM 16] LEMBERGE B., MOREL R., *Big Data and Machine Learning*, Dunod, Paris, 2016.

[LÉV 15] LÉVY-LEBLOND J.M. (ed.), *Lettres à Turing*, Edition Thierry Marchaisse, Paris, 2015.

[MAH 11] MAHONEY MICHAEL S., *Histories of Computing(s)*, Thomas Haigh, Harvard University Press, Cambridge, 2011.

[MOH 15] MOHANTY H., BHUYAN P., CHENTHATI D. (eds), *Big Data. Primer*, Springer, New Delhi, 2015.

[WUY 01] WUYTACH L., BREZINSKI C., *Numerical Analysis: Historical Development in the 20th Century*, Elsevier, Amsterdam, 2001.

From Sample to Big Data: Competing or Complementary Paradigms?

The 20th Century was characterized by sampling and surveys. Thanks to massive data, the 21st Century is returning to the exhaustivity that was the normal paradigm of scientific observation until the end of the 19th Century; the massive collection and processing of data has increased our objective knowledge of contemporary society. This is favorable to telecommunications operators, useful to the media and prepares us for the revolution of the Internet of Things (IoT) that will impact health, homes, vehicles, finance and insurance, clothing, etc. Big Data will undoubtedly be a factor of growth and new jobs. Major scientific developments are linked to the massive processing of data and the algorithms that allow them to be exploited.

This chapter addresses three questions. The first examines the methods by which data can be exploited: sampling and exhaustive observation are sometimes comprehensive and can even be combined. The second question is circumstantial: is big data a trend or will it last? The third question is about the personal data of those whose habits and behaviors are massively analyzed through the traces they leave online: can they trust the intrusive practices that have already been trivialized by search engines, commercial websites and large public systems such as social security, health and education? Can we still ensure a certain discretion regarding personal data in this era of the Internet and social networks, and how[1]?

Chapter written by Philippe TASSI.

1 This chapter is derived from the lecture given by the author at the close of the ECAIS Big Data Day in November 2014 at the IUT in Paris. We thank the author and organizers of this scientific day for their support.

Sampling and big data: useful synergy

From the first Sumerian tablets of the country of Sumer to the end of the 19th Century, the world can be considered to have lived under the almost exclusive reign of exhaustivity. In the mid-18th Century, there were some approaches to sampling: with John Graunt and William Petty's school of political arithmetic in England and with the advances of Sébastien Le Prestre de Vauban and Jean-Baptiste Colbert in France[2]. However, these innovative attempts were not generalized. The standard remained as an exhaustive vision; the most statistically[3] developed countries were already managing censuses of population, companies, industrial establishments and agricultural land.

From the sample...

The 20th Century was marked by a slow decline in exhaustivity and the increasingly assertive rise of the sampling paradigm. The founding act can be considered to be the communication from Anders N. Kiaer, Founding Director of the Central Bureau of Statistics in Norway, at the Bern Congress of the International Statistical Institute in August 1895[4]. Entitled "Observations and Experiences of Representative Enumerations", it opens with an initial and long debate on sampling, biting the bullet: *pars pro toto*. At the most general level, the first four lines of the introduction to the presentation, which are pertinent and visionary, should be particularly appreciated:

> "At different times during the evolution of science, certain ideas have prevailed to such an extent that they have obscured other ideas, which were of too great importance but were hardly emphasized, either because they had not yet broken through or because no one was paying attention to them" [KIA 95].

Following this presentation and its subsequent communications, not very well received by the scientific world at the time, and then at other interventions taking up these ideas in a theoretical and experimental way, the IIS created a commission in May 1924 to study the validity of these representative techniques. It was presided

---

2 In 1686, Vauban published a book entitled *Easy and General Method for Doing the Census*. For a historical view, see [DRO 90].

3 "Statistics" comes from the Latin word status, one of the meanings of which is "attitude, posture, position, state" but also has a broader meaning of "government, state".

4 IIS: International Statistical Institute [IIS, 1985].

over by the famous Adolph Jensen, author of the well-known eponymous inequality and included celebrities such as Corrado Gini, Arthur Bowley and Lucien March. The works of this commission would confirm the scientific value of the approach. Anders Kiaer, who died in 1919, was no longer present when Jensen derived two submissions at the IIS biennial congress in 1925: "Report on the Representative Method in Statistics" and "The Representative Method in Practice"; these conclusions were published in the Bulletin of the International Institute of Statistics [JEN 25]. In a few words, Kiaer's representative approach was validated. The development was then rapid: in 1934, the reference paper on survey theory was published [NEY 34]. A rather rare occurrence in the scientific field at the time, this work quickly found its way into operational applications.

In economics, following J-M. Keynes' articles in the early 1930s, the first consumer and distributor panels started appearing in France in 1935, operated by companies such as Nielsen in the United States, GfK in Germany[5] and later Cecodis, the Centre for Consumer and Distribution Studies in France; still in 1935 in the United States, George Gallup launched his company, the American Institute for Public Opinion, and made himself known to the general public by predicting, with the help of a sample of voters, Franklin D. Roosevelt's victory over Andrew Landon in the 1936 presidential election. Jean Stoetzel created the French equivalent in 1937, the French Institute of Public Opinion (*Institut Français d'opinion publique*, in short: IFOP), France's leading opinion research company.

After the war, sampling became the benchmark in terms of speed of operation and reduction of poll costs, in the context of strong progress in probability, statistics and information technology, in addition to the generalization of fields of application in economics, official statistics, health, marketing, sociology, media coverage, political science, etc[6].

...to Big Data

Therefore, most of the 20th Century has statistically lived under the sampling paradigm; the exhaustive censuses have retreated. Whereas in the 1960s, in terms of official statistics, there were still: the demographic census, the agricultural census and the industrial census, observational systems which no longer exist today! Since the late 20th Century and the beginning of the 21st Century, digital convergence has

---

5 The German company GfK was founded by economics professors from the University of Nuremberg.
6 For more information, see [DRO 90].

favored the automatic collection of observed data on increasingly large populations, creating databases with a growing mass of information and thus heralding the graceful return to exhaustivity. In addition, the switchover to digital technology has made it possible to put historically distinct and heterogeneous information in the same form, such as quantitative data files, texts, sounds (audio), still images and moving images (video), which is as fundamental a revolution as if human beings all started speaking the same language! This is what is now called Big Data (also called massive data or metadata), a name recommended since August 2014 by the National Terminology Commission[7]. On a serious note, Big Data has two major parameters that help define its volume: quantity and frequency of acquisition. You can write it:

Volume (of data) = *Quantity* (of data) × *Frequency* (of its collection)

The quantity can be collected until exhausted; and the frequency up to real time. We also usually associate terms in V to Big Data, in chronological order, 3V first; then 6V. The three primitive 3V's are volume, variety and velocity:

– *volume*, for the quantity of data exchanged (collection, storage and processing);

– *variety*, for the diversity of formats (text, audio, image, video), sources (sites, social networks, telephones, Radio Frequency Identification (RFID), Global Positioning System (GPS), etc.), and origins (internal, structured, external, unstructured data);

– and lastly, *velocity* for data collection and processing, more or less in real time.

Three other V terms have been recently added, inspired more by marketing because they are some of Big Data's strengths that have made themselves familiar and recognized [TIS 14]:

– *veracity* to induce user confidence in the information collected;

– *visualization* for the processing and presentation of data and results to non-specialists (for decision support, for example);

– and lastly, *value* to qualify the creation of value for the company.

---

7 Let us note in passing the humor of this Commission, which not only shows its firm and legitimate determination to fight against the English term "big" but also Latin terms, since 'data' is none other than the plural version of the A form of the supin of the verb *do, das, dare, dedi, datum*... which means "to give" in Latin. *A priori*, or rather at first glance, it is a bold extension of its field of competence. Let us hope that the Commission does not realize that the English term 'Big' has been translated from the Greek prefix "mega", probably as reprehensible as Latin!

Big Data raises various issues, sometimes old and sometimes new, concerning processing methods, storage, property rights, etc. These questions have not yet been given an optimal answer, and we must be aware of that and remain cautious. Applying the policy of ostracism and ignoring these issues cannot be a satisfactory option for a scientist, so it is necessary to choose:

– What statistical processing to apply to the data, is it these algorithms that we see appearing in the daily media?

– What is the status of the data and the status of its author/owner?

– Is a regulatory or legislative framework appropriate and applicable?

– Or realistically, if the law is running behind social practice, is it evolving as fast as statistical practice and databases?

Homogeneous or massive data?

There have been some passionate discussions for some time now about the processing of massive Big Data. Seeming to oppose the advocates of homogeneous data, resulting from sampling carried out according to the "rules of art", are those who advocate taking advantage of heterogeneous data from unstructured but massive collections. On a completely different level, this reminds us of the endless debates in the 1960s, which have become quite sterile with the passage of time, between the advocates of geometric data analysis and the defenders of probabilistic or statistical approaches. Above all, this ridiculous game must be avoided: just as in the 1990s, mega-databases (then in declarative trend, controlled by companies such as Claritas or Axiom) did not kill sampling. The victory of Big Data and the full disappearance of surveys are, in the medium-term, very unlikely.

Nevertheless, since the early 2000s in many sectors of activity, there has been a return to exhaustivity thanks to new communication technologies and digital convergence. In telecommunications and in the media, this is linked with a feedback data that devices transmit instantaneously on the network, such as: smartphones, tablets, connected televisions, ADSL connection boxes and consumer loyalty cards, without also forgetting the widespread use of sensors and the appearance of connected objects, which are multiplying rapidly[8].

For use and processing, the answer is simple, even if it can be very complicated to implement. Let us refer to the "philosophy" of leading statisticians and surveyors such as Jean-Claude Deville and Carl-Eric Sarndal: when we have data or auxiliary

---

8 Editor's note: see Figure 2.2, Chapter 2.

information, we must use it. Excellent principle: it is up to the statistics (so to us all) to find intelligent mathematical answers. It is even our *raison d'etre* as scientists!

Going towards hybrid measures: concrete cases

To illustrate this, let's take a look at the significance of this hybridization between sources that mixes sample data and massive data of different granularities in the media sector:

– observation of fine behaviors from panels of individuals on the one hand;

– collection of information on the status of a "box" or other "devices", on the other hand.

First of all, an object is not an individual: most connected devices have several users. Gathering comprehensive data on the state of a device does not mean that it is "error-free" or "perfect". This is obvious, but it is what some non-specialists frequently believe; it is not easy to make it clear, for example, that quantity or exhaustivity is not necessarily the Holy Grail. This brings us back to Anders Kiaër in 1895 and Jerzy Neyman in 1934, or Gallup's straw votes in 1936, and therefore to the foundations of survey theory.

Let's point out two illustrations on this subject: in television, an ADSL box remains active on the last channel watched, even when the television is turned off. The information provided by this device is hence complete, but utterly false. This skews the observation by a few hours on the duration of viewing! For the Internet, the average number of visits created by robots or other contact technologies is considered to be around 50% to 60% (source: *Le Journal du Net*). This near exhaustive data must therefore be processed and filtered. After this cleanup, numerous scientific presentations have shown that the hybrid approach to separate sources holds promise for the future [MED 10].

In the field of media marketing, two techniques of hybridization have been developed: the first one is called "panel up". As its name indicates, it improves the individual data resulting from a panel; it is a "recovery" approach. The other technique, called "log up", individualizes the state of a device; it is a modeling approach. Thus, the behaviors of a panel of Internet users have been compared with the enumeration of all visits and pages viewed on sites. With the market agreement, the hybrid approach (the "panel up") has become the benchmark for measuring the Internet audience by microcomputer for the French market since summer 2012.

It was inevitable that television would follow this example. Already on an exploratory basis for some thematic pay-tv channels, the individual behavior of the audience of people living in a home equipped with a CanalSat box could be estimated by working on the recordings of boxes (elementary log information). This was enriched by elements provided by a television panel, thanks to an entirely new algorithmic model developed by Médiamétrie's scientific management, using the general framework of the theory of hidden Markov chains to get past the state of a device, to the individuals who make it work[9].

Hybrid results contain a greater amount of information and they ensure much better overall consistency than the results that would be achieved by each of the two observation systems, taken separately. However, this being said, when the French census institute INSEE elaborated on the "unified system of business statistics", the data provided by the samples of the annual business surveys were compared with exhaustive tax data and sometimes even with data contained in the reports of the board of directors; wasn't that already a hybridization between several sources?

To conclude, here is an image: A few years ago, we observed a phenomenon through a sample; we, therefore, had a brick of observations composed from a homogeneous material. Now, it is as if we have several bricks at our disposal and our goal is to build a wall: the solidity of the bricks is important, but the quality of the cement is also important. The bricks are similar to devices that produce data; while statistical design and modelling are similar to the cement. This cement is the job of specialists in observation, surveys, mathematical statistics, modelling and more generally, the use of mathematical techniques. This mixture of data of different natures is, in the broadest sense of the word, a fabulous opportunity for these scientific professions. It is a vision totally opposite to that of those who claim that the profusion of data will dispense mathematics and even intelligence!

Is this an ephemeral or sustainable phenomenon?

Massive data is not a passing fad. The real question should be: how many years can this new paradigm of juxtaposition of sources live on? Not only are these investments temporary, but there is also a real policy choice for the companies concerned. In the introduction, we considered that digitalization gave weight to methods, models and technologies. That does not have the appearance of stopping,

---

9 Andrei Markov (1856–1922) was the originator of models for the probabilistic description of transition from one system state to another. Markov's hidden model dates from 1965; its applications were developed from the late 1970s and 1980s. This hybrid approach to television was rewarded with i-com's Data Creativity Award in May 2015 [DUD 14].

not only because many industries are developing this type of source[10], but also because it is a hope for economic growth and jobs.

Advantages

It is obvious that we are only at the beginning of the exploitation of Big Data. Each day provides new examples in fields of activity that are constantly evolving: medicine, epidemiology, health, insurance, sports, marketing, culture, human resources, etc. Admittedly, the general public and the media may consider that a line is sometimes crossed with certain target marketing approaches; but beside these mistakes, how much progress is possible? By comparison, has the banking system been abolished because of rogue bankers, toxic financial products and the existence of robberies? The current North American approach is indicative of this state of mind, summed up in this extract from a report submitted to President Obama:

> "In any case, there are benefits and risks [...]: in terms of health, obvious risks of indiscretion, but also information for insurance companies; for trips tracked by GPS: optimizing traffic flow, anticipating traffic jams, locating an individual, etc." [PCA 14]

Three recent examples, taken among many others:

– in early January 2014, Amazon filed a patent to anticipate the orders of its customers before their final click of validation and to start sending parcels even before the confirmation of the order;

– Netflix developed algorithms to predict what subscribers wanted to watch on its film and series distribution service;

– Swiss researchers developed a method for predicting a person's next travel destination.

The enumeration would be long and, by nature, incomplete. A note from France stratégie, the former General Commissioner for Strategy and Foresight, provides a good summary [HAM 13]. Drawing up a list in prevention would be of no use, as the daily newspaper illustrates the added value that modelling, algorithms and machine learning bring when applied to big data; this field is in full expansion, from Alan Turing's genius to Arthur Samuel, Tom Mitchell, or Vladimir Vapnik and Alexei Chernovenkis [VAP 95-98].

---

10 To set these ideas down: in 2014, the world created 1.7 million billion bytes of data per minute, the equivalent in content of 360,000 DVDs!

An interesting brainstorming session

When you are not involved in it permanently it's hard to imagine the current intellectual abundance in this field. We could say that this enhances the conference market. This is not false, but there is a fundamental reality behind this abundance of communications. During the first three weeks of November 2014, there was:

– in Berlin, The Falling Walls Conference 2014, meetings between researchers and start-ups focusing on breakthroughs in scientific thinking;

– in Paris, two simultaneous conferences: the Digital Innovation Summit, held under the aegis of the Electronic Business Group (EBG), brought together more than a thousand participants working on digital data in France: academics, researchers from start-ups and established companies (Orange, Danone, Coca-Cola, Criteo, Dassault Systems). The second conference was focused on Data Management, with themes on cloud, data, quality, corporate governance; it brought together more than 250 participants (GfK, Schneider, CNRS, Accor, etc.).

Clear political guidelines

The guidelines were clearly announced: everyone has read or heard about the 34 proposals to relaunch industrialization in France (François Hollande, September 2013); the report of the Innovation Commission 2030[11], in addition to the government roadmap on digitization (February 2013) and the training plan presented by Minister Fleur Pellerin (July 2013). There was one thing in common with all these announcements: data. The Lauvergeon report particularly highlighted the acknowledged quality of French mathematical and statistical courses. In addition to these political governance guidelines, there were many other initiatives. A first example: INSEE launched, at the beginning of October 2014, a strategic discussion targeting the year 2025. This work has several themes, one of which is entitled "open data". It deals with access to private data and its use for public statistics, and thus questions:

> "[a] potentially large volume that would nevertheless be a shame to sample [...] unstructured or poorly structured data [...] of privacy issues..."

Another example: on October 13, 2014, a Memorandum of Understanding was signed between the European Commission and the Big Data Value Association, a

---

11 Commission chaired by Anne Lauvergeon: Seven ambitions for France, October 2013.

structure bringing together European companies and research organizations. This BDVA included the universities of Bologna, Duisburg-Essen, the Technical University TU Berlin, the Polytechnic University of Madrid, and companies: ATC, IT Innovation, IBM, Sintef, Nokia Solutions and Networks, Thales, Siemens, SAP Engineering, TIE Kinetix, Answare, Software AG, Orange, Atos, Indra, ITI, VTT and Fraunhofer. The purpose of this protocol was to establish a public-private partnership (PPP) for a total amount of 2.5 billion in order to "search for revolutionary ideas on metadata"[12]. Another link with research: academic chairs in Big Data flourish: without claiming to be exhaustive, ENSAE and ENSAI announced a partnership with LCL in October 2014; the Ecole Polytechnique also announced a similar partnership with Orange, Thalès and Keyrus on a similar subject, without forgetting the precursors that were Télécom Paris-Tech and ESSEC. Finally, on September 18, 2014, the French government appointed Mr. Henri Verdier as its Chief Data Officer, the first data administrator in France put in charge of open data (a first in Europe), a job consisting of opening up public data, drawing up an inventory, ensuring that it is good, encouraging its circulation and above all, developing new methods of analysis in the service of public policy[13]. Open data is a movement towards free access to public data, generalized at the beginning of the 21st Century. It consists of considering public information as a common good, parts of which are even guarantors of democracy (law, jurisprudence, public accounts, evaluation of public policies, etc.). Open data is based on digitization, and even seems to grasp the concept of opening administrative files to private data[14].

The Internet of Things

Connected objects will be Big Data's next evolution [NEM 15]. Its widespread use will generate multiple databases in increasingly diverse fields. Incidentally, let's mention an area that may surprise: sport. In January 2014, the SFdS (French Society of Statistics) organized its first half-day seminar entitled: "When statistics meet sport." Some presentations highlighted the use of data, if only for the fight against doping. It is fortunate that the scientific world has a role to play in ensuring that the

---

12 The European Union would contribute 20% of the budget, i.e. €500 million from the 2020 rolling framework programme.

13 Editor's note: access to public data has been the subject of much work in France since the mid-1990s, due to disputes concerning the press; access to administrative documents, in the broad sense, has been regulated since the law of July 1978, which established the Commission of Access to Administrative Documents (CADA), which is still present today. For an update on the subject, see: CADA Annual Reports and [CHA C13].

14 Data is to be taken lightly, because it may as well concern results and even documents.

data that will be derived from it are used effectively. On March 5, 2015, the National Research Strategy was published, setting out guidelines, challenges and action programs on five thematic issues[15]. The seventh among 10 challenges is entitled "Information and Communication Society". The first action program states this:

> "Big Data: an exceptional source of knowledge and growth. The volume of digital data produced by our society (companies, public institutions, health systems, scientific experiments, social networks, connected devices, etc.) doubles every two years. This digital universe is expected to represent 40,000 exabytes of data by 2020, one billion times the volume of data collected by the Hubble telescope in its 20 years of observations of the universe. The information present in this digital world constitutes an immaterial capital of great value for knowledge and a formidable source of economic development: the Big Data plan of the new industrial France is targeting a 9 billion euro market and a potential of about 140,000 jobs, 80,000 of which will be new jobs.
>
> France has mastered hardware and software technologies throughout the entire value chain, from their collection, indexing, storage, visualization and knowledge extraction to their exploitation. Today, Big Data technology represents an issue for a large number of economic sectors and for most scientific disciplines (health-biology, environment-climatology, particle physics, human and social sciences, etc.). The objective of the program is to contribute to the full realization of our country's potential in the field of massive data, by focusing on the acceptance and appropriation of these applications, and data security, an increasingly important economic and social issue.
>
> This program has to mobilize multidisciplinary teams associating researchers in digital science and technology (knowledge engineering, hardware and software technologies, networks and telecommunications, cybersecurity), mathematicians, SHS researchers and experts in potential application fields."

All of this constitutes an opportunity for training, research, development and employment: it is estimated that at least 300,000 data scientist jobs will be created in

15 These orientations include: connected objects, exploitation of large masses of data, the collaboration of man-machine, fifth generation infrastructures, data availability and knowledge extraction, resilience of security systems, etc.

Europe by 2022. France strategy's report with DARES "Jobs in 2022", published in July 2014, estimated that 292,000 engineer jobs will be filled in France in IT, research and development, including retirement replacements.

How can data confidentiality be guaranteed?

Data and statistics, held and compiled by administrations and enterprises, have generally been constructed on the basis of personal information, which raises the issue of source protection, that is to say privacy. Given the constant progress of science and treatment processes, how can we build and maintain the confidence of the general public, our number one stakeholder, while at the same time respecting the balance between the promise of confidentiality and the fair use of collected data?

In response, two complementary approaches are needed: one is regulatory, as countries have long recognized the need to establish legal safeguards. The other aims to build on technology by setting up technical barriers to prevent the unwilling dissemination of data.

An already significant regulatory framework

First, it should be noted that there is a major difference between sample and metadata. An individual who agrees to participate in a sample grants his or her consent implying the voluntary disclosure of information, which is not necessarily the case for the acquisition of massive data. It may be considered that being part of a sample or panel is a voluntary act implying a contract between the panelist and the company organizing the sample, a contract regarding the personal or behavioral data of the panelist. A statistic is compiled from observed data. If a database is representative of a population, in the specific sense of the term "representative", its purpose is to infer (in the sense of [FIS 22]), meaning to acquire reliable knowledge of the population as a whole, or subsections of that population, while respecting the privacy and intimacy of the individuals in the sample within the existing framework (statistical secrecy, telecoms law, "computing and freedoms" law).

Confidentiality and secrecy are present in many areas: business confidentiality, banking secrecy, medical confidentiality. In statistics and for the corresponding databases, a legislative framework exists in many countries, including France, which even played a pioneering role with its "computing and freedoms" law of 1978. The French Act 51-711 of June 7, 1951 on the legal obligation, coordination and confidentiality of statistics defines statistical secrecy as an "impossibility of identification" in the context of official statistics (censuses, surveys). Thus, the communication of personal, family and private data was prohibited for 75 years. For the production system (companies, shops, etc.), cumulative results may not be published for a perimeter composed of no less than three companies, or if a company represents at least 85% of the accumulated object indicator[16].

Second legislative framework: The Post and Telecommunications Code (Law 84-939 of October 23, 1984, amended several times) which deals with the processing of personal data in the context of electronic communications services, in particular via networks that support data collection and identification devices.

In addition to the previous regulations, several professional codes of ethics are in force, including those of the directors of INSEE [AIS 84, PAD 86, 91] and those of the European Society for Opinion and Market Research [ICC 95]. The latter, created in 1948, is regularly updated and specifies "good practices" for conducting market and opinion research. One of its objectives is to trust this type of study, with the public being a major stakeholder. To this end, this code defines voluntary participation, the rights of respondents and their anonymity.

Information technology and freedom

The French law that is best known to the general public is probably Act no. 78-17 of January 6, 1978 on information technology, data files and civil liberties, entered into language as the law on computing and freedom (*Informatique & Libertés*). It specifies the rules that are applicable to personal data. What is personal data? Article 1 of the 1978 Act states it as: "information relating to a natural person who is or can be identified, directly or indirectly, by reference to an identification number or to one or more factors specific to them. In order to determine whether a person is identifiable, all the means that the data controller or any other person uses or may have access to should be taken into consideration." Such personal data may be kept raw or stored after processing. The law stipulates that processing includes "any operation or set of operations relating to such data, regardless of the method used, and in particular the collection, recording, organization, storage, adaptation or

---

16 Exceptions are sometimes allowed for the purposes of scientific research, following the advice of the Committee on Statistical Confidentiality, a body within the perimeter of the National Council of Statistical Information (CNIS), which in 1984, took over from the National Council of Statistics that was created in 1972.

modification, extraction, consultation, use, communication by transmission, dissemination and any other form of making available, approximation or interconnection, as well as locking, erasure and destruction". This is important, since Big Data is "massive" in both senses of the word mentioned above: quantity and variety (the 6 V's) and also by extensive analysis, which can infer calculated data.

The "Fisherial" inference of classical statistics, broadens the observations made on this sample population to the entire observed population: one learns about it by observing one of its parts. Mega-bases collecting personal data, on the other hand, can generate an inverse inference: from the database to the individual, this inference can be "perverse" because the processes, models, algorithms, data mining, not only deliver elements from the cumulative observation of a set of individuals, but also data resulting from processes carried out on the database data, that is these estimated variables consort, within the database, with the variables actually observed. What then is the status of data that was not collected, but calculated?

A well-known example is profiling, which consists of estimating the socio-demographic characteristics of an individual based on his or her behavior. Thus, if their characteristics are well known, a bland decomposition into conditional probabilities makes it simple enough to evaluate the profile of Internet users who visit websites: S, S', S". The very purpose of the sites visited induces an estimate of the visitor's interests, and associates them with a particular category, even if it is "ephemeral". Lastly, it is important to integrate into our analysis that our reflections take place in an evolving context: the continuous progress of science constantly creates new models and new algorithms that we will be tempted to apply to existing databases, leading to new inferences through the increase of processing and calculation capacities. The "computing and freedoms" French act already addressed this subject, its Article 10 explicitly mentioned that:

> "No judicial decision implicating an assessment of a person's conduct may be based on automatic processing of personal data intended to evaluate certain aspects of his or her personality. No other decision having legal effects in respect of a person may be taken solely on the basis of the automated processing of data intended to define the profile of the person concerned or to assess certain aspects of his or her personality". On the other hand, "decisions taken in connection with the conclusion or execution of a contract on which the person concerned has been given the opportunity to present his or her observations shall not be regarded as being taken solely on the basis of automatic processing".

Among personal data, there is another special category qualified by law as sensitive data, the collection and processing of which is, as a matter of principle, prohibited. Sensitive information is considered to be information which reveals, directly or indirectly, racial or ethnic origins, political, philosophical or religious opinions, trade union affiliations, health and sexual life (Article 8). This notion of sensitive data has been extended by case-law. Tracing the fact that someone is injured or sick on leave is sensitive data. More generally, biometric and genetic data (fingerprints, DNA, etc.), offences, convictions and security measures, INSEE and social security numbers and any assessment, comment or observation concerning social difficulties are also sensitive. In addition, some data is considered sensitive in a certain context: accounting or financial corporate data, for example; but this data is not necessarily personal within the context of the 1978 law.

What guidelines for the future?

They are difficult to predict[17]. There are many thoughts on privacy and algorithmic processing, and it is important to keep a close eye on them, if not contribute to them, as they are likely to have an impact on various professions. A report published on the Buzzfeed website (Nov. 10th, 2014), reproduced below, shows the inevitable evolutions:

> "Facebook will transmit the data of 185 million Americans to Buzzfeed and ABC. Buzzfeed will use Facebook data as a survey tool in the 2016 U. S. presidential election. The entertainment media site will have access, like the ABC channel, to data on the feelings and political opinions of 185 million Americans registered on Facebook. The analysis of this data, called Sentiment Analysis, will be provided directly by Facebook: 'We think that this may be the most important source of political data,' writes Buzzfeed, who points out one flaw: sarcasm is difficult to detect at the moment."

Facebook has also modified its privacy policy by appropriating the data posted by its users: this came into effect on November 20, 2014. On a completely different front, the French Senate approved the inclusion of two questions in the French population survey, refering to the country of birth of the ascendants and previous nationality.

---

17 Editor's note: The EU General Data Protection Regulation (GDRP) enacted April 27th 2016 is now binding and applicable to all Members States of the Union from May 25th 2018.

Reflections of the French Conseil d'Etat

This Council published an impressive work on Digital and Fundamental Rights, containing 50 proposals to put digital technology at the service of individual rights and general interest. Let's extract a short segment of it concerning "predictive algorithms" and the five proposals of the State Council that concern them [ROU 14]:

1) "To ensure the effectiveness of the prohibition to base a decision on the mere implementation of automated processing, confirming human intervention in the decision must be real and not only formal. Indicate in a flexible legal instrument the criteria for appraising the effective character of human intervention.

2) Impose an obligation of transparency on the authors of decisions, based on the implementation of algorithms regarding the personal data used by the algorithm and the geo-reasoning followed by it. Give the person who is the subject of the decision the opportunity to make representations.

3) Within the framework of Article 44 of the law of January 6, 1978, and with due respect for industrial secrecy, to develop the control of algorithms by observing their results, particularly in order to detect unlawful discrimination, to this end by strengthening the human resources available to the CNIL.

4) Analyze and sanction price differentiation practices based on the use of personal data, measure their development and determine which ones should be characterized as illegal or unfair commercial practices.

5) Encourage consideration of cultural diversity in recommendation algorithms used by websites distributing audio-visual and musical content".

The first proposal refers to Article 10 of the above-mentioned Law of January 6, 1978. Without explicitly mentioning them, this article refers to algorithms and models. The Council notes that it is necessary to "avoid that systems, presented as aid under the terms of the decision, almost always follow and command the decision, human intervention only being apparent".

The second proposal aims to enable people suffering the consequences of a decision based on an algorithm, to defend themselves. In order to "benefit from similar guarantees as those of an adversarial procedure", the victim should therefore access certain data and receive explanations. But, again, can such a system be set up simply? If a strengthening of the CNIL (proposal 3) can only be positive, we should nevertheless see how to apply the first two proposals.

Culture and media: the Avignon Forum

Created in 2008, the Avignon Forum is a think tank bringing together personalities from the cultural, media, economic and digital sectors. In November 2013, this forum proclaimed: "cultural personal data [...] is worth gold." This Forum found that the mass of digital traces is sufficient to track and model rational and coherent "digital beings" and addressed digital cultural data, its trends, uses, and its protection. The Avignon Forum unveiled an interesting contribution that proposed eight digital human rights:

– digital DNA: the personal data, particularly digital data, of every human being reflects his or her cultural values and private life. They cannot be reduced to a commodity;

– ethical and equitable: reasonable use of data is an opportunity for the development of research and general interest. It must be overseen by a universal ethical charter protecting dignity, privacy, the creation of each human being and the pluralism of opinions;

– private life: every human being has the right of respect to their dignity, privacy and creations, and may not be discriminated against on the basis of access to their personal data and the uses made thereof. No entity, public or private, shall use personal data for the purpose of manipulating access to information, freedom of opinion or democratic procedures;

– right of scrutiny: every human being must have a right of scrutiny, confidentiality and control over their personal data, including those produced as a result of their behavior and objects connected to their person. They are entitled to the protection of their anonymity whenever they wish;

– consent: any use of the data as the creation of any human being presupposes their prior, free, informed, time-limited and reversible consent;

– transparency of use: users of personal data, regardless of their level of responsibility: countries, public and private authorities, companies and individuals, must demonstrate total transparency in the collection and use of personal data and facilitate access to the traceability, confidentiality and security of each individual;

– research and general interest: open research and innovation, based on the agreed and anonymous sharing of data of every human being, with respect for their dignity and cultural diversity, are favorable to general interest;

– co-operation, data-driven society: the cooperation of civil society and business is necessary to put human beings back at the heart of a society of trust, assisted by a reasonable use of personal data produced and inferred.

The digital transformation of the economy

The report of a mission entrusted to Philippe Lemoine by four ministers [LEM 14] tackled digital technology as a whole, a much broader field than metadata; it had the merit of highlighting the digital transformation and presenting more opportunities than risks. Some of his statements are thought-provoking:

> "In this way, we could assert everyone's right to their personal data, opening up the possibility of storing their data in a personal cloud [...] the sovereignty of the data must be given back to individuals..."

The principle would be to trust citizens by giving them control over the personal data relating to them. Is this route socially feasible without dividing the population, having groups at different speeds depending on their level of mastery over technology?

Published in the J.O.R.F on October 8, 2016, this law was prepared by a public consultation on the Internet which had some echo: more than 21,000 participants, 8,500 contributions and nearly 150,000 digital opinions were expressed! After a series of fairly numerous amendments, both in the National Assembly and the Senate, the final text was adopted on 28 September. It contains three main parts that affect successively:

1) access to public data (open data);

2) the protection of personal data (data protection);

3) territorial coverage of broadband networks.

This text incorporates various stipulations that make for a rather rich reading.

In principle, two independent administrative authorities will be involved in the implementation of this law: the National Commission on Computing and Freedom (CNIL) for the protection of personal data and ARCEP for the provisions relating to electronic communications. It will be confronted with the EU Regulation (GDRP) enforced May 2018 (refer to footnote 17).

Box 3.1. The French "Digital Republic" *law, 2016*

Protecting personal data

The relationship between computers, privacy, personal data and databases is a field of research that has been discussed since the 1970s. Respect for privacy is a principle on which everyone seems to agree, but we know that "the devil is in the detail": beyond the regulatory framework, how can we ensure this is the case on the technical side? The emergence of massive data is provoking consideration that borders on the big gap: can privacy be respected without slowing down the economic potential promised by digital technology?

In the United States, the Presidential Council for Science and Technology (cited previously) strongly believes that "the benefits will be incomparably greater than the risks" [PCA 14]. If this is true, it would be in the highest interest to guarantee the confidentiality of personal databases in order to live digital life in confidence. Two trains of thought are expressed: the first, essentially European, is based on legal safeguards[18]. The second, North American, is more open to self-regulation. Beyond the prohibitions, can technical solutions satisfy the need for confidentiality? Here are some answers to accommodate the use of personal data with credible confidentiality. First, there must be a clear distinction between computer security (or cybersecurity) and the protection of privacy itself.

Encryption[19]

Cybersecurity and encryption methods have evolved well since their inception over three millennia ago. These methods make a document – in the broadest sense of the term – unreadable (that is to say incomprehensible) to anyone who does not have the encryption key[20]. Julius Caesar encrypted the messages he sent to his generals; the "Great Cipher" from Louis XIV's black cabinet, acquired world celebrity in the 17th Century thanks to the Rossignol des Roches family (Antoine, Bonaventure the son and Antoine-Bonaventure the grandson). Everyone has heard of the coding used by Claude Chappe's telegraph at the end of the 18th Century, and that of Samuel Morse's electric telegraph, a few years later[21].

In this regard, it is worth mentioning the recent work of two professors at MIT on semantic security (pre-print in 1982, then [GOL 84]). Both of them designed the

18 Rather French in its inspiration, given the international role of the CNIL in the G29, the European group of European regulators for the protection of personal data.

19 Cryptography, the science of encryption, is the prerogative of the police; cryptanalysis, the science of decryption, is the terrain of thieves!

20 An encryption technique is called symmetrical when the same key is used to encode and decode. It is asymmetrical if two different and independent keys are needed: one to hide the message and the other to unmask its contents.

21 Editor's note: the Chappe brothers' optical telegraph operated in France from 1793 to 1855; Morse's electric telegraph, more efficient than the British Cooke and Wheatstone's system which had preceded it by a few years, was put into service in 1845; it originated from the Western Union, which exploited its patents. Since the definitive abandonment of the telegram in 2006, this American company has continued to exist in a new form dedicated to the international transfer of funds. For an analysis of this slice of industrial history, see [BER 81].

first probabilistic encryption system proven to be absolutely secure. They received the Turing Award from the Association for Computing Machinery (ACM). However, despite advances in encryption protocols and even in the case of perfect cybersecurity, data may be at risk for other reasons, whether by chance, accident, inadvertence, human failure, etc. Attempts to intrude or misuse by third parties are possible. Cybersecurity, therefore, as a necessary condition for protecting privacy, may not be seen as a sufficient provision to maintain trust: it must be combined with other precautions!

The vision of Tore Dalenius

In the context of databases as they existed prior to 1980, Swedish statistician Tore Dalenius set out principles of ethics, privacy and confidentiality. His article stated the following principle:

"Accessing a database should not allow you to learn more about an individual than what could be learned without accessing that database" [DAL 77].

He added: $X(i)$ being the value of the variable X for the individual i, if the publication of a statistical aggregate T allows to determine $X(i)$ precisely, without accessing T, there is a breach of confidentiality. This principle seems acceptable. Unfortunately, it can be shown that it cannot be general: third parties who wished to collect personal data on the individual i can do so by taking advantage of ancillary information that is accessible to them outside the database!

We can illustrate this by an example: suppose that we have a database the size of adult men of several nationalities, including the Italian nationality; and that we also have auxiliary information on an Italian individual, Mr. Z...: he measures two centimeters higher than an average Italian adult. The database is used to calculate the average size of an Italian adult male; the auxiliary information we have on individual Z, who measures two centimeters higher than the average Italian, allows us to know his real height: it is equal to the average size (from the database) plus two centimeters! And yet, the only auxiliary information does not say much about Mr. Z... Moreover, this result remains valid regardless of whether Mr. Z's personal data is stored in the database or not[22]!"

---

22 Strictly speaking, the impossibility of the Dalenius principle can be written as follows: given S, a protection mechanism of a database; and F, a flaw in this protection. There might always exist some auxiliary information Z, such as: 1) Z alone has no use for who wants to

Anonymization

A first and, in theory *a priori*, intuitive data protection technique would be to make personal data anonymous. This would mean removing all variables that would identify a particular individual from the database. Here we'll find the notion of personal data mentioned by the French *Informatique & Libertés* 1978 Act[23]; a physical person will be identified by his or her name, but also by other characteristic variables such as a registration code, an address (postal or IP address), telephone numbers, a PIN (Personal Identification Number), photographs, biometric components such as a fingerprint or DNA and more generally, by any variable that makes it possible, by crossing or cross-checking in order to find an individual in an ensemble (for example: his or her place of birth, the date of birth or the office where he or she votes). It is a less perfect and slower identification than by their surname, but a very credible identification, which takes us significantly away from complete ignorance.

For more than a decade now, information and communication technologies have been creating numerous data sets that can be exploited by a former type of analysis, for example, when making a telephone call from a mobile device or an Internet connection. All these "computer traces" are easily exploitable thanks to advances in software and search engines: they are logs[24]. At first sight, anonymization can be a simple concept to understand and implement, but it can be complex because it can also remove useful and relevant variables from the database. In addition, the number of breaches in confidentiality is increasing with scientific progress and the probability of identifying an individual in a personal database is increasing too, even after anonymization. This is therefore, ultimately, not a sufficient method to truly protect personal data against indiscretion.

Destruction or aggregation of data

Another method would be to delete the data beyond a certain period of time during which it would remain operational. However, since the duplication of a database is always possible, this attractive but temporary concept is, in practice, misleading. In addition, deleted data can be of value long after its "active life" period; for historians or researchers, for example. Using the principle of the 1951

---

break through the secret of the base; 2) but Z, combined with some of the protected data, makes it possible to find a fault F with a probability that tends towards 1.

23 Article 1: data is considered personal as soon as it relates to an identified or identifiable individual, directly or indirectly (see above p. 90).

24 The name given (for several centuries) to the information collected in the ship's logbook.

Act for Statistical Confidentiality of Enterprises, individual data could then be aggregated and, after a certain period of time, disclose only aggregated results. Would that also condemn microeconomic analysis that takes advantage of individual data? Furthermore, some mathematical models can neutralize this approach by allowing an individual inverse inference. Here are two examples to illustrate these limitations:

– a first example of a highly successful inverse inference appears in a publication that describes how to indirectly identify individuals from the traces left by their DNA. Here is the crucial part[25]: "[...] we demonstrate that it is possible to seriously and robustly [...] extract from a mixture of DNA traces that of a particular individual (and thus prove his or her presence) even if this [individual] trace constitutes less than 0.1% of the total DNA traces found [...] it suggests that further research [in this direction] is needed and that the composite statistics [data aggregated] on a cohort do not mask the identities of the individuals [of which it is composed]";

– a second example relates to genomics [SWE 13]; working on a major American project (Personal Genome Project), these authors can correctly identify 84% of the individual profiles (within an experimental cohort). This rate rises to 97% if we eliminate the notion of strict identification by first name, by accepting diminutives such as Jim for James or Andy for Andrew!

Obscuring data

Data obscuration (also referred to as darkening)[26] is the process of preserving the confidentiality of data by "altering" it voluntarily. This can be done indirectly, by

---

25 Editor's note: our condensed version of the following summary: "We use high-density single nucleotide polymorphism (SNP) genotyping microarrays to demonstrate the ability to accurately and robustly determine whether individuals are in a complex genomic DNA mixture. We first develop a theoretical framework for detecting an individual's presence within a mixture, then show, through simulations, the limits associated with our method, and finally demonstrate experimentally the identification of the presence of genomic DNA of specific individuals within a series of highly complex genomic mixtures, including mixtures where an individual contributes less than 0.1% of the total genomic DNA. These findings shift the perceived utility of SNPs for identifying individual trace contributors within a forensics mixture, and suggest future research efforts into assessing the viability of previously sub-optimal DNA sources due to sample contamination. These findings also suggest that composite statistics across cohorts, such as allele frequency or genotype counts, do not mask identity within genome-wide association studies. The implications of these findings are discussed", available at the online address: http://dx.doi.org/10.1371/journal. pgen.1000167, August 29, 2008.
26 Or neologism obfuscation, from the Latin verb *obfusco, obfuscare*, or *obfundo, obfundere* meaning: darken, obscure.

plunging the data into larger spaces, following a principle of diluting significant data; or directly by transforming the data to render them insignificant – coding is far from this! In the first group of methods, for example, we can create additional variables that increase the size of the data vector and thus create a "fog" that masks what we hold. In the second group of methods, there are non-intrusive techniques: masking the value of certain cells in a results table, removing variables concerning certain individuals, sharing a sample of data extracted from the database, combining certain categories for modality variables, etc.

There are also, and above all, directly interventionist methods on data that make it possible to generate noise, or in the broader sense, to modify certain variables by rounding them up or blocking them by truncation at maximum or minimum thresholds. Variables can also be transformed by applying a homomorphism ($X_{1,...}$, X_K) $\rightarrow \varphi$ ($\varphi 1$ (X_1)$_{,...}$, φ_K (X_K)), switching the value of the same variable between two individuals (which scramble tracks!), or disturbing the data by adding a random noise $X_k \rightarrow X_k +$ $_{uk}$. Applied to the original data, some transformations (e.g. permutation, rotation) will leave linear statistics invariant; others will not. This method was born from work on missing data, and is particularly interesting for synthetic data [LIT 93, RUB 93, 03].

A new approach: differential confidentiality

Since the mid-2000s, another perspective has been opened up to protect privacy; one of the leading figures in this approach is a Microsoft researcher [DWO 04, 06, 06a]. Her philosophy is strongly inspired by Dalenius' philosophy and can be synthesized as such: "The probability of any negative consequences for individual i (e.g. being denied credit or insurance) cannot increase significantly because of the representation of i in a database."

The adverb "significantly" should be weighted because it is very difficult to predict what information (or what combination of information) could have negative consequences for the individual in question, if that information were made public. Especially since this information cannot be observed, only estimated by a calculation; and also, that some consequences that are considered negative for one may seem positive for another! This approach, which could be called "privacy" or "differential confidentiality", is based on probabilistic and statistical assumptions. Maybe it will develop? The idea is to quantify the risk of a possible breach of confidentiality, while measuring the effect of effective data protection on privacy, in statistical terms. An open field of research to analyze the data after the original has been obscured, altered or modified in order to preserve its confidentiality. This method can be summarized as follows:

1) promising an individual that a third party (the adversary) will not be able to learn anything specific about him or her if he or she agrees to participate (for example, in a survey or panel);

2) accurately measure the effectiveness of the protection mechanism for personal data collected;

3) maintain the confidentiality of the data, even if the third party has ancillary data on the individual concerned.

A statistic or a random function f guarantees differential confidentiality at the level $\alpha > 0$ if and only if, for all related datasets D and D' and for all T's belonging to Im(f), image of f, one has:

$$e\text{-}\alpha \leq P(f(D) \in T)/P(f(D') \in T) \leq e\alpha$$

where two data sets are said to be neighboring if they differ from one, and only one, individual[27]. The smaller the size of α, the better the confidentiality. Nevertheless, the question arises as to the choice of α. The definition of f is to be taken in the broadest sense (common statistical index such as: an average, a variation, a proportion, the coefficients of a model, a set of synthetic data). A link then exists between the differential confidentiality and the synthetic data mentioned above.

How to conclude?

Unless we confine ourselves to data collection alone (while ignoring the context and processes) we will finally find the three well-known fields of statistics, which are related and interconnected, and therefore have three main functions: data collection, data processing and the use of results. However, the survey specialist, whether a theorist or a practitioner, who is properly focused on the upstream side of the value chain never loses interest in the downstream processing of survey data: exploiting and using it.

Since the apparition of Big Data, new scientists have been interested in statistical mathematics, probabilities, surveys, databases, algorithms and computing. The statisticians of tomorrow will need cross-cutting skills more than ever: shouldn't hybrids of lawyers and cybersecurity specialists be made given that we're seeing the development of law reviews and scientific reviews of the same subjects? Tomorrow

---

27 This is similar to the Jackknife technique created by Pr. Quenouille in 1949 and 1956, which in terms of logical estimation, worked on samples from which he retrieved an observation.

can't wait! But, in the end, hasn't it always been so? What could be more immutable than changing subjects and finding answers? To illustrate this permanent *coup d'état* following us, here is a short text:

> "A disorder of which the term cannot be imagined is now observed in all areas. We find it around us, in ourselves, in our daily life, in our appearance, in the newspapers, in the media, in our pleasures and even in our knowledge. Interruption, incoherence and surprise are the usual conditions of our life. They have even become real needs in many of us, whose minds are fed only by sudden changes and constantly renewed excitements. The words of everyday life paint our times. And, great innovation, we can't stand to wait any longer, we can't stand the duration."

Who is the author of this premonitory text on breakages, disruptions, and even "real time"? Which genius of the new digital economy, among Jeff Bezos, Bill Gates, Steve Jobs, Larry Page, Mark Zuckerberg and many other contenders wrote it? None of them. These lines, so real, are barely more than 80 years old; they are by the Sète poet Paul Valéry, the famous author of *Le cimetière Marin*. They are excerpted from a lecture dated 16 January 1935: the author then occupied the chair of poetics at the Collège de France. Let's leave the last words to Valéry:

> "The wind is rising... we must try to live
> The immense air opens and closes my book."

Bibliography

[AIS 84] AIS, Association des administrateurs de l'INSEE, Code de déontologie statistique, 1984.

[BER 81] BERTHO C., *De Valmy au microprocesseur*, Livre de poche no. 5581, Paris, 1981.

[CHA 13] CHAMOUX J.-P, BOUSTANY J. (eds), "Données publiques, Accès and Usages", *Cahiers du numérique LCN*, vol. 9, no. 1, Lavoisier, Paris, 2013.

[COL 13] COLLECTIF, "Marketing: challenges and perspectives", *Décisions Marketing*, no. 72, October–December 2013.

[DAL 77] DALENIUS T., "Towards a methodology for statistical disclosure control", *StatistikTidskrift*, vol. 15, 1977.

[DOM 04] DOMINGO-FERRER J., TORRA V. (eds), "Privacy in Statistical Databases", *Proceedings CASC Project*, Springer, New York, 2004.

[DRO 90] DROESBEKE J.-J., TASSI P., *Histoire de la statistique*, PUF, Paris, 1990.

[DUD 14] DUDOIGNON L., LOGEART J., "Mesure hybride de l'audience TV", *Actes, 46ᵉ Journées de statistique de la SFdS*, Rennes, France, 2014.

[DWO 04] DWORK C., NISSIM K., "Privacy-preserving data mining on vertically partitioned databases", *Advances in Cryptology, Proceedings of Cryptography Conference*, Springer, Berlin, 2004.

[DWO 06] DWORK C., "Differential Privacy", *Proceedings of the 33ʳᵈ International Colloquium on Automata*, Languages and Programming, Venice, Italy, 2006.

[DWO 06a] DWORK C., MCSHERRY F., NISSIM K.. *et al.*, "Calibrating noise to sensitivity in private data analysis", *Proceedings 3ʳᵈ IACR Cryptography Conference*, Santa Barbara, USA, 2006.

[FIS 22] FISHER R.A., "On the mathematical foundations of theoretical statistics", *Philosophical Transactions of the Royal Society*, no. 222, 1922.

[GOL 84] GOLDWASSER S., MICALI S., "Probabilistic Encryption", *Journal of Computer and Systems Sciences*, no. 28, 1984.

[HAM 13] HAMEL M.-P., MARGUERIT D., Analyse des Big Data, quels usages, quels défis, Note d'analyse no. 08, France stratégie, 2013.

[ICC 95] ICC/ESOMAR, International Code of Marketing and Social Research Practice, 1948, latest edition 1995.

[IIS 85] IIS (Institut international de statistique), Déclaration sur l'éthique professionnelle, 1985.

[JEN 25] JENSEN A., "Report on the Representative Method in Statistics", *Bulletin de l'Institut international de statistique*, vol. 22, no. 1, 1925.

[JEN 28] JENSEN A., "Purposive Selection", *Journal of the Royal Statistical Society*, vol. 91, no. 4, 1928.

[KIA 95] KIAER A.N., "Observations and Experiences with Representative Enumarations", *Bulletin Institut international de statistique*, vol. 9, no. 2, 1895.

[LEM 14] LEMOINE P. *et al.*, La transformation numérique de l'économie, Report, November 2014.

[LIT 93] LITTLE R., "Statistical Analysis of Masked Data", *Journal of Official Statistics*, vol. 9, no. 2, pp. 407–426, 1993.

[MÉD 10] MÉDIAMÉTRIE, Livre blanc sur la mesure hybride, 2010.

[NEM 15] NEMRI M., Demain l'Internet des objets, Note d'analyse France stratégie no. 22, January 2015.

[NEY 34] NEYMAN J., "On the two different aspects of representative method: stratified sampling and purposive selection", *J. Royal Statistical Society*, vol. 97, no. 4, pp. 558–625, 1934.

[PAD 86] PADIEU R., "La déclaration de l'IIS et le code de déontologie de l'AIS", *Courrier des statistiques*, April 1986.

[PAD 91] PADIEU R., "La déontologie des statisticiens", *Sociétés contemporaines*, no. 7, 1991.

[PCA 14] PCAST, Big Data and Privacy: A Technological Perspective, Report to the President, May 2014.

[ROU 14] ROUVROY A., "Des données sans personne : le fétichisme de la donnée à caractère personnel à l'épreuve de l'idéologie des Big Data", in *Le numérique et les droits fondamentaux*, Etude annuelle du Conseil d'Etat, La Documentation française, Paris, 2014.

[RUB 93] RUBIN D.B., "Discussion: Statistical disclosure limitation", *Journal of Official Statistics*, vol. 9, no. 2, pp. 461–468, 1993.

[RUB 03] RUBIN D.B., "Discussion on multiple imputation", *International Statistical Review*, vol. 71, no. 3, pp. 619–625, 2003.

[SIN 99] SINGH S., *The Code Book*, Fourth Estate, London, 1999.

[SWE 13] SWEENEY L., ABU A., WINN J., "Identifying participants in the Personal Genome Project by name", Harvard College, White Paper 1021, April 2013.

[TIS 14] TISSIER-DESBORDES E., GIANNELLONI J-L., "Repenser le marketing à l'ère du numérique", *Décisions Marketing*, no. 73, January–March 2014.

[VAP 95] VAPNIK V, *The Nature of Statistical Learning Theory*, Springer, New York, 1995.

[VAP 98] VAPNIK V., *Statistical Learning Theory*, John Wiley & Sons, New York, 1998.

4

Researching Forms and Correlations: the Big Data Approach

In less than 30 years, the databases of banks, distribution and scientific laboratories have undergone profound changes of nature and ambition: their size has grown enormously. The variety of data has increased considerably. The updating of these databases is constant, near to "real time". Only very powerful specialized computers equipped with suitable software are able to exploit these massive stocks, which are (for example) assembled at all times by search engines; the same is true for social networks and for the scientific instrumentation that equips particle accelerators or telescopes. There is little commonality between the data collected for any of these activities, but the operating methods are similar.

Gathered together by an automatic and systematic process, the Big Data referred to here is rarely collected with a single and precise purpose. Many iterations are therefore necessary before you can spot the "needle in the haystack" of a mega-database. In order to carry out such a search within an acceptable period of time, these computers are both more powerful and different from conventional computers: they simultaneously perform a large number of parallel calculations, look for significant details among scattered elements, try to extract a meaning from them and try to recognize a hidden form or correlation within a formless multitude. Their programs derive from algorithmic methods described in the two preceding chapters. This chapter compares this approach to a complex puzzle; it also presents analogies with its exploitation of gold sediments that manipulate tons of sand in order to retrieve just a few grams of gold!

Chapter written by Gilles SANTINI.

Deconstruction and accumulation of data

The massive availability of data today (Big Data or massive data) is the result of the process of deconstructing and accumulating digital data. Indeed, if binary coding has allowed for the exact and universal expression of any data[1], it is only by the possibility of breaking down imagery, sound and displacements into elementary data that its expression has been made possible in stored form. The deconstruction of an image into a matrix of elementary visual elements was already used by Luis Duclos and Charles Cross in 1869, which influenced Georges Seurat and his postimpressionist school of pointillist painting.

The work of the mathematician Joseph Bastide Fourier (1768–1830) had certainly already made it possible to break down the waves into constituent elements, but in a form unsuited to a massive accumulation of digital data: it was probably the invention of mp3 coding, by Karlheinz Brandenburg[2] and his research team at the Fraunhofer Institute in Erlangen, that actually allowed its development after 1993[3]. As far as location and travel data are concerned, even though our current systems are based on very old work[4], it was the introduction of GPS (Global Positioning System) into civil use from 1983 onwards that made its ubiquity possible.

The automatic acquisition of massive data (or Big Data) is an essential condition of its existence, because the collection of such data is generally passive; however, the frequency of capture will increase with the introduction of the Internet of Things (or IOT): data will be captured, transmitted and stored without mankind keeping control over this accumulation process.

Massive databases

The establishment of databases useful for the management and operation of companies has greatly influenced the evolution of work carried out in the latter. ERP (Enterprise Resource Planning) software is dedicated to maintaining the uniqueness

---

1 Gottfried Wilhelm von Leibniz (1646–1716) had foreseen it in 1703 in his report of the Paris Science Academy entitled "Explanation of binary arithmetic which only uses the characters 0 and 1".

2 Title of his thesis: Digital Audio Coding, University of Erlangen-Nuremberg, 1989.

3 Standard ISO MPEG-1.

4 Those of the Flemish cosmographer (of Germanic origin) Gerard de Kremer, known as Mercator (1512–1594), inventor of the Earth's cartography bearing his name (Mercator projection).

of recorded information and guaranteeing that its origin is known; they have been able to make the most of it. However, it is important to understand that massive databases are profoundly different from previous databases. Less structured than previous databases, massive databases differ in many aspects. Taking a section of the Beckman Report's[5] conclusions, we can go deeper into what distinguishes massive databases from what is considered typical today [ABA 16].

Massive databases must meet the requirements of the 3V's (volume, variety and velocity); it takes advantage of the progress of traditional database systems to quickly manage large volumes of data[6]; but its gigantic size and high renewal frequency often lead to remote management in the cloud, which requires knowledgeable changes and new operational schematics. On the other hand, the need to process various types of data, forming a heterogeneous corpus, not only raises the question of their form, but also that of their variable frequency and unequal quality, not to mention the management of any rights attached to them in view of the disparity of sources.

In order to store and process massive data, it is therefore necessary to have infrastructures that allow heavy work to be carried out quickly. These infrastructures most often use either distributed or virtualized devices:

– in the case of distributed architectures, the use of standard processors is possible thanks to adapted programming models such as MapReduce, developed by a Google.inc team and widely used within the open source platform Hadoop;

– the development of new specialized processors is also of great interest, especially for processing ultra-fast data streams. New technologies are enabling us to control the storage costs of an ever-growing volume of data[7].

Moreover, in order to exploit massive data (it being considerably more varied than in previous databases), it is necessary to have the computer means that allow the processing of a great mass and a great diversity of data at the same time, the aim being to control a chain of operations transforming raw data into knowledge. It is, therefore, necessary to integrate applications designed to implement very different treatments and to produce syntheses of results from multiple sources. The successive and joint use of different programming languages and several processing models is

---

5 Work of the study group convened in October 2013 on the University of California-Irvine campus, to discuss the evolution of database tools.

6 Editor's note: see Chapter 3 pp. 80–81.

7 Micro-SD cards can now store 128 GB; some new multilayer nanoscale optical disks promise 360 TB; one gram of artificial DNA could store one Petabyte = one million gigabytes in the future.

essential in this context, as well as the provision of application software (Datamining, Data Visualization, Business Intelligence, etc.) offering great ease of use and complete automation.

Lastly, it is crucial to take into account that operations linked to massive databases require seasoned data technology specialists (Data Science) in order to master them. The lack of human resources with this level of qualification is well known; filling this gap requires considerable effort, especially since this data science is not only based on the mastery of computer science, statistics and applied mathematics, but also on a praxis that takes a long time to acquire!

Playing games with the devil?

Some of the difficulties we encounter in processing massive data are reminiscent of a puzzle game: reconstructing an image that we ignore from a set of small pieces. This game is usually easy to play and is based on the form, colors and drawing elements that can be seen on each pieces of the puzzle. The difficulty of such a game varies according to the number of its pieces. To train, it is good practice to try to reconstruct the puzzle by turning the pieces over, thus renouncing the information provided on their face side. This rather difficult practice underlines the extent to which the knowledge of parcel elements drawn from the examination of the faces (drawings and colors) makes it possible to link the pieces together and infer the meaning of the puzzle, in other words to mentally reconstitute the image. If all the pieces were square, it would not be possible to reconstruct the puzzle backwards, because the information available to reconstruct the image would be void. On the other hand, it would still possible to reconstruct the image of the puzzle with square pieces whose face side is visible. So, can we say that:

– on the one hand, the shape of the pieces allows a reconstruction of the puzzle if these shapes are well differentiated;

– and that knowledge of parcel visual attributes (drawings and colors) provides sufficient information to effectively guide the reconstruction of the image.

Similar considerations apply to the processing of massive data: the notion of structure (of data) replaces the notion of form (of the puzzle); and descriptive attributes (of data) play a role analogous to that of facial details (of the pieces of the puzzle)!

Let's imagine now that a prankster devil is roaming around us in order to complicate our game. This devil could, for example, mix two boxes of puzzles; it wouldn't interfere with our game, but it would increase its complexity by having twice as many pieces as before. This devil could also intentionally misplace a few pieces; but again, besides the fact that the reconstructed image would be incomplete, it wouldn't be too bad!

On the other hand, if the devil mixed two puzzle boxes representing the same image, but cut in two different ways, our task would become very difficult, because the visual attributes on the face side of the pieces would be deceiving. Our best strategy would be, without a doubt, to turn all the pieces over and reconstitute the two puzzles upside down, ignoring the visual attributes on the face side of their respective pieces so as to avoid being deceived by similarities.

Are we too clever for the devil? Unfortunately not, because pursuing his evil endeavor, this devil could still mix two neighboring images (different, but very similar) that are cut in the same way: the shape of the pieces would then be insufficient and misleading, even given the redundancy of their shapes and visual attributes that would make the identification of the matching pieces more difficult. Nevertheless, with sufficient effort, it would be possible to overcome the devil's deceitful attempts by combining our research with the simultaneous use of forms and correlations between the pieces of the two puzzles.

Big Data doesn't owe its complexity to the devil; as if to reconstruct a puzzle, it is necessary to combine the study of forms and correlations to overcome the difficulty. In fact, in most massive databases, data is either uninformed or heterogeneous: to overcome the difficulty, it is necessary to identify forms in order to structure the corpus of data. Additionally, each piece of information being very poorly characterized in isolation, it is also necessary to combine a large amount of data when processing measurements, in order to reveal a similarity between the items on which data is carried.

A case study

To illustrate this combined approach between forms and correlations, let's consider a case study from the world of mass distribution. A grocery store operator wants to promote new products by sending advertising messages to consumers in their catchment area, that we will refer to as their target. To do so, these messages must not only correspond to consumers' tastes and customs, but also reach them at the right time to trigger a potential purchase.

It is assumed that this operator knows the purchase history of the customers who have subscribed to his loyalty card: these are his members, and that he also asked a panel recruited from among his members to gather additional information on their interests and attitudes. This provides three sets of data on potential customers:

– general data on the target, including socio-demographic data (A);

– data on the past purchases of members, loyalty cardholders (B);

– data provided by the survey from the panel of members (C).

Data (A, B, C) are available for all panel members; but only (A, B) are known by members; and only (A) is available for the target. Operations on the database will be carried out in two stages:

1) messages to members and study of their new purchases;

2) determination of the appropriate recipients for each type of message and mass dispatch of said message types[8].

The first step is to determine which types of messages to send to members. This is done on the basis of data provided by the panel survey; each member (non-panelist) will then be assigned the data of a panelist who is similar to him or her and who could have the same type of consumption. Without going into the statistical techniques, commonly referred to as injections, fusion, or reconciliation of data implemented during this operation [LEJ 01, SAN 05], the essential part of it can nevertheless be understood:

– a consumption profile is determined for each of the members: each member is classified as Big, Medium, Small or Non-consumer of the product studied;

– the sequence of these codes (B, M, S, N) constitutes, for all the products studied, what is termed as the consumer's consumption DNA.

Each member (known as the recipient) is assigned one or more panelists (known as donors) whose consumption DNA is similar[9], and then each recipient is assigned available survey data on his or her donor(s)[10].

---

8 The transmission of messages to the concerned Internet users is generally entrusted to specialized service providers (Ad Servers) who know how to take into account the characteristics of individuals to determine where, when and how often messages should be placed.

9 Also ensuring that a donor is not used too often, in order to preserve the diversity of information observed among panelists.

10 An operation globally referred to as Data Ascription. This operation means assigning to each member not observed, but plausible data, which is attributed to him or her by analogy with those observed on one or more members of the panel. This is achieved by using complex

Having extended the information gathered by the panel to all members in this manner, promotional messages about new products are sent to these members, and their purchasing behavior is then observed for a period of time: have they changed? Did they take any action? And within what timeframe? Did they repeat the purchase and express their satisfaction? From this data, lessons are drawn: in which subgroups does a high purchasing probability appear? Do certain information and messages increase the likelihood of purchase?

In more mathematical terms, this means modeling the response (purchase) according to the form, content of messages[11] and individual characteristics known to members, which can be exploited operationally when sending messages to the target[12]. It is possible to refine this modeling according to the context that is defined by data from open access sources outside the survey itself (open data on weather, road traffic, holiday calendar, economic morale, etc.). Therefore, identifying promotional messages likely to favor the desired purchasing behaviors.

The protection of privacy

As can be seen in this example, the use of form-based and correlated parcel data from a variety of sources allows large-scale customization of the relationship with the customer. This practice does not infringe legality: the panelists are warned in advance and agree to respond to the surveys. The members have willingly subscribed to the loyalty program and have accepted the terms of their relationship with the operator in their contract; the consumers who constitute the target are anonymous recipients who have, at least formally, agreed to be contacted in advance.

However, there are cases where privacy protection imposes more severe barriers; it is then necessary to blur the trace of an individual that some data (or a combination of data) would easily find. To do this, Big Data providers often use so-called "differential privacy" techniques, which randomly alter an individual's data[13].

---

algorithms that not only take care to ensure that the donor and recipient have identical socio-demographic characteristics, but also that their resemblance, measured by a statistical index based on information known to both members and panelists, is great.

11 These are the explanatory variables in the statistical equation of the model.

12 The so-called co-variables of the response model.

13 We can also consider replacing the personal data of an individual with that of another individual whose behavior is similar: this method has the advantage of little disturbance to the processing of forms and correlations carried out on massive data (see also Chapter 3, pp. 99–100).

Automatic processing

Automatically going from available data to the desired response without human intervention is the claimed ambition of Big Data operators. However, this response must be adequate and educated. This is where the progress made by Deep Learning[14] techniques can play a role. These techniques, based on progressive improvement through unsupervised learning, seek to automatically recover objects whose deconstruction has produced Big Data. Such ex-post identification of images, words and forms is dazzling, but the advanced modeling of the phenomena on which the data seized was based is still moderate!

Based on a set of operating units (called neurons) that are divided into layers that can interact with each other, Deep Learning (DL) systems modulate how these neurons modify the digital and logical information that passes through them. This modulation is carried out without human intervention, according to consecutive intermediate states until a stable state emerges, providing a significant response. The more the operation is easy to evaluate in terms of the identification of a form, the more the relevance of an inference based on a model is difficult: it would be risky to promise too much, the risk being to make a decision on the basis of false inferences, which was what feared Karl Pearson, the one who came up with the term "spurious correlation" in 1897, to designate misleading correlations resulting from inadequate statistical analyses.

Great vigilance with regard to this risk is all the more important, as massive data growth inevitably leads to blind processing, based on Deep Learning, which can now be carried out by massively parallel processors developed from graphics processing units and have paved the way for cost-efficient HPC (High Power Computing)[15].

Conclusion

Thomas Nelson Winter [WIN 99] established the beginning of Big Data in 1951 when the US Bureau of Census, the statistical institute of the U.S., acquired its first UNIVAC computer; and when IBM decided to help Robert Busa, a young Jesuit whose ambition was to produce a general index of the works of St. Thomas Aquinas. Thirty years later, the 56 volumes of the Thomisticus Index were published. A

---

14 DL in short: methods that allow for an automatic endogenous modelling of data with minimal human intervention.

15 Estimated price: US 1.5/TFLOPS - 10^{12} floating point transactions per second. Editor's note: such processors have been developed for video games, see Chapter 9, p. 208.

decade ago, in 1988, Sergey Brin and Lawrence Page published their seminal article "The Anatomy of a Large-Scale Hypertextual Web Search Engine" at Stanford and Tim Berners-Lee created the World Wide Web in 1989 at CERN, making the Big Data we know today possible. But, at the time, data and its processing remained distinct, as in 1951.

The data we now handle are less structured, more massive than before; and the available computing architectures are less rigid and more powerful. The Deep Learning algorithms allow us to adapt data processing; but the computing architecture precedes the processing. So, what evolution can we expect in the future? No doubt real-time self-adaptation of computational structures to data, an advance that would be necessary for the emergence of a new form of intelligence of objects.

Bibliography

[ABA 16] ABADI D. *et al.*, "The Beckman Report on Database Research", *Communications of the ACM*, vol. 59, no. 2, February 2016.

[LEJ 01] LEJEUNE M., *Traitements des fichiers d'enquêtes : redressements, injections de réponses, fusions*, Libres Cours, Presses universitaires de Grenoble, 2001.

[SAN 05] SANTINI G., "Mathematical Models and Methods for Media Research", *Data Processing Models*, G.S. IT Services Ed., 2005.

[WIN 99] WINTER T.N., "Roberto Busa, S.J., and the Invention of the Machine-Generated Concordance", *Faculty Publications, Classic and Religious Studies*, University of Nebraska-Lincoln, 1999.

5

Bitcoin: an Innovative System

The advent of the Internet has not yet created as profound a shock in insurance and banking as we have seen in electronic commerce or "uberized" transport. But the decentralized and ubiquitous blockchains could change this: scattered all over the world, they are accessible everywhere, without resorting to savings, without former stock market quotation. It is the full set for an application that mainly manages money!

Bitcoin is an innovation for which the main application is financial, for the time being: with its own monetary symbol, this blockchain allows payment, exchange, placement, investment and even lending. Could it be an actual threat for banks and financial companies? Not yet, or not quite yet, because the scope of this new type of organization is limited. Accused of all the evils in the financial world, Bitcoin is already useful to the assets of countries in which neither the banking infrastructure nor modern means of payment have taken root. Just like micropayment by cell phone, which has replaced the failed banking network on the African continent!

Bitcoin therefore serves niches here and there; the volume of transactions and the cyber-currency money supply it manages are several orders of magnitude lower than the amounts exchanged in Europe, Japan and North America through banking services, the stock exchange and the various modes of credit, insurance and exchange. But, in a few years, wide avenues of growth could open up, which could be quite threatening for traditional finance and even for commercial intermediation.

Until recently, this tool has been poorly known, little described and not really understood, even in professional circles. This original and documented chapter sheds light on a subject that has many black holes for the honest man. It assesses the

Chapter written by Gérard Dréan.

scope, function, potential, limitations and competitive advantages of the implementations that manage money today. It focuses on the general mechanisms for building a block-chain; Chapter 6 will develop the purely financial transactions and open perspectives, which are mentioned here in an introductory way.

Since its launch in January 2009[1], bitcoin has been both a popular payment tool and a leading media topic. As of December 2016, the Bitcoin system was processing 250,000 transactions per day; the total value of outstanding bitcoins was 12 billion USD and the price had risen from a few dollars in 2012 to 1,000 USD, after reaching a peak of almost 1,200 USD in January 2014 and then falling back to 200 USD in 2015. Beyond the quick rise of bitcoin rate of exchange against the US $ witnessed in 2017 (BTC low 1.000 $ Feb. 2017, high 18.000 $ Dec. 2017) the volatility of BTC pricing over time stays however within much stricter limits than most poeple think: since late 2016, 60 days BTC volatility index ranged between 1% low (Dec. 2016) and 7% high (Jan. 2018), a much smaller range than earlier volatility index ranging between 1.5% low (Jun. 2012) and 14% high (Jun. 2011) during the period Sept. 2011 to Aug. 2014! see for instance: www.buybitcoinworldwide.com/volatility-index/.

As an alternative currency, bitcoin is the subject of much discussion, ranging from the denunciation of "the greatest scam of all times" to the announcement of an economic revolution that is comparable to the Internet. But too much discussion is still based on a lack of knowledge of the system. Those who are more economists than computer scientists transpose their positions on money to bitcoins: the overwhelming majority of them are blinded by the 20th Century belief that money is the business of countries, while Bitcoin is a radically new object, far beyond a monetary symbol alone. On the other hand, computer scientists are often unaware of the real terms of monetary competition. It seems that accepted knowledge leads to many mistakes because the principles on which Bitcoin is based, as well as the mechanisms it uses, are beyond our usual references. This chapter briefly describes the underlying system and technologies, the potential of which goes far beyond the monetary area. It also offers a tour of the unusual environment in which it developed, that of free software, of which the rules and practices are probably shaping the future of computing.

Bitcoin and *bitcoin:* some key concepts

The same term refers to two meanings: Bitcoin (a proper noun, written with a capital letter) is a peer-to-peer electronic payment system; and the unit used in this system, the bitcoin, a common noun written with an article and a lower-case letter[2]. A payment system is a device that transfers units from one user to another. Users can accept these transfers in exchange for services or goods, which gives these units a money role.

---

1 By the mysterious Satoshi Nakamoto, probably a collective pseudonym.
2 Editor's note: This writing convention will be observed in this chapter and in Chapter 6.

In computing, a peer-to-peer system is a set of machines linked by a communications network, where each node of the network is equipped with the functionalities corresponding to all possible roles. Each user can freely offer the services he/she wishes and freely choose the services he/she wishes to use without any function being reserved in an authoritarian way for certain participants. Each user can therefore be a user and a service provider at the same time. Such a system is therefore characterized by the absence of a central point to which participants would be forced to apply for certain functions. It can be designed in such a way that a large number of nodes work together to provide the same services, that these nodes control each other and provide mutual assistance when necessary, thus ensuring the system is almost completely secure and tamper-proof[3].

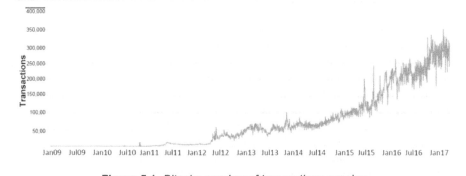

Figure 5.1. *Bitcoin: number of transactions per day*
Source: https://blockchain.info/fr/Graphique nombre de transactions

The Bitcoin system

Its central function is to validate and record transactions, produced continuously by many sources, in a public file protected against alteration. Secondary functions prepare the transactions and provide access to the validated transaction files. All of these functions are performed by freely downloadable software that can be installed on a wide variety of computers. These software programs create accounts and transactions and maintain the transaction ledger by monitoring the validity of transactions issued.

An elementary transaction consists of transferring a certain quantity M of units called bitcoins from user A to user B. This transaction is only legitimate if it is issued by A, who must have previously received M units (at least), a fact that any

---

3 Incidentally, this definition is not very far removed from that of a free society or a free market; it is therefore no coincidence that the promoters of Bitcoin claim liberal, and even libertarian, positions.

other user can verify. If this is the case, this movement is irreversibly and publicly recorded, which then authorizes B to transfer all or part of these units to C. Similarly, B may accept the transfer as compensation for a service rendered to A or an asset that he has assigned to him, and C may also accept the transfer in return for a service rendered to B or an asset that he has assigned to him. Thanks to the mutual trust of users and the trust they place in the system, the accounting unit, the bitcoin, becomes a means of indirect exchange, that is money.

This psychological mechanism is neither mysterious nor exceptional: it is the same that makes us accept a payment by check/cheque, banknote or credit card. There is, however, a novelty: this currency can only be used within the payment system, a limitation that should not be forgotten in any discussion of this form of money. In short, it is a local currency used by the members of the Bitcoin network and by them alone. That being said, all Internet users, in other words a few billion people on the globe, can join this network free of charge in just a few minutes and without any formality. The heart of the system is formed by the complete history of legitimate transactions and all the computing processes that construct it. In this history, transactions are recorded in plain text and can be read by anyone, but they cannot be edited or deleted.

The "accounts"

Each user can create any number of accounts, between which bitcoins can be transferred. An account consists of a pair of cryptographic keys, each of which encrypts messages and decrypts messages coded with the other. One of the keys, the public key, may be shared with third parties, published in a directory and included in official documents; it allows other users to communicate with its owner. The other, the private key, must be kept secret by its holder; it serves as his signature[4]. In reality, it is not the actual public key that is issued, but a "hardened" version of it which includes its own protection system, and is improperly called "account number". These identifiers are 160 bit numbers, containing a control key, represented in an esoteric form of which here is an example:

1Lke9VyQHixh8zxteh7mENSr4wsX5N6BeN

---

4 This function is based on cryptographic signatures and uses asymmetric double-key cryptography. If I send a message that is known to a correspondent by encrypting it with my private key that he doesn't know, he will be able to verify that I am the author of this message by decrypting it with my public key. I can thus sign the transactions I create and allow all other users to verify that I am the author. Formulas for this form of electronic signature can be found in many books describing the RSA algorithm (Rivest, Shamir and Adleman), published in 1978 in the United States, see for example: [MEY 82].

The holder of this identifier may, for his own use, designate it by a symbolic name of his choice (for example "Jules" or "my account"), which will not appear in the registry or in other public files. What is called an account in Bitcoin is therefore only a pair of keys that allow you to create and exploit transactions. No balance is ever shown in the central registry.

Users usually keep these addresses in a wallet[5] that also offers functions for creating and exploiting transactions. There are many wallet management software packages available, which can reside on a shared computer, on the user's computer, on a smartphone or even on a magnetic card. Regardless of the medium, each user must protect his wallet in order to maintain anonymity and prevent a third party from associating his identity with his accounts, except for the one he chooses as a public key. For this purpose, wallets are often protected by sophisticated cryptographic devices.

Each user can have any number of accounts, in other words key pairs. The number of possible separate addresses is expressed by a number of 48 digits. That would allow each human being on Earth to have several billions of billions of billions of billions of accounts (or 10^{36}) which, on a human scale, is a good approximation of infinity. For security reasons, it is strongly recommended to use a new address for each transaction, which some wallets do automatically.

Transactions

When a user has created a wallet and accounts and acquired bitcoins by, for example, selling a good or service, or in exchange for a conventional currency, the user may issue transactions to transfer all or part of his bitcoins from one or more of his accounts to one or more other accounts, for himself or for another user. These transactions are anonymous: only account numbers are included. Users can keep the links between themselves and their accounts secret, preventing a third party from going back from an account to its owner.

Each transaction is signed by its sender. It can group together amounts issued from several previous transactions and distribute the total amount to several outlets. A transaction therefore has any number of inputs and any number of outputs. Each input refers to an output from a previous transaction. Each output specifies an amount and the conditions under which another user may appropriate it[6]. In the

---

5 Like the word "account", the word "wallet" is inappropriate, since it is a simple keychain that does not contain bitcoins, but contains the keys that allow it to interact with the system.

6 The amounts are expressed in *satoshi* (one hundred millionth of a bitcoin), which at the current rate, allows payments of about 1/10,000 EUR.

simplest and most common case, the issuer indicates the account number to be credited and expects the recipient to provide a cryptographic signature proving that he or she is the holder of that account.

In reality, for each output of a transaction, this condition is defined in the form of a program (an output script) written in a specific language, which is an integral part of the transaction. This program expects its data from the input that will refer to it. The account holder who wants to benefit from the transaction must therefore include a program written in the same language (an input script) in the input of his own transaction, which produces that data. The validity criteria of a transaction are written into the scripts of its outputs and inputs, which makes the Bitcoin system potentially capable of handling a wide variety of different types of transactions.

When a transaction is validated, the script of each of its inputs is executed, and its result is immediately used as data by the output script designated by that input. If the result of this calculation is "false" for one of the inputs, the transaction is rejected. Before entering a transaction in the history, the system checks that its issuer is authorized to use the amount of the transactions it has received. It also verifies that the total of the amounts shown in its outputs is less than or equal to the total amounts made available by its inputs[7]. In practice, making a simple transaction is as easy as paying with a credit card. The customer only has to type the amount on his mobile phone and "flash" the merchant's account number. The wallet software will include the customer's account number, search for available outputs covering the transaction amount, format the transaction, sign it and send it over the network. However, the wallet can be programmed to build more complex transactions, as we will see in Chapter 6.

The transactions register

Each transaction is first broadcast to all the computers on the network, which verify its integrity and legitimacy compared to previous transactions. Generally speaking, the Bitcoin system applies a principle of generalized distrust: as a principle, every node in the network is considered as capable of committing fraud and therefore each node verifies the integrity of everything it receives from others. An illegitimate transaction is ignored; a legitimate transaction is placed in a local queue, passed on to neighboring nodes, and then passed from one node to the next through the entire network. Each node therefore contains all the transactions issued.

---

7 Editor's note: this procedure verifies that the balance of the paying account is sufficient to honor the transfer issued.

Block construction

The following operations include two steps: in the first step, transactions are assembled into intangible blocks, as if they were written on registry pages in indelible ink. In the second stage, the resulting blocks are assembled to create the complete history (known as the blockchain), which is analogous to a tamper-proof binding of the created pages.

The first step consists of extracting a certain number of pending transactions from the local file (typically between 1,000 and 3,000 operations), organizing them in a tree structure to facilitate subsequent consultations and adding a header that characterizes the block. In particular, this header contains a checksum or hash, a usual method of data protection[8].

The calculation algorithm ensures that two blocks with different contents always have different checksums. In this way, the checksum of a block can be used as a unique identifier. The header of each block contains the identifier of the previous block[9]. It is therefore possible to go back up to the initial block of the chain from any block and check its validity at each step. This linking system is designed so that any modification forces you to not only recalculate the control sum of the modified block, but also that of all subsequent ones in the blockchain. If the perpetrator of the modification has also changed the block header by recalculating its new checksum, he has also modified its identifier. The blocks that referred to it no longer have any predecessors and the blockchain is broken. Inserting a modified block into a chain forces you to modify the headers of all subsequent blocks, an operation that is all the more expensive as the block is older, which quickly becomes prohibitive.

In order to make the blockchain tamper-proof, Bitcoin imposes conditions on the checksums that make their calculation extremely demanding in terms of computing resources (calculation time and/or memory). The creation of a block is set so that the calculation of an acceptable control key takes an average of ten minutes for the most powerful computer or computer pool in the network. As it is very demanding in machine time, this step can only be carried out by specialized nodes whose owners are rewarded with bitcoins: this is why they are called "miners". The operation itself

---

8 Remember that a checksum (hash or fingerprint) is a number, calculated from the contents of the block, such that it is impossible to reconstitute the block from its checksum: it is a one-way function and the slightest modification of the block modifies the checksum in an unpredictable way. In Bitcoin, it is a 256 bit number whose value is expressed by a number of 78 digits. This checksum is systematically recalculated at each subsequent access in order to detect any modification of the block after its construction. The header of each block also contains an evaluation of the work done to build it.

9 Which is its checksum.

is called "mining". This remuneration is only granted to the miner if the block is accepted in the chain at the end of the next step[10].

Chain assembly

When a miner succeeds in assembling a valid block, he or she passes it on to neighboring nodes, which in turn check its validity and that of each of the transactions it contains, before adding it to the local blockchain and passing it on to their neighbors, who in turn carry out the same checks. Each transaction is thus verified countless times before being definitively recorded into the multiple copies of the blockchain.

Unlike in the previous case, this second step in the construction of the blockchain is carried out by a large number of nodes in parallel (called full nodes). Each of these nodes maintains its own copy of the transaction register. With each new block it receives, the computer of a full node executes a protocol with three possible outcomes: reject the block if it has already been received, or if it is invalid, or if it contains a transaction that is already present in the local chain; add it to the end of the local chain after a final check of all the transactions it contains, or else put it on hold. Since each block contains the identifier of its predecessor in the blockchain of the miner who built it, this predecessor is usually also the terminal block of the local chain to which it will be added, after a final check of its validity. Otherwise, it is put on hold in a secondary branch of the blockchain.

In order to ensure that all copies of the blockchain are identical, albeit independently constructed, this protocol incorporates a "consensus" mechanism: this is a vital component of the system. The rule is to retain the chain that required the greatest amount of construction work for the blocks that make it up. If, after adding a new block, a secondary chain has required more work than the current main chain, this secondary chain must become the main branch. To do this, the program goes back to the branch point on the main branch, successively revalidates each block put on hold and the transactions it contains, adds this block to the end of the chain under construction if the checks are satisfactory, but abandons this process at the first error.

This critical and complex protocol is the heart of the system. It provides some additional services, such as rebuilding the local network after a computer or network

---

10 Initially set at 50 Bitcoins per block, this premium is halved every four years. It is currently 12.5 Bitcoins and will become zero around 2140. Since this is the only way to create new bitcoins, the total number of bitcoins in circulation will then be constant at 21 million; miners will then only be remunerated by commissions paid by the issuers of transactions.

shutdown. It imposes a very large footprint in secondary memory. This is why we have recently seen the appearance of "thin client" servers that do not need to keep the complete register up to date and rely instead on full nodes, which they access by means of a secure protocol.

At the end of this second phase, each of the thousands of copies of the blockchain that exist on the full nodes have been extended by a block chosen by each node from among the proposals made by miners, applying the programmed consensus rule. If all these full nodes implement the same validation rules, this additional block is the same for all nodes, and therefore all copies of the blockchain are identical[11].

Overview

Ultimately, transactions created by hundreds of thousands of users are recorded in thousands of identical files, on many different sites, in the form of unalterable and freely viewable blocks. Let's emphasize the fact that these files are built by different operators and independently of each other. Thus, contrary to what is often read, the chain of blocks is not "distributed", which would imply that different nodes would carry different parts of the same chain; nor is the chain "replicated", which would imply that it would be built at a central point and copied by the other nodes.

This construction is broken down into stages and executed by different operators. The miners build the blocks and only add them to their own copy of the chain. Full nodes accept these blocks and add them to their copy of the chain, provided they have validated them, but without the ability to modify them; everyone checks what the others have done. These operations are carried out in parallel by thousands of sites that are managed by independent operators around the world; anyone is free to play any role in the system, including the most central ones. The system is based on the assumption that it is constantly targeted by a large number of potential fraudsters, all of whom are highly competent.

In total, Bitcoin therefore consists of several layers:

– at the center, a network of complete servers operating on a peer-to-peer basis; several thousand people perform the same functions in parallel and independently of

---

11 Different nodes can sometimes carry different copies, either temporarily (soft forks) or permanently (hard forks). A typical case is where two miners produce two different valid blocks almost simultaneously. Depending on the propagation times across the network, these blocks can then reach the other nodes in a different order. Each node will retain the first block that arrived and put the other one on hold, creating a temporary fork that will (normally) be resolved after the arrival of the next blocks.

one another. Each manages a local copy of the basic database; they monitor each other and help each other if necessary;

– a network of lighter servers that do not contain the blockchain, but use full servers to access transactions;

– among all the precedents, some of them are miners, often grouped together to combine their computing power (pools);

– all the above is surrounded by input points (the wallets) ranging from a simple app on the computer (for an individual) to a local management function on a commercial site, company or financial institution.

The true originality of Bitcoin (and the systems that derive from it) is to be implemented on an open peer-to-peer network. Open because any computer owner can, at any time, join the network without anyone else's permission; peer-to-peer because everyone freely chooses the function(s) they perform, including the most centralized ones. In such a network, there is no central control or privileged node.

These principles of openness and decentralization make it impossible to know the number of operators in each role. However, the number of wallet holders (therefore bitcoin holders) is estimated at several million, a few hundred thousand of which are actually active. Nodes are counted in tens of thousands[12]; miners can group themselves into cooperatives (pools) to combine computing resources and profits while sharing a full node, which makes a pool look like a single miner. A dozen cooperative pools, with an indeterminate number of miners, provide 95% of the blocks admitted to the chain. The evaluation of the number of full nodes, that is to say the number of copies of the blockchain (which, as we have pointed out above, may not all be identical), is very risky: the estimates range from 5,000 to 30,000, spread over 85 countries, across all continents.

Reliability and safety

Extreme redundancy of the master file and the construction of this file ensures a continuous 24-hour service. Each computer can disconnect or fail without compromising the overall operation. If it is a full node, the software protocol will automatically reconstruct the missing portion of the blockchain with the help of neighboring nodes when the node server becomes operational again. As long as the user has Internet access, he or she will always find a node to accept and relay a transaction; there are always enough miners and full nodes to register it and make it

---

12 The only number measured continuously by specialized sites is the number of "listening nodes", in other words those that are able to receive and transmit new transactions at the time of measurement; this number varies between 5,000 and 11,000.

accessible in the blockchain. All transactions, even those created in a country without any Bitcoin nodes, are relayed and processed by computers located elsewhere in the world; they can be viewed at any Internet access point. The only way to stop this system is to stop the Internet.

This same redundancy, together with the "precautionary principle" whereby each node checks the validity of everything it receives before exploiting it, prevents the spread of fraudulent transactions. Errors and frauds are possible on a particular computer, because of the operator or hacker who manipulates this site. They may even spread locally through contagion or collusion. However, it is virtually impossible for this pollution to spread to a significant percentage of the block chain, let alone to the entire network.

On the other hand, any device whose functions are not duplicated remains vulnerable. This is the case, for example, with individual keychain wallets, which hold the correspondence between account numbers and the identity of their holders and with portals for inputs/outputs, such as currency exchange sites and interconnection sites for corporate computing. The security and confidentiality of these peripheral systems are the responsibility of their operators. Hacking a wallet or exchange site can therefore have dramatic consequences for their users (by way of example, this is the only way to "steal" bitcoins), but it has no effect on the Bitcoin system itself, just as stealing someone's wallet does not endanger the banking system. So far, all frauds and security breaches have involved local applications, exchange rate systems and not Bitcoin itself, the robustness of which is amply demonstrated by the facts[13].

While offering its users a high degree of security, the multitude of copies of the blockchain poses a problem for them: in application of a "precautionary principle", it cannot be assumed that all copies are identical, so which one should be taken as a reference in case of disagreement? It is up to each user to define the consultation protocol of his choice according to the use he makes of it. A typical example is to randomly interrogate nodes until a certain number of them, which have been defined in advance, give the same result with an overwhelming majority. The user can also use trusted nodes, or any combination of these two approaches. It is up to him to choose the method.

All transactions recorded in the blockchain, including the public keys of their issuers, beneficiaries and associated scripts, are visible to all interested parties. Although the identity of users does not appear there, it is not entirely impossible to

---

13 When the activities of an illicit trading platform such as Silk Road (which closed in November 2014) come to an end, it is, proportionally speaking, as if we were dismantling a mafia; contrary to what we have read in the media, Bitcoin is only getting better.

trace public keys back to the identity of their owners, which gives some possibilities of controlling and auditing. Users concerned about confidentiality can set up cryptographic procedures using the peer-to-peer network to prevent this "re-identification", which can only be carried out by experts at the cost of a real police investigation.

Software changes

So far, we have implicitly assumed that all computers on the network use the same software for each of the roles they play. There are standard software packages for the community; but operators have complete freedom to use others, whether for local needs or on an experimental basis, for fraudulent purposes or simply by mistake or negligence. So, what happens then? As long as the software installed on the nodes implements the same transaction and block validation protocols, and the same consensus mechanism, regardless of their other differences, the two essential steps in building the blockchain run in the same way on all nodes and produce identical copies of the chain. This enables countless experiments and variants in terms of user-friendliness, performance and ancillary functionality, without affecting the system's core functions. The only truly critical functions are:

– the transaction validation protocol used in transaction distribution, block construction and blockchain construction;

– the block validation protocol (which itself uses the transaction validation protocol) and the consensus rules implemented for building the blockchain. If different nodes use different validation protocols, each node only retains and redistributes the transactions it recognizes as valid. If a node serves one or more miners, they only incorporate the transactions validated by that node into the blocks they build. These blocks are distributed to all nodes, but each one is only accepted by the nodes that apply the same rules as those of the miner who built it. The network is then divided into several populations that build and use different blockchains. The same applies if the blocks have different formats or if the consensus rule is different. Since each node retains the blocks that it has not incorporated into its blockchain in one or more secondary branches, this situation (called a fork) causes a split in the node population, which then uses different blockchains.

Owning bitcoins means having access to transactions that credit my account. Since everyone can only access transactions entered in the blockchain of the population to which they belong, and can only record transactions on the same blockchain, transactions between different populations are not possible. We now have two different currencies between which exchange is only possible by means external to the Bitcoin system. In other words, different protocols define different currencies. If the protocols are sufficiently distinct that the transactions and blocks accepted by each of them are rejected by the other, each node only accepts the blocks produced by the miners of its own population. The split is then complete (hard fork), constituting of two networks that record transactions using different currencies separately, with the system sorting them.

Another particularly important case is that of an evolution of the software. In this case, the transactions recognized as valid by the existing protocol are generally also valid by the new protocol, but the new protocol can also validate transactions that were not accepted by the old protocol. In population B (that uses the new protocol), the chain contains all transactions. In population A (who retained the old protocol), the blockchain only contains transactions according to the old standard; regarding the "mixed" blocks produced by the miners of B, population A keeps them on hold. Even if such an alteration is consensual, a transitional period will be necessary for it to be applied by all. In this interval, as soon as an A node installs the new version of the software, it will accept the first valid block of a miner from B. Since it is very likely that the chain that leads to this block will have required more work than the current branch, the blockchain construction protocol then reconstructs in this node the new branch of the blockchain and substitutes it for the old branch. This is aided by the fact that each node keeps all the well-formed blocks it has received in a secondary branch of the blockchain, including those coming from miners from the other population; but without checking the transactions they contain, which it will only do at the time of the changeover. If this validation succeeds, this node will thus rejoin population B. Such a temporary fork, which is automatically corrected at the time of the software change, is called a soft fork. A non-consensual modification, which divides the network permanently, causes a hard fork.

Fraud and control takeover

Any attempt at fraud requires that critical software be replaced by a permissive protocol on a sufficient number of nodes, otherwise a disputed transaction could not spread across the network. But fraudulent transactions are only accepted and retransmitted by the nodes that have adopted this software; the effect of these fraudulent transactions will therefore be limited to fraudsters only.

Similarly, the only way to take control of the system, for whatever purpose, is to take control of a majority of miners and a majority of full nodes. To create fraudulent transactions, there must be miners to include them in complete blocks and nodes that add these blocks to their chain. Regardless of the number of these miners, their blocks will only be accepted by the nodes themselves fraudulent; the majority of full nodes will remain the same. The majority of full nodes is the determining factor, in other words the majority of users, provided that the population of full nodes is sufficiently large and representative of the user population.

Extensions

We have seen that transactions contain scripts that define their conditions of validity. Some limitations are written in the general Bitcoin protocol, including the size of scripts (10,000 bytes), the size of each transaction (100,000 bytes) and the size of blocks (1 Mb); any script with less than 10,000 bytes will be accepted without verification. By developing appropriate scripts and wallets to create transactions that use these scripts, it is possible to introduce new types of transactions into Bitcoin (without modifying the system itself), that perform quite complex financial operations and transactions of a non-financial nature, where critical information is kept and made publicly accessible without anyone being able to modify it. Examples of these are given in Chapter 6.

Evolution of Bitcoin and peer-to-peer payment

To form a prognosis on the future of Bitcoin, it is necessary to take the prospects of evolution of the software itself into account. There is indeed such an abundance of initiatives and creation of additional software, corrections, improvements and alternatives to the Bitcoin system, that the context of alternative currencies is constantly changing. These developments are facilitated by open source software: not only are the software free and freely usable, but the source code itself is public and everyone has the right to modify it and distribute modified versions. There is therefore a population of voluntary developers and testers around Bitcoin who identify problems and opportunities for expansion, devise solutions and produce modifications and extensions to existing systems, or even completely new alternative systems.

This activity is supported by a few specialized sites (the most important of which is GitHub) that provide the necessary tools to coordinate and integrate a multitude of decentralized and autonomous initiatives, including exchanging ideas, discussions, managing developments and versions, tests and modifications, publishing work in progress, and lastly, building, distributing and maintaining operational systems. Several types of objectives can be distinguished from these developments.

The first is obviously, as with any software, to solve common problems: eliminate malfunctions, plug security holes, improve user-friendliness and performance. In the long term; reduce resource consumption, process more transactions, reduce response times and accept a very large number of nodes in the network without exceeding the physical capacities of computers (scalability).

A second way is to add new functions and services to the existing system, still on a peer-to-peer basis, in order to match and surpass the offerings of specialized establishments. These developments can exploit the open platform of transactions by defining new scripts that create services within Bitcoin, such as conditional payments, crowdfunding, blocked accounts, etc. Other, more ambitious ones, are aimed at adding new financial interactions such as offers and requests, credit, foreign exchange, contracts of all kinds, etc.

A third way is to have the uses of an indelible public register not be limited to financial transactions, but extended to other classes of information: reference texts, contracts, titles of ownership, patents, access rights, expert reports, literary works, etc. It is then a question of programming application functions specific to different information classes in the form of scripts. These applications can be either stand-alone or coupled with a payment system. In the latter case, the system would manage both informational goods, their transfer between users and the monetary counterparts of the services, that is to say its trade, in addition to that of the goods and services, whose access would be controlled by information recorded in the blockchain.

Such efforts may take the form of a new version of the basic software (the current version, after eight years of existence, bears the number 13); or additional software of optional use, especially for wallets and light servers. Several independent teams are developing extensions to the Bitcoin system to form an under layer, capable of handling complex transactions such as decentralized exchange between virtual currencies, savings and credit[14].

The rules of free software allow everyone to take the ideas and developments of others and incorporate them into their own products. Therefore, there are variants of the same software, where only a few parameters have been modified, in particular those governing the accounting unit. Some of these variants coexist with Bitcoin on the same network and the same blockchain as alternate chains (alt-chains); others use a separate blockchain. Litecoin, launched at the beginning of 2011, is a Bitcoin clone that offers the exact same functionality with some differences in the discipline of unit creation and a different method of blockchain protection, which is less time-consuming and therefore can support a larger volume of transactions with a better response time, suitable for small transactions. It is the only clone with a significant market share, far behind Bitcoin. In contrast, these same rules of free software allow Bitcoin to integrate all or part of the developments produced by its competitors.

---

14 There are currently more than 100 BIP (Bitcoin Improvement Proposals) formalized and active.

Lastly, there are total reconstruction projects. The most important ones are Ripple and Ethereum, discussed in Chapter 6.

In summary

Taken separately, at a strictly technical level (prior to any competition) each of these projects will be able to succeed or fail, live as an independent project or disappear by seeing their functions more or less taken over by others. The free flow of ideas and pieces of code, which is the hallmark of free software, allows us to treat everything as a whole in which different systems maintain relations of competition and mutual enrichment, resulting in extraordinary reactivity and very lively creativity. Competing with and complementary to one another, each of these systems is a test bed that can benefit everyone.

Bitcoin was a prototype; for the moment, it is the dominant realization; the common problems it poses are and will be identified and quickly solved, including some residual security flaws. Thanks to an active community and the rules of open source software, today's criticisms will be obsolete tomorrow and the improvements will be somewhat spectacular for revolutionary applications in the fields fundamental to society: testaments, accounting, intellectual rights, rights of use or enjoyment, etc. The future is open; experimentation continues at a great pace.

Bibliography

[ANT 15] ANTONOPOULOS A., *Mastering Bitcoin*, O'Reilly, Sebastopol, 2015.

[BIT 17a] BITCOIN, http://bitcoin, 2017.

[BIT 17b] BITCOIN, https://en.bitcoin.it/wiki/Protocol_rules, 2017.

[BIT 17c] BITCOIN, http: //bitcoin.org//bitcoin.pdf, 2017.

[BIT 18] BITCOIN, http://www.bitcoin.fr/, 2018.

[BLO 17] BLOGCHAINCAFE, http://blogchaincafe.com/, 2017.

[BLO 18] BLOCKCHAIN, http://blockchain.info/fr/, 2018.

[COI 17] COINDESK, http://www.coindesk.com/, 2017.

[MEY 82] MEYER C., MATYAS S., *Cryptography*, Wiley Interscience, New York, 1982.

[WIK 17a] WIKIPEDIA, http://fr.wikipedia, 2017.

[WIK 17b] WIKIPEDIA, https://fr.wikipedia.org/wiki/Logiciel_ libre, 2017.

Tactics and Strategies

Introduction to Part 2

Several of the contributions in the first part of this volume highlight the universal, almost invasive character of digital applications, in that everything seems to have been working together to give these devices a more prominent social role up till today. As subtle and impressive as they may seem, the techniques that are used cannot be lessened to that of the mega-social machine stigmatized by Jacques Ellul. Certain behaviors are almost certainly pathological and addictive[1]. But common practices confirm Michel Crozier's intuition that society treats the technical system as a foreign body, invading it without making society itself become a machine!

Commercial propaganda obviously focuses on the positive, imperative and irresistible character of digital applications: let everyone lead their lives with the help of a digital assistant and they will reap the rewards until the cows come home! Such an approach is purely tactical: it seeks a concrete operational result, selling machines and services to as many people as possible. Others, however, pursue a long-term objective, inspired by something other than an immediate result; by some sort of utopia, they aim to win the public's trust and change their behavior. They are strategists.

This second part illustrates the concomitance of these two behaviors: some are tactical, others strategic. The burgeoning health and care sector, whose growth is constantly increasing thanks to technical progress and to the health action pursued over the last two centuries, still merits a real strategy. However, the field underlines that tactical considerations, which are still too heterogeneous to come together

---

1 Addiction to video games, television and social networks, for example. See quotations from Ellul and Crozier in *Le système technicien*, Cherche Midi reprint, 2012, Paris, pp. 26–31, 2012. [First edition 1977, Calmann-Levy, Paris; English translation by J. Neugroschel: The Technological System, Continuum, New York, 1980].

around a single strategic vision, prevail in this vast sector. For the time being, the information industries have a wide, profitable and multifaceted scope of application. But without any overall strategy!

A cooperative peer-to-peer organization that builds and maintains a chain of blocks like Bitcoin intends to transform the issuance, circulation and exchange of monetary symbols on a global scale. It shares a strategic objective with other projects such as Ripple, Ethereum, Omni, and many others who share the same vision: to adapt finance to the digital world. The same is true of the transhumanists who put the intellectual, financial and industrial resources of the very large companies they manage at the service of social projects such as: extending life, eradicating senescence and a possible synthesis between biology and electronics; offering wide strategic perspectives for the artificial intelligence of tomorrow.

Let us beware of assimilating digital objects and their technical system to a social being or a god; its presence and its practical uses are mere experience.

6

Bitcoin and Other Cyber-currency

"An effective currency is at the condition of human freedom.
Believe me, today as yesterday, man's fate is at stake on the currency."
Jacques RUEFF, *L' âge de l' inflation*,
Payot, Paris, p. 15, 1963

*The following text extends the previous chapter and develops an important part
of the implementations that exploit the "blockchain" technique on the scale of cross-
border service. The author presents and comments on the broad spectrum of
financial and currency applications that this technology allows; he precisely
documents the extension and functionalities that this new technology promises, with
a precision and detail that goes far beyond the comments and information published
to date, at least by the major media and management literature.*

*From the outset, Bitcoin's inventors have sought to organize a payment system
without intermediaries, thereby bypassing some of the functions performed by banks
and other financial establishments. The author proves, by way of example, that these
peer-to-peer trading methods, which are entirely dependent on the Internet, can
have a revolutionary effect in the monetary field; and that their impact on financial
services is already noticeable, in much the same way as the established paradigm of
real estate services and car transport services being disrupted by AirBnB and Uber.*

*In addition, the new Bitcoin services are challenging the monetary monopoly of
modern states. Announced as an experiment and kept confidential for several years,
this system has been operational worldwide since 2013. It is growing steadily, which
at least proves its feasibility and robustness: peer-to-peer payment is decentralized,*

Chapter written by Gérard DRÉAN.

which was incidentally the objective of its inventors. The success of this innovation, which has matured to adulthood in recent years, has aroused many emulations and competitors. In this way, Bitcoin is the ancestor and star of a family of blockchains who use their own account unit, ensuring instantaneous exchange of all circulating currencies and between cyber-currencies[1] themselves. What does its future look like? What kind of reception does it get from professional circles? How do the monetary authorities of our time deal with this mode of exchange that disturbs established customs?

---

1 This term is adopted by the Commission of Enrichment of the French Language, preferred to "crypto-money" which evokes secrecy and concealment, whereas in these systems, transactions are kept in plain text in a public registry that remains visible to everyone.

Introduction

There are currently more than 700 cyber-currencies in circulation, and they appear and disappear almost daily. This family of cyber-currencies rely on a very active community of high-level developers, including many start-ups. Bitcoin and cyber-currencies have also become a journalistic phenomenon that produce their usual batch of errors, approximations and hasty judgments. Lastly, by posing itself as an alternative to banks, these heavily cross-border systems spark interest and concern to key financial players and governments alike.

Why do so many competing achievements coexist? How do they differ from each other? What would be their likely impact on the sovereign monetary system? These are issues addressed in this chapter.

Bitcoin, the first cyber-currency

To answer the questions above, it is necessary to take the time to assimilate the innovative techniques that establish the Bitcoin system and its derivatives; and to do so, to go back to its very definition and underlying functionalities.

The true nature of bitcoin

Bitcoin is generally associated with the blockchain[2] principle. However, this technique is not specific to monetary or financial mechanisms such as Bitcoin. It is only a storage mode that allows any type of entries to be recorded, in a form that is publicly accessible and unmodifiable. What characterizes Bitcoin, and more generally payment systems, is the nature of the records, namely the financial transactions that credit and debit accounts.

As we have seen in the previous chapter, a Bitcoin transaction consists of any number of inputs composed of the identifier from one of the outputs of a previous transaction and a program (input script), and any number of outputs, each consisting of any number of bitcoins and an output script. To allow an input to appropriate the amount of the output it designates, the system executes the script of this input and of the designated output, and checks that the combined result has the "true" value. In the simplest and most common of terms, the output script verifies that it receives a

---

2 For a definition of the blockchain and its construction techniques, see Chapter 5.

cryptographic signature corresponding to the account to be credited; the input script that vindicates this output will have to provide this signature.

A transaction can only be recorded in the blockchain and therefore be considered executed if all its inputs have been matched to their designated outputs. To avoid double payments, each output can only be used once.

At any given moment, there are outputs in the blockchain that have not yet been referenced by subsequent transactions. These unspent outputs, which are available for future transactions, are stored in a list kept up to date by each node in the network (unspent transaction outputs or UTXO)[3]. When a new transaction has been entered in the blockchain, the system removes the outputs used by the transaction from this list and adds its own outputs that then become available. The cumulative amount of all available outputs constitutes the system's money supply.

For each account and for each wallet, an analysis of the transactions involving it allows you to calculate a balance. This balance does not appear anywhere in the blockchain, but it can be calculated and kept up to date in the holder's wallet. The only way to use this credit is to create transactions that reference the outputs credited to the account holder. Therefore, bitcoins have no existence of their own, they are only units of account attached to transactions; they cannot be used outside the Bitcoin system.

This system is analogous to a primitive system of exchange in which everyone retains the memory of all services rendered as well as those rendered to them, either explicitly or in the form of a conventional value attached to those services. Such a system remains existent in primitive communities, with few participants and a limited variety of mutual services[4]. Paradoxically, the latest computer and telecommunications techniques revert to a primitive system, thus making it operational on a global scale, to the benefit of an indefinite number of participants that are unknown to each other, and allowing all the goods and services of the modern world to be exchanged between them. By putting these ancient principles back into effect, Bitcoin's stated objective is to do without intermediaries by building trust on the consensus of many independent operators, like in primitive exchange.

---

3 This list currently contains 46 million outputs. It can be reconstituted at any time from the blockchain.

4 In modern societies, the idea of concretizing value units by means of tokens given to the service provider by the beneficiary of an exchange, dispenses with the need to keep the memory of all previous exchanges, which makes it possible to extend the exchange to a large number of people and an infinite range of services. These tokens have been given the name "currency".

All in all, Bitcoin is essentially a faithful and lasting record of the value of exchanges. Since such a mode of payment can be accepted in exchange for a good or service, its unit of account essentially plays the role of a currency, which cuts short the idle debate around the question: is bitcoin an actual currency[5]? Symmetrically, bitcoin is nothing more than the unit of account of this system, whose central functions are a transaction validation protocol and a block validation protocol. Therefore, if two analogous systems use different protocols, they define different units of account and therefore different currencies, even if they are based on the same network and use the same software. Any comparative analysis should focus first on the payment systems implemented and subsequently, where appropriate, on the units of account used by each of these systems.

The itinerary of a transaction

A transaction is built by a wallet[6]. It enters the system through a network node that verifies its form, the existence of the outputs referenced by each of its inputs (either in the blockchain or among the pending transactions) and the amount actually available to execute it. If the transaction is valid, it is placed in a local list of validated transactions and passed on to neighboring nodes that perform the same process. Otherwise, the process is abandoned and the transaction is left on hold.

Eventually, miners draw transactions from their local list of validated transactions and group them into a block. To do this, they repeat the same checks, but this time only taking into account transactions that are already present in the blockchain. If these checks are satisfactory, the miners include the transaction in the block under construction. Otherwise, the transaction remains on hold until all inputs are validated[7]. The new block, completed with its header, will be sent to all the nodes of the network, which will in turn repeat these same checks before adding this new block to their local chain if all these checks are satisfactory.

---

5 A question, which in reality, amounts to a semantic debate on the "true nature" of money; see [RIB 73].

6 A wallet is the software that ensures communication between a user and the system. It creates accounts, maintains the holder's own information such as the list of its accounts and the list of inputs available to it, prepares transactions on the holder's initiative by incorporating appropriate scripts. There are many variants of wallets that can be used either manually on a smartphone or microcomputer, or even incorporated into the management system of any company or organization.

7 In a transaction, it is also possible to specify a time period during which it will remain on hold and can still be modified, but in a limited way.

Between its creation and its recording in the blockchain, a transaction can be put on hold either on certain nodes that have not validated it in relation to their local list of available outputs ("orphan" transactions), or on full nodes that have validated it in relation to their local list, pending validation by miners.

Simple and complex transactions

The recipient account of an output is determined by the script of that output. It can therefore result from a calculation for which data is provided by the input script that uses this output. Ultimately, an output may not specify any account and accept, as the recipient of its amount, the account indicated to it by the first transaction that refers it. For example, this recipient could be the winner of a contest. To this end, the output script will contain the cryptographic hash of information known to the operator of the transaction, for example the solution of a crossword puzzle; the first competitor who completes the grid and proves it by including the hash of the solution in the input of a transaction will then be credited with the amount of this output.

Complex conditions can be applied, including the use of multiple signatures (multisig). Some wallets make it possible to create accounts in which transactions must be authorized by multiple signatures that the output script can verify. This is called an M on N type transaction (requesting M signatures taken from a list of N authorized signatories). For example: a transaction of type 1 out of 2 may involve the joint account of a household, a 2 out of 2 transaction may involve the savings account of the same household, a 2 out of 3 transaction may specify a list containing the issuer, the recipient and an arbitrator in case of a disagreement between the contractors; a 7 out of 12 transaction may represent a payment requiring the signature of the majority of a board of 12 members, etc. On these bases, it becomes possible to invent new forms of transactions by writing appropriate scripts, which are inserted into the inputs and outputs of transactions and then executed in the standard Bitcoin system.

It is finally possible to create more or less complex "contracts" consisting of a set of interdependent transactions that can be prepared by exchanging messages between the parties concerned, before being submitted for registration in the blockchain, possibly after the specified time limit. These messages may contain partially signed transactions, submitted to other agents for signature[8].

---

8 When an agent transmits an (incomplete) transaction to another agent, it authorizes the latter to complete it and submit it to the system for final registration in the blockchain, which is the equivalent to executing it.

When executing the scripts that are contained within the messages, transactions can use specialized servers such as "notaries" of Open Transactions[9], who ensure the validation of transactions by an independent third party, or "oracles" to whom the signature of a transaction can be delegated, provided that a certain expression, written in a language that the oracle can interpret, takes on the value "true"; the oracle can in turn access reference servers, such as the registry office. Among the applications of these techniques are: loans between individuals, fund raising, guardianship, betting and insurance contracts.

New tools of exchange

In a script, as in any computer program, it is possible to introduce constants that can characterize a particular input or output, as long as the scripts are programmed to interpret them. Such a constant can define a particular unit of account, hence the English term "colored coins" for this technique. The possibility to create and use these colored coins is offered by some wallets, such as: Chromawallet, Coinprism (2014) and Colu. Such a unit of account is created by a particular transaction that defines, among other things, the issuer's commitments, such as the obligation to provide a certain good or service upon request. This token can thus represent any asset defined by the creator (an actual good, a certificate, a title of ownership, a financial instrument, a sovereign, private, complementary or alternative currency, a right of access, etc.). At the time of processing of this transaction, these commitments will be publicly recorded in the blockchain in a non-modifiable way.

Such a token can then be transferred between users, exactly like ordinary bitcoins, including under contracts as described above[10]. It can be exchanged for other tokens, in particular for ordinary bitcoins, which are "colorless". Lastly, it can be accompanied by a computer key that opens an available document on the Internet: a text, music, a film, a computer service; or give access to an apartment, a vehicle or any other object with an electronic lock. The user credited with such a token receives his access key at the same time. This brings us to the "Internet of Things", which is rapidly developing internationally.

---

9 To avoid making this chapter heavier, references to the systems mentioned have been omitted. Interested readers are invited to consult the Internet for more complete descriptions. The following terms are metaphorical: notary, oracle, etc. The main idea is to submit transactions to a "trustworthy third party" within the meaning of the French law and the Civil Code (Art. 373 ff.).

10 These transactions (or more precisely their outputs) generally have a very low value in bitcoins, the value of the token being that of the associated asset.

It should be noted that all these functions are implemented in terms of wallets, or even with a simple messaging system, without modification to the core of the Bitcoin system itself. On the other hand, writing the necessary scripts and wallets to process them is an expert matter and mobilizes many young companies with unlimited imagination. Many of these developments compete with each other; it is too early to predict which ones will succeed, but it is clear that the expansion and perfecting of the Bitcoin system is still in its infancy.

The problem of growth[11]

Bitcoin's most critical problem is its growth capacity. With the current equipment, this system is approaching its maximum capacity (in transactions per second) even though it only accounts for a very small part of the transactions carried out in the world. Even relying on significant progress in the power and capacity of the hardware involved, it cannot claim a major place in the world of payment systems, unless software changes dramatically improve its performance. The proof of work mechanism, by its very principle, consumes a tremendous amount of computer resources and energy. By design, a new block is produced on average every 10 minutes, with a maximum of 5,000 transactions per block, in other words less than 10 transactions per second; whereas the averages for a system such as the VISA payment card are around 50,000 transactions per second! Without an improvement by at least a factor of 100, as a settlement system, Bitcoin would be doomed to occupy only a tiny niche in the world of modern payment systems.

The first idea to improve performance is to increase block size, which would allow more transactions per unit of time, but would increase the cost of building a block, making mining and preservation of the blockchain even more expensive; and would consequently risk reducing the number of miners and full nodes, leading to a centralization of critical functions, which is contrary to Bitcoin's philosophy. There has been considerable controversy over this proposal. The majority position seems to be to raise the maximum block size in a gradual manner, while experimenting with other ideas to improve the performance of the Bitcoin system.

One of these ideas, called SegWit (for segmented witness) was recently made available and has already been adopted by just over a quarter of the nodes. Its principle is to store separately the information relating to the transactions themselves, which must remain indefinitely in the blockchain and the information that determines whether the transactions are valid, which becomes useless when a block is definitively integrated into the blockchain. This system has an immediate

---

11 Editor's note: this concerns scale effects or scalability.

advantage: it turns out that these testimonials (witness) are not taken into account regarding the limitation of the block size, which doubles the number of transactions per block. Moreover, in a future version, it will be possible to delete this temporary data after a certain period of time.

A more radical solution is to adopt other disciplines to build blocks and build consensus between full nodes. In the current system, the choice of blocks in the chain, among all those proposed by the miners, is based on the judgment of the full nodes on the involvement of the miners in the functioning of the system; and this interest is expressed by the expenses that each one has made to build a block. We can imagine less expensive ways of expressing this interest and speeding up the production of blocks, like in Litecoin (one block every 2.5 minutes) or in the similar Dogecoin (one block every minute). These approaches also solve another inherent problem in the standard Bitcoin system: the delay for confirming a transaction that is, by design, at least 10 minutes or even a multiple of that time for the confirmation to be final. Other testimonies of interest could be the assets in bitcoins, security deposits, the number of transactions carried out, etc. This is the spirit of the various methods of proof of stake proposed by systems such as Ethereum, Bitshare and NEM.

All these variants are considered more democratic given that the requirements imposed on miners are lighter (in terms of work and computer equipment in particular), which could lead to the disappearance of specialized miners. However, they risk undermining the level of security afforded by the current regime; and they would undoubtedly open up the possibility of permanent forks[12].

Lastly, another way of increasing the system's capacity would be to reserve it for large transactions by processing small transactions with faster and less computer-intensive means, particularly for recurring transactions such as payment for parking or supermarket shopping (micropayments), even if they are less secure. This could be done by using a side chain mechanism to temporarily transfer bitcoins to another blockchain that uses a different discipline than the main system. The Lightning extension, which is currently under development, promises to create "micropayment channels" between two parties, on which transactions will only require the agreement of these parties, while in Bitcoin all transactions are verified by all full nodes[13]. These micropayment channels could be networked and allow for quick

---

12 That is to say, divisions within the system that lead to its fragmentation. Some systems are also considering hybrid solutions where the blocks, validated quickly by proof of stakes, would be periodically revalidated by proof of work to resolve these forks before they prolong dangerously.

13 The use of the Bitcoin channel and its consensus protocol would remain optional, at the request of one of the parties or in the case of a disagreement between them.

settlements without loading the system. All these functions make extensive use of multiple signatures (multisig).

The issue of anonymity

A final problem is the anonymity of transactions. On a blockchain, all transactions are readable in plain text, but without revealing the identity of the account holders. However, it is possible to identify the accounts of the same user and, to a certain extent, identify the user of each account through an elaborate analysis. Of course, this "re-identification" can be made more difficult by using a new account number for each transaction, as some wallets do automatically; but a commercial site must generally adopt and publish a permanent account number, making it possible to identify its accounts.

For more demanding users, some specialized sites such as Dash (formerly Darkcoin) and Zerocoin offer to "mix" transactions with elaborate cryptographic techniques; or indirect routing of transactions by a random path as already done by the TOR system. Monero is a Bitcoin rewrite that adds advanced privacy and security features to ensure the complete anonymity of transactions.

Towards a refoundation?

Over the years, Bitcoin has become an extremely active ecosystem with a plethora of ideas, projects and achievements that are more or less ambitious. In addition to the extensions that superimpose on the Bitcoin system, strictly speaking leaving it unchanged, other developments aim to solve certain fundamental problems either by proposing new versions involving more or less definitive hard forks; or by proposing entirely new systems, which can reuse certain parts of the Bitcoin software. Among these foundation projects, the two most important ones are Ripple and Ethereum, which demonstrate two opposing trends.

Ripple and Omni

Ripple, launched in 2012, was intended to be an alternative to Bitcoin, capable of dealing with all the currencies present and imaginable, including the exchange between these currencies and a wider variety of financial transactions. Unlike Bitcoin, which is developed by an informal community, Ripple is produced by a private company of the same name, which, since 2013, has been concentrating on the clientele of financial establishments. Instead of bypassing financial establishments, Ripple serves them by giving them a privileged role.

Unlike Bitcoin and the systems which it derives, following the principle "no one trusts anyone", each Ripple user can explicitly create trustworthy relationships with the accounts of their choice by specifying the amounts agreed to be entrusted to that user. As a whole, these links form a network of trust between accounts. For a settlement between two accounts to be possible, there must exist a "path of trust" between them, through which the settlement will pass. A function of the system is to dynamically search for these trust paths for each transaction.

Unlike Bitcoin, where account balances do not appear in the blockchain, Ripple's central file keeps the status of all accounts, their balances and trust relationships. All of it is recorded periodically in the form of a timestamped "ledger". The time interval between two successive ledgers is a few seconds. The transition from one book to the next is achieved by applying a set of transactions selected from the pending transactions, by consensus between particular servers (the "validators"), who play a similar role to that of miners in Bitcoin. The sequence of validated ledgers plays the same role as the Bitcoin blockchain, but the validation of a transaction only uses the latest released ledger and the next ledger that is being validated, which speeds up the process considerably.

The network communication with the outside world is provided by gateways, which specifically supply the system with currency units, accept deposits and make payments. Approximately 150 of them are automated financial entities that strive to comply with existing regulations and must be licensed by Ripple.

Any Ripple user can offer an exchange between currency A and currency B. The system registers these offers and explores the network to look for a counterparty among nodes that are linked to the requesting node by a trusted path. In the absence of a direct counterparty, the system proposes to split the exchange into an indirect exchange of A for a domestic currency called Ripple (XRP), then an exchange of XRPs for B.

The Ripple system's internal unit of account is either used as a central currency in foreign exchange transactions, or used to collect commissions due on each transaction and pay service providers. Created once and for all, it does not involve mining[14]. Its exchange rate, floating in relation to other currencies, is determined by supply and demand, particularly against the bitcoin for which a Bitcoin Bridge converts instantaneously in both directions. Overall, Ripple is a system of its own,

---

14 Additional issues may be carried out by Ripple.

very different from Bitcoin in its technological solutions and completely at odds with its objectives and principles. It is supported and used by a consortium of banks, for both their own needs and those of their customers; it wants to be a robust and reliable interbank settlement system, operating between a limited number of selected participants.

The Omni system (formerly Mastercoin) essentially uses the same ideas, but carrying them out in the form of a software overlay added to Bitcoin. This illustrates two concurrent attitudes in the face of Bitcoin's limitations: either to develop successors and competitors, or to consolidate its current supremacy through extensions.

Ethereum

In Bitcoin, the settlement and management functions of the blockchain are intertwined. In 2013, its creators thought that the underlying technologies could be used by a variety of non-monetary applications; some of them launched the Ethereum project to build a separate infrastructure capable of supporting a wide variety of applications. The first version of this system was released in July 2015.

In the Ethereum blockchain, each block not only contains the validated transactions, but also the status of the accounts modified by these transactions. Ethereum uses a proof of work system that is less time-consuming than that of Bitcoin and less favorable to the use of specialized equipment, which is therefore more democratic, because it allows a greater number of miners that are representative of the users' population. The time between the creation of two successive blocks is generally less than 30 seconds[15]. In this new system, the scripting language becomes a general (Türing-complete) language called Solidity, which allows the writing of any algorithm[16]. Like Bitcoin scripts, programs written in this language, which are called "contracts" in the Ethereum language, can be entered into the blockchain by means of specific transactions; in this manner, they become publicly accessible and unmodifiable. The execution of such a contract is

---

15 Developments currently under study include a block validation system combining proof of work and proof of stakes, as well as the possibility of assigning validation work a priori between miners according to their stakes, instead of letting them all build blocks to select afterwards.

16 Bitcoin scripts use a very limited instruction directory to prevent infinite loops, or large and complex scripts that would block the system or open security holes. In particular, this language does not include loops or go-to instructions; it is executed in a strictly sequential manner. These restrictions, which severely limit the variety of actions that can be executed by a script, are lifted in Solidity.

triggered by transactions, issued either by user accounts or by other contracts. It is the miners who execute the contracts when processing these transactions. The results of these successive executions can be entered in the blockchain.

To protect the system from dangerous programs, running a program consumes an internal resource (called gas, the "fuel" of the system, by analogy with the automobile). At the beginning of every program execution from the blockchain, a certain amount of gas is allocated to it by the applicant, and then decremented with each executed operation and memory allocation. If the program calls a subprogram, it transmits a certain quantity of gas to it. When the gas allocated to the program is exhausted, it stops. This makes it impossible for a badly written or malicious program to run indefinitely.

Ethereum uses an internal unit of account called ether. Each unit of fuel required to run a program must be purchased with ether, at the price set by each miner. The ether consumed by the execution of a program is credited to the miner who executes it and whose block is included in the blockchain. The ether can pay for all system operations, thus resolving the problem of motivating service providers in a peer-to-peer system. Just as in Ripple, ether is a simple internal unit of account; but like in Bitcoin, new ethers are created by mining at a fixed rate of 5 ethers per block, or about 14,000 ethers per day. Ethers can be exchanged for bitcoins and any other currency, especially those that manage implementations hosted by Ethereum.

For the application developer, Ethereum presents itself as a virtual machine that works continuously; it is accessible from anywhere, at any time, records programs and results irrevocably, making them universally readable and executable. On this basis, many applications have been developed and are in progress in the form of standard Ethereum contracts. These include: financial applications such as settlement and foreign exchange in various currencies, including sovereign currencies and private currencies created by users; participative financing, derivative products, savings, as well as registration services of generic names or trademarks, identity management of persons or objects, voting, insurance, transfer of rights, access keys to goods or services such as computing power and memory capacity, online betting, etc.

An extreme form is that of Distributed Autonomous Organizations, of which all forms of interaction with all stakeholders, as well as accounting, financial and management policies, are formalized by contracts coded in the blockchain. Transactions and their results, including any changes in operating policies, are recorded publicly and permanently. Such an enterprise can collect royalties, pay fees and publish accounts without human intervention.

Ethereum is moving at a swift pace. Its capacity is three times that of Bitcoin (25 transactions per second compared to 7 for Bitcoin), but still processes only 30,000 to 40,000 transactions per day compared to 200,000 to 300,000 for Bitcoin. The number of full nodes in the network passed that of Bitcoin in May 2016 and the number of miners can be compared: like Bitcoin, a group of ten miners produce 95% of the blocks. Features of the Ethereum virtual machine have recently been introduced in Bitcoin as an extension called Counterparty, which makes it possible to execute contracts in Bitcoin that are written in the Solidity[17] language.

A similar and even more ambitious project, Dragonchain, was unveiled by the Disney group. In addition to functionalities similar to those of Ethereum and interfaces with other blockchains including Bitcoin, it provides several modes of block validation (which may differ depending on the blocks), different levels of certification and a hierarchy of chains and validation bodies. It is a multi-currency system, without an internal unit of account. A first version of the software largely reuses Bitcoin software; it was released in September 2016 as open source software.

The future of cyber-money

Although there are more than a thousand e-money accounts, the few cited in this chapter account for 95% of their total value. Most of the other cyber-currencies are either experimental in their nature, or have limited use geographically or by the nature of the goods and services they provide. Given that there is no reason for this abundance to dry up, it is likely that systems will continually emerge to solve problems of all kinds as they are identified, experiment with new approaches and satisfy different needs and preferences through new monetary tools. Even though most of them are ephemeral or marginal, a wide range of electronic payment systems and the e-money associated to them will always be available.

Almost all these systems are developed with open source software: all programs are released and freely available. Each developer can freely incorporate pieces of code extracted from the work of other developers into his own software, the only condition being to mention the origin. When a software solution is found to solve a particular problem, it can then easily be taken over by competing systems, which makes it possible to consider all these payment systems as branches of a single project. In addition, each of these systems allows for the easy exchange of their own units of account for bitcoins and conventional currencies.

---

17 It is the same idea as Omni: instead of suggesting a new system, Bitcoin benefits from the new functions introduced by its competitors.

Bitcoin continues to occupy a privileged position in this abundant landscape, largely due to its long history, which explains its dominant position and the extent and dynamics of its technical ecosystem. It will thus continue to absorb most of its competitors' progress and can only be superseded by systems that offer both revolutionary non-transposable advances and attractive migration tools.

In fine, we can imagine that all experiments, whether based on Bitcoin or in separate systems, will reach their ultimate operational implementation on a general basis such as Ethereum, and that Bitcoin accounts will gradually migrate to this new base. However, it is also possible that different systems will continue to co-exist in the long term.

Cyberspace and sovereign currencies

Peer-to-peer systems and e-money are permanently established in the international financial landscape; they all offer alternatives to the services offered by existing companies, in particular by banks, as well as a partial substitute for national currencies. To explore the potential economic and social consequences, we obviously move onto the register of personal appraisal and prognosis. Of course, it would be presumptuous to formulate a definitive forecast. Therefore, we will simply set the scene, remind ourselves of the rules of the game, introduce the protagonists and outline possible paths to the future.

When a new technology competes with an old technology, it offers advantages to some users, but it is opposed by those who live off the old technology, in particular those who exploit it. The greater the impact on the existing situation, the more resistance to change is likely to be strong. The rate at which a new technique is adopted depends on the arbitration of the conflict between those who see benefits, whether as users or as entrepreneurs, and those who primarily see threats to their own situation. Here, the possible opponents are not only some or all of the banks and other financial establishments, but also the countries where cyber-money risks threatening the monetary monopoly that they have enjoyed over several centuries; on which they establish, to a large extent, their economic power, a monopoly that constitutes a tool for monitoring the movement of funds and an auxiliary for the taxation of wealth and income.

It can be assumed that companies, whether financial or non-financial, will only use "normal" competition tools and policies to defend their interests. On the other hand, it can be assumed that states, under the pretext of defending national sovereignty and the interests of citizens, are tempted to resort to authoritarian measures. It is pretty clear that peer-to-peer systems are already reliable and can, if necessary, be made even more reliable so that nobody without exorbitant powers can prevent systems from functioning or take control of them; but it remains possible that some states may be tempted (if they consider their sovereign privileges threatened) to resort to large-scale retaliatory measures of a legal or police nature, as some have begun to do, like China and Russia.

Let us temporarily leave these threats aside and examine the choices that are repeatedly offered to users as well as their probable decisions, in order to identify the possible path(s) of evolution, in such a changeable environment that any abstract reasoning around the notion of e is rendered ineffective. We will be careful not to paralyze our thinking with the belief that prevailed in the 20th Century: that money is necessarily a matter of states alone, a belief that prevents us from thinking properly about monetary issues and that the very existence of cyber-currencies challenges.

Currencies and payment systems

We have seen that bitcoins are just amounts attached to transactions recorded in the blockchain, which can only be used by using this system to record transactions that refer to previous ones. The bitcoin, as a cyber-currency, exists only by and in the Bitcoin system. In general terms, any currency can be considered as the unit of account of one or more payment systems. In their scriptural form, the current currencies are the means of various payment methods, usually computerized tools; in the form of coins and banknotes, they are the tools of a primitive payment system by person-to-person exchange.

An easy exchange system makes it possible to dissociate the choice of a currency, from the choice of a payment system. For a currency such as the euro, each user is at any time free to choose between several payment systems; on the contrary, a multi-currency system allows the user to choose the unit of account for each transaction. Peer-to-peer allows the internal unit of account (e.g. ether) to be exchanged for bitcoins or conventional currencies (the euro, dollar, pound, yen, etc.), either through specialized sites such as Ripple gateways, or in peer-to-peer mode in Ripple or Ethereum.

In the absence of direct obstacles from governments, peer-to-peer payment systems will allow for multi-currency transactions; those that do not will shall *ipso facto* be relegated to a marginal place. Each user will be able to pay for their purchases or accept a payment in any currency, specifying the chosen currency for each transaction: paying a Vietnamese supplier by dong from an account in dollars or Swiss francs will be as easy as paying in euros for a purchase at the local supermarket. On the other hand, anyone can accept any currency, while requesting that the credits be automatically and instantly converted into the currency of their choice.

Competition between payment systems

Under a free exchange rate system, the unit of account will no longer be a consideration for choosing between payment systems, provided that the recipient of the transaction can reasonably accept that currency within hours or even minutes following the transaction, either for a new exchange of goods or services, or in exchange for another currency. This choice will mainly take into account the good or service in question, the interlocutor and the nature of the service, as well as the features, availability, ease of use and performance of the system. The unit of account will no longer be a major criterion of choice, but a consequence of the chosen payment system.

Similarly to all payment systems, cyber-money primarily competes with previous telepayment systems such as the Blue Card, American Express and, more recently, Paypal, Apple Pay, Google Pay, as well as with the many fintech companies that offer services that rival those of banks, but using existing conventional currencies.

For the simple user who only carries out basic transactions, the primary advantages of Bitcoin are the ease of access: to use the system, you only need to download a small application free of charge, without formulating an application or filling in a file, and without a registration deadline[18]. The wallet software (electronic wallet) can be installed on an existing computer or smartphone. Thereafter, each transaction will only take a few clicks and will be carried out at no cost. For some users, global coverage, anonymity and the absence of any intermediary may be additional benefits.

The major disadvantages of the new payment methods are their weak adoption by commercial sites, which is still limited; and the use of a specific unit of account that requires foreign exchange transactions. In addition, the time taken to confirm a transaction, which is currently at least 10 minutes, makes Bitcoin unsuitable for in-store payments for which the maximum acceptable delay is a few seconds. This is part of the reason why Bitcoin insures only a very small part of commercial transactions. In addition, this system usually operates on an open circuit: dealers who accept bitcoins rarely pay their suppliers in bitcoins; and very few users

---

18 Only registration on a foreign exchange platform is subject to the formalities required by current banking regulations.

themselves are paid in bitcoins. The usual sequence of events is therefore: buying bitcoins on the foreign exchange market – settlement of the transaction in cyber-money – resale of bitcoins on the foreign exchange market. It is estimated that actual commercial transactions, in other words those which do not involve a foreign exchange site, represent less than 15% of the total volume of transactions, with a slight upward trend. The main use of bitcoins is still either a militant move or a speculative investment. This situation explains the volatility of the price of bitcoin, which is not based on any real goods.

For this to change, the bitcoin would either have to be developed as a trading tool, at least in a major sector of the economy, until this cyber-currency circulates in a closed circuit within this sector and the price of goods and services become expressed in bitcoins, which would provide a foundation on real goods; or that the exchange with other currencies, within the system itself, becomes as trivial as a bitcoin transaction, which is currently only the case for Ripple.

For bitcoin to be adopted by the public, it would have to also be adopted by a sufficiently large number of dealers; for it to be adopted by dealers, they would have to have a sufficiently large audience. However, from a commercial point of view, accepting payments in bitcoins costs almost nothing. We can therefore expect that some people will take the risk of accepting payments in cyber-money along with Paypal, cards or money-transfer. It is likely that as soon as a major distributor has done so, others will follow for fear of being cut off from the market or a competitive disadvantage: merchants will most likely be the driving force of this adoption, especially purchase/resale sites such as eBay and Leboncoin that sell and buy to the same population of users and could therefore operate only in bitcoins without any inconvenience.

The complexity of the system is often put forward as an obstacle to its daily use. This ignores the fact that an ordinary user only perceives the system through his wallet, which is as simple to use as a credit card or any other payment by computer, like Apple Pay. To use Bitcoin, you don't have to be a computer scientist, let alone an expert: just as you don't have to be an electronics technician to make a phone call or an agricultural engineer to eat potatoes.

It can therefore be predicted that there will always be a large number of payment systems. However, at the same time, they will be close to each other in terms of functionality and performance; the benefits of peer-to-peer systems are likely to grow with their development dynamics. It is probably the network effect that will play the largest role in separating them, either giving the advantage to the first installed, or to the most widespread, that is to say to the systems established in conventional currencies. Furthermore, Bitcoin will probably be very different from what it is today, evolve continuously and absorb most of the improvements introduced by its competitors; this will prevent users from making any effort to convert or migrate, even if the unit of account changes its name during the process.

Economists are quick to get rid of the question of a possible coexistence between currencies by referring to the transaction costs associated with exchange rates, fluctuation and uncertainty of exchange rates; they conclude that competition between currencies would be neither desirable nor sustainable. This objection does not stand up to examination, however quick. When different currencies coexist, foreign exchange services are developed, as is the case of cyber-currencies. There is no technical difficulty when withdrawing cash from a distributor from an account in another currency; nor is there any technical difficulty in having a cash deposit immediately credited to an account in a different currency, even in a flexible exchange rate system where exchange rates are constantly the result of supply and demand. In everyday life, the multiplicity of currencies will not be a problem: in systems such as Ethereum and Dragonchain, anyone can choose the currency or currencies they want to use for each of their transactions without this being a real constraint. Choosing a currency for a particular purchase is easy and inconsequential: you can get it on demand and only hold it for a few hours or even minutes.

We have seen that the deposit function, the core of the banking business, is carried out by the blockchain itself and that other functions of deposit banks are (or can be) carried out by Bitcoin. In addition, the developments that make use of the scripting language included in Bitcoin transactions allow all users to establish financial relationships that are much more complex than simple payment, without intermediaries. Ultimately: any particular person who knows the scripting language could invent a financial tool, write the corresponding scripts and create a wallet that simplify the use of this tool, then introduce it on the network. A potential impact of peer-to-peer payments includes bypassing a large number of banking functions and depriving states of a means of observation, controlling cash flows and taxation.

We have also seen that blockchain technology is susceptible to many implementations whose development and adoption are *a priori* independent of cyber-money and are based only on peer-to-peer functionality. These include the registration of documents (patents, titles, diplomas), rights of access to documents, publications, premises and vehicles, computer resources (Filecoin, Maidsafecoin). Transfers of rights to these objects will most naturally be made in exchange for a currency managed by the Internet. The Internet of Things will include the use of cyber-money. At the same time, the diversity will favor the coexistence of different systems, and therefore different units of account, since two payment systems compete only to the extent that they address the same uses and users.

This adoption will profoundly change certain professions, for example that of notaries, who will have to evolve towards a greater proportion of advice and interpretation, to the detriment of their traditional tasks of registering, preserving and returning documents. However, the fact remains that the drafting of contracts is a matter largely for specialists. On the one side, if the carrying out of operations is increasingly automated and "uberized", professionals will not only focus on consulting and analysis, but also on specialized services within general infrastructures such as Bitcoin, Ripple and Ethereum.

Competition between units of account

The choice of payment system is a circumstantial choice that may differ for each payment; the choice of currencies that each individual agent, company or other organization, chooses to keep in its accounts ("custodial" or "reserve" currency) is a patrimonial decision that commits the future. The ease of immediate exchange thus puts currencies in direct competition with each other in their value reserve function, regardless of the payment system used.

This situation is new and its theory remains to be articulated, as we are so accustomed to living in disjointed monetary zones within which the only currency in which all prices are expressed circulates; exchange rates remain localized at the borders and are closely controlled by banks and States. For the most part, even economists consider the monetary monopoly to be self-evident[19]; some find theoretical justifications for it, even though it was only universally imposed less than a century ago and the world has lived for three millennia with numerous, competing currencies in each territory[20]. However, these currencies were only different forms of the only real currency: gold. The decision on whether or not to accept a particular currency depended on the trust placed in the authority which, by its seal, had certified the title of each minted coin. Economists who have approached monetary competition have always done so by primarily dealing with international competition between national currencies, with assumptions significantly different to that of the conditions projected in this chapter. As for the controversies of the 18th and 19th centuries over bimetallism, they are not applicable today, because they presupposed the authoritarian fixing of parities.

---

19 A notable exception is the economists of the "Austrian" school. See, for example, the Analysis of Competition between Currencies [SAL 90].

20 Editor's note: for example, in the Hellenistic period, each city was freely emitting currencies; in addition, the rulers introduced an abundant amount of royal coinage in which their effigy appeared and from which they benefited; gold coins were widespread, but it was mainly silver that was used for international transactions (tetradrachmas). See [CHA 81].

The situation studied here is of a different nature: in the same geographical area, we have several currencies covered by different payment systems, more or less communicating with one another, all of which are accessible to each economic agent accepting several currencies, some of which circulate between several payment systems. Prices and exchange rates are formed independently between the systems, depending on supply and demand. Currencies are therefore in competition with each other for each of their functions, like any other goods. The fate of each currency is therefore subject to an analogous natural selection, as Hayek[21] suggested.

Since the choices of an exchange currency and a custodial currency are independent of one another and facilitated by the fluidity of exchange rates, it can be assumed that any currency that is suitable for at least one of these two uses, will be able to last. The choice of an exchange currency is linked to payment systems; it is carried out at each payment and can lead to the coexistence of several currencies adapted to different payment conditions. For example, for small hand-to-hand payments, existing currencies are likely to continue to be used, as creating new physical monetary symbols would be costly and of little interest. It is therefore likely that a fairly large number of currencies will coexist in the long term, even within a given geographical area. Neither bitcoin nor its successors will likely ever become a single global currency: given that manual payment systems will never disappear, national currencies will continue to exist.

On the other hand, an inflationary currency exposed to the risk of depreciation as a result of a discretionary issuance regime, will survive only to the extent that it will serve as a unit of value in a payment system, particularly suited to a context such as direct cash payments[22]. If a currency is used in a payment system but refused as a custodian currency, its holders will quickly require either its conversion into another currency deemed more suitable for the reserve role, or the delivery of the counterparty promised by its issuer[23]. If this issuer is unable to meet this demand, his/her currency will soon no longer be accepted as a payment currency either.

National currencies are under the control of the State, central banks or private banks, which are heavily regulated and controlled to the extent of accompanying the

---

21 See [HAY 90]: this book was written urgently to propose an alternative to the single currency; it was more a manifesto than an in-depth analysis of the monetary competition mentioned here.

22 Editor's note: this is a classic situation in Africa, ever since the multiplication and fairly common adoption of payment by mobile phone.

23 If the issuer has not promised any counterparty, its currency will not be accepted in the presence of currencies guaranteed by such counterparty.

implementation of the State's monetary policy. In practice, this policy steers the supply of money with the purpose of achieving macro-economic objectives such as: interest rate stability, exchange rate stability, price stability and growth, full employment and external balance. According to Keynesian theses, this economic policy often involves the creation of *ex nihilo* money, which reduces the value of money. States have the freedom to act with discretion in this field, depending on the context and political objectives.

On the contrary, the creation of cyber-money is ultimately programmed by an intangible algorithm, unless the majority of its users decide otherwise. In the Bitcoin system, new units are created every 10 minutes to remunerate the formation of blocks by miners (and only in this way). Initially set at 50 bitcoins per block, this remuneration is currently 25 bitcoins, resulting in an annual growth of around 10% in the mass of bitcoins. This remuneration will be halved every four years, which limits the money supply to 21 million, which will be reached around 2140 (but 99% of this limit will have been reached by 2032). In Ripple, the internal currency is created once and for all. In Ethereum, it is created with 5 ethers per block. The value of all cyber-money is hence bound to grow over time, a competitive advantage as a value reserve.

Changing these settings, as with any major change, means circulating a new version of the software that each user is free to install or not. As we have seen, as soon as a user installs the new version, the user population splits into two subsets and the blockchain splits into two branches, thus defining two different currencies between which users can choose. In this manner, they can either opt for new rules of money management, or stick to the old ones by concrete action (staying in the chain or leaving it for an alternative channel) and not by a simple vote.

It is therefore to be expected that an overwhelming majority of users will select the cyber-currencies over which they have the most reason to believe that their value will not diminish over time[24]; bitcoin is a good candidate according to this criterion, perhaps just as favorable to other cyber-currencies. Some would prefer currencies based on a material commodity such as gold, or even currencies guaranteed by a country. The other currencies will revert, more or less rapidly, to their issuers and disappear from circulation, along with the payment systems on which they are based.

---

24 This is a subjective assessment of the money issuer's promise and ability to generate confidence. As cyber-currencies fall in with Ludwig von Mises definition of fiat money "consisting of mere tokens which can neither be employed for any industrial purpose nor convey a claim against anybody" their value mainly relies upon trust. See Chap. XVII, Section 9: mises.org/humanaction/library/human-action-0. [Original edition: *Human Action, A Treatise on Economics*, Yale University Press, 1949].

It should be noted that the coexistence of several currencies protects the public against the loss of value or disappearance of one of them. At the first signs of depreciation, savers can convert their assets, which accelerates the decline of a fragile currency, but avoids ruin. The position of each currency issuer is therefore fragile: they must be quick to react to the first signs of depreciation, which limits the risk of a bank crash. However, the multiplicity of issuers limits the consequences of failure from one of them: the new cyber-money system should therefore, as a whole, be rather reliable.

In this cyber-environment, at the same time that national currencies will be put in competition[25], a variety of settlement methods and new disciplines of monetary creation will be offered to users, from which the most satisfactory solutions will emerge. The current debate between metal-currencies, virtual currencies and state currencies will thus be decided by the users themselves. However, it is likely that this process will leave inflationary currencies with no chance of surviving and will make it very difficult for those currencies to remain.

If competition between currencies remains free, countries wishing to retain a national currency will have no choice but to maintain its value and thus renounce the ease of monetary creation; this will deprive them of what they still consider to be an essential tool of economic policy. Faced with the prospect of such a surrender of sovereignty, impeding the use of cyber-money is tempting and easy thanks to the power of coercion, which makes it possible to build up regulatory barriers under the pretext, for example, of protecting consumers. Without any technical means to prevent peer-to-peer systems from functioning, they can either declare them illegal and defer to the police and the courts, or request a prior declaration, with or without compulsory authorization, and probably tax their use. Today, attitudes differ between countries, ranging from indifference leading to inaction, to near total prohibition (Russia, China). Nevertheless, it can be expected that some countries will maintain (or even increase) regulatory barriers for foreign exchange transactions, something that would maintain a certain coupling between competition of payment systems and competition between custodian currencies.

Conclusion

Peer-to-peer payment and cyber-money are firmly established in the economic landscape; they will become increasingly important and will contribute to the disruption brought about by digitalization in many areas. It is a rich and dynamic

---

25 This could inevitably lead to several of them giving up.

world where technical problems are solved as they appear. There are numerous achievements; the relationships between the different systems are new, the combination of competition and cooperation means that competition is not strategic for users who maintain freedom of choice. On the other hand, in the face of such a shift in economic paradigm, it is to be expected that strong resistance from governments and financial establishments will probably translate into regulatory action, due to a lack of technical capacity.

In the Bitcoin camp and derivatives thereof, we can already see two postures. The first, faithful to the intentions of historical promoters, is to fight head-on against attempts at government control, in order to further strengthen the anonymity of users, invulnerability and the closed nature of the system, even at the cost of less user-friendliness and increased consumption of IT resources; this trend is distinct for Dash, by way of example, or similar projects such as Zerocoin and Monero, which aim at absolute anonymity. The other trend, illustrated by Ripple, which is more conciliatory with the public authorities, is quite the contrary, seeking good repute by complying with regulatory constraints and giving operators the means to satisfy the constraints applicable to the role they have chosen. Are there the beginnings of a schism from which two families of systems would emerge?

I will not make a prognosis on the outcome of these tensions, the terms of which are numerous and subject to too much uncertainty. One can, in short, describe the landscape and the players without predicting the outcome of their interactions: either the peer-to-peer payment, launched by Bitcoin, helps to restore a healthy environment of competition between currencies[26], while inducing the removal of governments from the economic sector; or else governments manage to preserve all or part of their privileges, delaying and restricting the effect of decisive progress in the daily life of all. In the latter case, we can hold on to the hope that a set of rich new technologies, validated on a real scale thanks to the inventiveness and initiative of inventors and animators who have shown the way through these new systems, will remain at our disposal.

---

26 Editor's note: this reflection suggests an analogy with the deregulation process, which has profoundly renewed the conditions for the exercise of several public utilities, all essential to the modern economy: during the last 20 years of the 20th Century, air transport, communication, energy and financial services have been transformed under the effect of rapid technical progress, which has revolutionized supply and market conditions. See Walrave M. (ed.), *Les réseaux de services publics dans le monde*, ESKA, Paris, 1995.

Bibliography

[CHA 81] CHAMOUX F., *La civilisation hellénistique*, Arthaud, Paris, pp. 572–73, 1981.

[ETH 17a] ETHEREUM, https://www.ethereum.org/, 2017.

[ETH 17b] ETHEREUM,//www.ethereum-france.com/, 2017.

[ETH 17c] ETHERCHAIN, https://etherchain.org/, 2017.

[HAY 90] HAYEK F., *The denationalisation of money*, IEA, London, 1990.

[RIB 73] RIBOUD J., *La vraie nature de la monnaie*, RPP, Paris, 1973.

[RIP 17] RIPPLE, https://ripple.com/, 2017.

[SAL 90] SALIN P., *La vérité sur la monnaie*, Odile Jacob, Paris, 1990.

7

Health and Care: Digital Challenges

The field of healthcare has long been under strain for reasons that should be celebrated: the increase in life expectancy, ageing of the population and a growing demand for hygiene and comfort have been producing their effects for more than a century! It is therefore natural that the need for care should increase and that it should diversify as a result of advances in technology and pharmacopoeia, which are increasingly treating a very large number of illnesses. To continue this progress (which is not cheap), our countries have exhausted themselves; it is a general harm, almost independent of the social insurance model chosen by each nation, as shown below[1]. This is reflected in the medical world, in hospitals and in institutions that care for dependent elderly people, the disabled and the chronically ill, for example. In France, where health expenditure is financed by redistribution, the political authorities are directly involved; elsewhere, even if mutual societies or insurance companies manage benefits, the overall organization of health and care is also a matter of public policy.

Few computers upset the established habits of doctors and laboratories 40 years ago. Today, electronics, computers and imaging are everywhere; sensors, thermometers and dosimeters are all digital, all connected to the local network and even to the Internet. Digital applications are omnipresent in everyone's life: from

---

Chapter written by Isabelle HILALI.

1 Editor's note: see Ecalle F., "Vers un bouclier sanitaire?", *Lettre Présaje*, no. 33, October 2010, and from the same author, "Le bouclier sanitaire", *Futuribles*, April 2008. We can also refer to a very far-sighted analysis published in the United States more than 15 years ago: Christensen C.M., Bohmer R., Kenagy J., "Will disruptive innovations cure Healthcare?", Harvard Business School Publication, Boston, 2000, whose diagnosis was illuminating: "Powerful institutional forces fight simpler alternatives to expensive care because those alternatives threaten their livelihood".

management to diagnosis, from treatment to prophylaxis, healthcare is part of a digital world. All this comes at a price!

Money is scarce, needs multiply and trade-offs are unpredictable. Where is the dream? What is to be expected from reality? It is not easy to see clearly in a tangle of multiple, differing and often hidden interests; the following study, based on a solid knowledge of this field, sheds light on the stakes involved in the digitalization of all healthcare. From the pharmaceutical industry to public hospitals, everyone can hope that digital technology will solve some of their problems; it will take a long time, and everyone will have to contribute.

The term "digital health" raises many questions; when one thinks of health, we associate it historically with: human, organs, living...and we have to wonder if the word "digital" alongside the word "health" symbolizes a leap towards a dehumanized world governed by technologies, especially since we are speaking more than ever of remote medicine, robotics, artificial intelligence, etc.

What are we talking about?

Just as in all fields, it is up to us to define the rules for the application of technology, because (especially for the time being) behind each technology, human beings can choose to direct it and limit its possible applications. We will come back to this in the second part, but first of all, what are we talking about when we talk about the digital transformation of the health world and what are the associated benefits?

Major changes for physicians

The doctor's profession has often been defined as characterized by a very specific relationship between himself and his patient. The appearance of digital technology profoundly disrupts this relationship:

– first of all, by offering the patient the possibility of obtaining information in a very global way, notably thanks to more or less specialized websites[2] (the best known in France being Doctissimo), whose information is more or less reliable, and sometimes very bad. But it is conceivable that the maturity of the system will enhance the quality of the information available. The patient's access to a great deal of information, in addition to the dialogue with his or her doctor, has been widely criticized, in particular because of the fear that the patient might be exposed to erroneous information; but the practice seems rather positive and the feedback from health professionals as a whole is ultimately positive; a more informed patient who is better able to guide the health professional and apprehend the advice and instructions given to him or her;

– the development of telemedicine[3] disrupts the medical profession through all its implementations and allows a more collaborative delegation and practice. The

2 More than 40% of French people claim to use the Internet to share or search for health information. See Baromètre du numérique 2015, Conseil général de l' économie, ARCEP.
3 Definition of telemedicine: Act No. 2009-879 of July 21, 2009, as well as the Decree of October 19, 2010, gave a precise definition and set its regulatory framework: "Telemedicine is a remote medical practice using information and communication technologies. It connects, among

possibility of consulting remotely profoundly modifies the practice: the very basis of the doctor's profession was through human contact (touch, smell, etc.); it is difficult to replicate from a distance. However, it can be seen that teleconsultation is developing in a very significant way (when it is authorized) and it is generally integrated into the health care system, enabling some initial guidance. For example, in 2011, former UK Health Minister Andrew Lansley said that 70–80% of NHS[4] appointments were no longer needed, and that replacing even one percent of appointments with remote consultations would save 250 million GBP per year (about 300 million EUR). Several teleconsultation experiments are underway in the NHS: the Babylon Health start-up, for example, is offering remote consultations that are supported by the NHS. Remote expertise and remote assistance make it possible to obtain expert advice or assistance if necessary: magnetic resonance imaging (MRI), the interpretation of which would not be clear enough for the treating physician, can thus be submitted to a more experienced specialist. Remote monitoring also changes the doctor–patient relationship: for example, diabetes is a pathology that lends itself particularly well to remote monitoring, since it is easy for patients to follow their own tests and send their blood glucose readings to their doctor, which they measure several times a day or even on a constant basis. Two key points need to be examined: the responsibility of the doctor in such circumstances, which nevertheless restrict his or her direct apprehension of the patient, and the time management of the treating physician, given that it is not practical to overwhelm him or her with data; they must reach him or her at a convenient time and in the right format, which will allow him or her to economize on time and have a better knowledge of the specific cases, which is linked to the previous point.

Lastly, a third element that will also impact the physician's profession: the development of benchmarks on the quality of care. There are already many of them in the United States, such as Healthgrades (www.healthgrades.com) which allows the comparison of healthcare institutions on the basis of quality criteria defined by Medicare data and patient reviews; it has 11 million unique visitors, which shows the heavy interest of people in accessing this kind of information. We can imagine that French sites dedicated to taking medical appointments (DoctoLib, MonDocteur, etc.) could eventually develop advice in order to choose a health professional. There is also a strong desire from patient associations to see more transparency in the quality of care. This would of course imply a fundamental reflection on the very

themselves or with a patient, one or more health professionals, including a medical professional if necessary and, where appropriate, other professionals providing their care for the patient. It makes it possible to establish a diagnosis, to ensure preventive or post-therapeutic follow-up for a patient at risk, to request specialist advice, to prepare a therapeutic decision, to prescribe products, to prescribe or carry out services or acts, or to monitor the state of patients."

4 British Public Health Service initials: National Health Service. See White Paper, [HDI 15].

notion of quality, with sometimes complex comparisons: for example, it is quite obvious that a surgeon mainly operating on very difficult cases would have a naturally higher mortality rate than one mainly dealing with benign cases. But this is no reason to hinder the definition of quality criteria and make measures accessible to all potential patients and guide them in their choices. Like other issues, quality can help balance the physician/patient dialogue and lead to increased joint responsibility[5].

Five acts of telemedicine are currently recognized by regulation:

– teleconsultation: remote consultation between a doctor and a patient, who can be assisted by another healthcare professional;

– tele-expertise: enabling a medical professional to seek the opinion of one or more medical professionals at a distance, on the basis of their specific training or skills, based on medical information related to the care of a patient;

– medical tele-monitoring: enabling a medical professional to remotely interpret the data necessary for the medical monitoring of a patient and, where appropriate, to make decisions on the curing of that patient. The recording and transmission of data can be automated or carried out by the patient himself, or by a healthcare professional;

– tele-assistance: enabling a medical professional to assist another healthcare professional remotely during the performance of an act;

– the urgent medical response provided as part of the emergency services activities.

Box 7.1. *Five recognized telemedicine acts*

One of the impacts of health digitalization is the improved access to information, enabling everyone to play an active role in the management of their health, whether to prevent or manage their illness, especially chronic diseases. Citizens in general and patients (or non-patients) are eager for empowerment, just look at the number of sites created on the patients' initiative and the significant number of visits to these sites [CUK 14]. The patient-physician relationship will thus radically evolve over the coming years following the complete overhaul of knowledge sharing. Surgical procedures themselves should be partially demystified by the use of decision support tools and robotics.

---

5 Editor's note: quality of care is a recurrent concern in the socio-economic work in hospitals; major US analytical surveys were already documenting this problem, on a detailed empirical basis, more than half a century ago: [GEO 62]. Contemporary ethical considerations can be found in [XER 11].

The use of health data could also contribute to much greater transparency on the effectiveness and quality of care, in addition to enabling patients to participate more effectively in health-related decision-making, provided, of course, that the data is used in a context that protects privacy and that the analyses are carried out and accessible to all on dedicated sites or through applications, for example.

What about the patients?

Individuals value freedom of choice, the ambition to increase equal access to care and fellowship among patients, as well as the sharing of information between patients. A few examples can illustrate this desire to be an active participant in their own health and the role that digital technology could play in supporting them.

Between May 2012 and June 2013, Facebook's social network offered its subscribers the opportunity to share their organ donor status with friends and official organizations, resulting in 21 more registered donors in one day than on a regular day[6].

The Renaloo patients' association highlighted the social disparities in access to dialysis and transplantation[7]. Surveys by the General Kidney States and QuaViRein show that, whatever their age group and sex, dialysis patients are less qualified than transplant patients. This study was made possible by the access to data and data processing techniques, and was greatly facilitated by the digital technology[8].

New challenges for medication

Pharmaceutical dispensaries are one of the components in the health sector that could be strongly impacted by digital technology, as soon as the sale of medication online will be authorized in France, which is already the case in other countries. The sale of pills by unit would also disrupt economic customs and balances. In the United States, Amazon is a major contributor in the sale of medication. Uber Health in New York connects available nurses and doctors in order to carry out vaccinations on those who wish to do so, and delivers the necessary equipment and vaccine to the person concerned in a timely manner!

---

6 Published in the *American Journal of Transplantation*, June 2013.

7 Studies published in the journal of the French National Institute for Demographic Studies (INED), *Population*, vol. 71, January 2016.

8 Editor's note: we could compare this example to the argument in favor of access to public data, which is still in the embryonic stage in France – see our collective publication: "Données publiques, accès et usages", *Les cahiers du numérique*, vol. 9, no. 1, 2013.

Do pharmacies have a future?

Contrary to what is often mentioned, the sale of medication online could have real advantages for the patient, especially if a coordination between online sales sites and data collected on the patient was put in place, allowing users to monitor drug interactions, follow individual doses, establish a history of prescriptions; all of this data would be essential to organizing personalized advice to patients, in real time. Pharmacists will have a role to play in this context: they could return to the sources of their profession, to which a long and very specific training has prepared them: individualized preparation (old fashioned?) and local advice would take its place of importance in the digital world, particularly to provide personal advice and conduct preventive actions; the human accompaniment of chronic diseases and healthy aging at home will depend on it. We can also think of new features such as vaccination, as well as delegating the use of digital diagnosis tools to pharmacies, along with care and health applications.

What about the pharmaceutical industry?

The pharmaceutical industry is putting considerable resources into place, in order to have a better understanding of the needs of individuals; to have a closer proximity to patients, even though this is highly regulated; and to develop services to help patients manage their health and disease, the famous "beyond the pill" strategy (besides prescribing).

Blockbusters[9] continue to be an important target for large pharmaceutical companies, but research and development productivity is declining: the return on investment from pharmaceutical research has dropped by more than half, from 10.5% in 2010 to 4.8% in 2013, while the costs associated with research into new molecules are now approaching five billion USD. While 95% of new medications fail to be both safe and more effective than previous ones, pharmaceutical companies are considering new strategies and services to increase the overall effectiveness of their treatments and solutions. The laboratories are therefore developing applications to support patients, to help them better cope with their

---

9 Editor's note: a term borrowed from the jargon of entertainment to describe popular success stories; by analogy, here we mean drugs that generate very large scale sales of more than one billion USD in revenue.

illness and to be more observant of their treatments. Some also envisage a strategy of participation in start-ups and/or supporting patient initiatives aimed at developing support programs and focus groups.

For example, Bayer offers the Didget solution, a blood glucose monitoring system for diabetic children aged five to 14 years; Pfizer has developed a Recipes 2 Go dietary application for patients taking Lipitor. GSK has developed MyAsthma, an application that provides personalized daily advice for asthma patients and a 30-second control test. Other initiatives at a more upstream level include the partnership between the Roche France laboratory and La Paillasse research institute, through which researchers can access anonymized clinical data provided by Roche, a way of advancing co-innovation in health, in a very open manner[10].

An El Dorado for medical equipment?

All medical devices should be connected in the short term: it is estimated that 21% of devices managing heart disease were connected in 2015 and that 34% will be connected by 2020; and if 12% of masks used for sleep apnea are connected in 2015, half of them will be connected by 2020. Among American households equipped with broadband Internet: 32% have a connected scale; 26% have a connected blood pressure monitor and 12% have a connected blood glucose meter. As a result, manufacturers of medical equipment can already collect (or at least generate) extremely large amounts of data on the population that owns these connected devices. Many of these equipment manufacturers have embarked on a strategic contemplation of the future exploitation of this data:

– how to improve products and better use equipment?

– how to personalize the follow-up and possible treatment of patients?

– what services can we offer thanks to this new knowledge?

– what is the value of the data collected in this way?

– what would be the associated business models?

– to whom and under what conditions should this Big Data be passed on?

– what are the associated issues: acceptability for patients?

10 Editor's note: such a procedure is in line with the open data approach, which aims to liberalize access to the stocks of data held by public institutions and administrations, in order to encourage any initiative that would make it possible to take advantage of Big Data; see footnote 8 and Chapter 8.

– nature and ownership of property rights?

– intimate relationships and private life, etc.

Medical equipment manufacturers are therefore preparing new services. These include: Alere, which has developed a remote monitoring platform with nurses who check the data provided by the equipment on patients suffering from heart problems. A pilot study of 70,000 patients in the United States and Germany, funded by health insurance, is currently under way; it is hoped that this will support the value of its investment. In France, the same company launched the PIMP'S platform (interactive doctor-patient health platform) in partnership with a Parisian hospital.

Healthcare sites and mobile applications are also helping to change this industry and the competition between companies in this sector. Who would want to invest in heavy and expensive machines if the same result can be achieved with a mobile device and an online application? Although the disappearance of medical equipment in hospitals is far from being an option, many diagnoses will soon be carried out remotely, using mobile devices, medical sensors and an Internet application, particularly in areas where access to hospitals is difficult. The medical equipment will also be enriched with artificial intelligence to help diagnose the disease[11]. According to an article from May 2016 in the English newspaper The Telegraph, one in six NHS patients is misdiagnosed! It is therefore hoped that the new technologies will be able to support the authenticity of human diagnosis, consolidate the first level of diagnosis and guide the measures to be taken if necessary.

Hospitals, clinics and nursing homes

For healthcare professionals and establishments, identifying people at high risk during a surgical procedure would make it possible to concentrate the resources needed to accompany the operation and prepare patients returning back home, thus contributing to better and more effective care. Models that take advantage of health data that is also enriched from other sources on patients' lives (dietary habits, living conditions, addictions, etc.), would enable the development of valuable decision support tools. In New York, Mount Sinai Hospital has had a very advanced policy on identifying patients at high risk of re-admission, with the hope of reducing the rate of

---

11 The reading of an electrocardiogram, for example, will develop more and more autonomously and with new sensors. In some cases, it is also conceivable that a well-trained medical assistant might be called in, or the assistance of an artificial intelligence will be used (see Chapter 9).

re-admission by 43%, which they have achieved; increasing patient satisfaction and reducing mortality. This hospital is testing the Watson Artificial Intelligence System, developed by IBM to help its doctors diagnose and prescribe. This approach, applied to healthcare, is still in its infancy; however, if this principle were validated, bearing in mind that it would take about 160 hours of *ad hoc* training per year for a doctor to know all of the new developments in his or her field of activity, the interest of diagnostic assistance seems obvious! Incidentally, IBM is heavily investing so as to enrich its software either through internal work, or by acquiring specialized companies[12].

Diabetes, asthma, multiple sclerosis, cystic fibrosis, HIV, depression: one in five French people suffer from a chronic disease that requires lifelong medical monitoring and treatment. How will we cope with the burden of such treatments? To answer this type of question, the APHP (Paris public hospitals agency) launched the Cohort-compare program. Using this platform, researchers are expected to recruit 200,000 patients with long-term conditions and monitor them for 10 years. The aim is to try to understand, through regular questionnaires distributed online, how patients live and how they treat themselves. Another objective of the program is to bring patients together with other patients in order to break their isolation, through discussion forums, in particular. Another objective is to facilitate their participation in cohorts to speed up research, given that recruiting volunteers is a real challenge and slows down many clinical trials. The ConSoRe project, initiated five years ago by UniCancer, brings together some twenty cancer centers in France; this is also worth mentioning, as it aims to deploy a Big Data platform that will enable specialized researchers to explore cancer lists with highly advanced semantic research tools. For the Paris Curie Institute alone, the foundation already includes about 500,000 patients and nine million images.

Will we be able to insure health tomorrow?

This subject is fundamental for all establishments that cover health risk, in whatever capacity. The control of health expenditure is a key challenge for the coming years: the ageing of the population and the increase in chronic diseases are factors that increase expenditure. It is also generally less expensive to detect and prevent a disease than to treat it once it has occurred. It is now possible to take preventive measures before the disease sets in, for example, through early indicators (biomarkers).

---

12 See, for instance, the February 2016 purchase of Truven Health Analytics for 2.6 billion USD; this purchase gives access to 215 million patient profiles, hundreds of clinicians, epidemiologists, health consultants, etc.

There are three main payers in France: public health insurance, private insurers (e.g. AXA) and mutual societies (the first group is Harmonie Mutuelle/MGEN). All payers want to go beyond the reimbursement of health expenses already incurred before their intervention. Prevention will take on a key role, with the aim of supporting policyholders while they are still in good health. This would take the form of chronic disease prevention programs and services. Examples include: PRADO for the National Health Insurance Fund, AXA Prevention and Vivoptim at the MGEN. New technologies open up new fields for health insurers. The risks can now be better assessed thanks to DNA sequencing, the cost of which has been greatly reduced, enabling massive sequencing in the years to come, although it is not the sequencing of the entire genome of each individual that was originally envisioned, because the means required to implement it are far too great. However, the hopes placed in the sequencing of the genome must be dimmed due to the complexity of the human body. The deciphering of the genome is therefore only one element of health risk; other factors such as the environment and diet also have an impact on certain pathologies. Genome sequencing could thus lead to the emergence of predictive and personalized medicine, an evaluation of genetic predispositions to develop certain diseases, an anticipation of the risks associated with certain treatments and a better targeting of treatments. The use of these techniques should therefore improve knowledge of the risk to be insured and have a strong impact on the principle of solidarity, which guides public payers and mutual societies.

The fear that health insurers would discriminate against individuals on the basis of their health risks, has long been raised as an old chestnut: can we imagine not insuring an unborn child because of the prohibitive price associated with medical risks? These fears are fueled by automobile insurance models, as well as by programs initiated by some American insurance companies, which essentially offers bonuses – and sometimes penalties – depending on compliance with commitments made by individuals and companies in terms of prevention; for example, anti-smoking. In the United Kingdom, the PruHealth's Vitality program, launched by Prudential, rewards policyholders with a system of points for their preventive behavior. In Japan, some companies have introduced bonuses/penalties depending on the food their employees eat in the company canteen, in order to avoid overweight and cardiovascular diseases! Connected objects, medical or not, can also be used in such programs: an American company has set up a program with its insurance to encourage people to sleep more than seven hours a night during a reference period! In France, CNAM launched the Santé Active coaching site in November 2014 with three programs: active nutrition, back health and heart health. Each person is monitored for several months by a virtual coach, who gives personalized and adaptive information and advice (videos, quizzes, messages, etc.). AXA has also offered, in partnership with Withings, rewards to users who take a certain number of steps per day towards increasing physical activity. In this context, however, it should be mentioned that there are many barriers in order for insurers to use personal health data, which limits the ambition of this type of program: in addition to the fear of living in a world where everyone would be constantly monitored at a distance and could be denied any health insurance, access to data is overseen with a particular distrust of insurers. The latter set their own ethical limits; and naturally, important socio-economic boundaries limit ambitions, while technological limitations are not negligible, despite the immense technical progress that we have benefited from since the dawn of information technology! In addition, a long-term investment in a group of policyholders is risky because of the volatility of policyholders, since clients tend to change providers much more often than before, a trend that has become widespread in recent years; in this capacity, digitalization also plays an important role[13].

So, what would be the right strategy for health insurers? Insurance companies are undeniably moving towards a service provider approach; as such, they have the competence to develop prevention and support for chronic patients, and to help their policyholders to safeguard their health. It is also a matter of regulation, everyone must have adequate health insurance coverage; the premium scale can be regulated so as not to exceed a reasonable ratio with the insured risk[14].

The challenges of digital healthcare

Reflection on this subject is progressing slowly, due to a great lack of knowledge on the subject by most people and the fears associated with it. The contributions that could be expected from digital healthcare (abbreviated as eHealth) are, altogether, positive for everyone and the community; if there were real risks, they would have to be apprehended with all the knowledge necessary in order to take full advantage of the benefits and combat potential dangers effectively. The main key issues are as follows:

– quality of care thanks to preventive and personalized medicine;

– equal access to information and care;

---

13 Editor's note: the success of the banking and insurance services administered by websites is very clear; comparators facilitate the change of supplier, especially given that in order to protect the consumer, a certain number of clauses are easily transportable from one insurer to another (example: bonus point). This underlying trend is most probably sustainable.

14 Editor's note: the technical ratio measuring the balance of insurance is their loss/prime ratio; if it exceeds the unit, insurers are condemned to either reduce benefits or to increase premiums. This "technical" coefficient was sometimes offset in the past by financial products; at the time of writing this, negative rates and the very low financial return on safe investments are forcing insurance companies to monitor their technical ratio very closely.

– expanding health research;

– better management of public health.

Digital data and quality of care

Personalized medicine dates from Hippocrates' time, the doctor's role being to make a personalized examination, a diagnosis and a prescription. However, new technologies make it possible to access a multitude of data on each individual, in real time if necessary, to compare them with a multitude of references or precedents, and to mobilize diagnostic and decision-making assistance thanks to the numerous data allowing for better prevention, better patient monitoring and better care, whether for medication or for intervention.

Better prevention: one in 12 people worldwide is diabetic, 90% of them suffer from type 2 diabetes and half of type 2 diabetics do not even know they are ill! Around 60% of people at risk of developing type 2 diabetes could avoid it by following proper nutrition and exercise. By 2017, mobile health in Europe could prevent five million people at risk from developing type 2 diabetes[15]. In Mali, sending prevention SMS messages to pregnant women and young mothers has reduced infant mortality by 30%, according to an OMS source.

Better monitoring: the benefits of continuous patient monitoring are undeniable when compared to a one-off measure; in cardiology, for example, monitoring weight gain can anticipate the occurrence of a severe crisis. In the United States, the annual cost of hospitalization for a chronic cardiac patient was estimated at 4,500 USD, an expense to be compared with the cost of sensors enabling remote monitoring, which is estimated at only 300 USD worth of equipment (scale, blood pressure monitor, pill box, wristband, all connected!). In psychiatry, a specialty for which compliance challenges are fundamental, the new technologies of remote monitoring can help patients to take their treatments regularly and trigger an alert to the treating physician in the event of breaching compliance.

Better care: in areas of remote access, whether in developing countries or in the listed medical deserts in France, eHealth is clearly taking its place. In rural China,

---

15 See Socio-economic impact of m-health, an assessment, Report for the European Union, PWC, May 2013.

remote hypertension monitoring is extremely developed; in Egypt, prevention programs for diabetics have proven to be very effective during the Ramadan periods (with SMS counseling to diabetics during this period).

New stakeholders for new health research

Using health data makes it possible to build avatars, with which it will be much easier and faster to test new care protocols. The combination of clinical data, health data and omics data (e.g. from genomics) would provide a better understanding of some chronic diseases. It is already possible to exploit early indicators (biomarkers) that allow us to act before the disease even starts. Access to massive data stocks and powerful data analysis methods will enable pharmaceutical companies, particularly in clinical tests, to analyze thousands of indicators per patient (patient genetic profile, patient history, etc.), define and predict individual reactions to the treatments tested and finally adopt a personalized treatment for each patient.

Flatiron is a US start-up that collects clinical data from cancer patients in more than 200 American hospitals. Its objective is to design algorithms to determine the best treatments applicable to each pathology and each patient. Flatiron has just raised 100 million USD from Google Ventures. Google[16] is heavily investing in the health sector through Google X; Calico, a structure dedicated to understanding the mechanisms of aging and related diseases; and Verily (formerly Google Life Sciences) with hardware, software, clinical and scientific teams that work on platforms, products and algorithms designed to identify the root causes of diseases, and analyze the most appropriate treatments to better understand the underlying causes of diseases in order to better diagnose and treat them. Google also announced the Baseline project in 2014, which hopes to build a map of a perfectly healthy human being, in partnership with the American universities of Duke and Standford. Participants are volunteers, recruited by applications set up by Google.

Equal access to information and care

One of the values associated with healthcare, in France as in many other countries, is equal opportunities to live in good health and with equal access to care. As in other areas such as education, this principle is routinely abused. Digital technology should enable wider access to information and, in this manner, help reduce unequal access to care. In the United Kingdom, the NHS Choice website provides access to many benchmarks on the quality of facilities, patient feedback

16 New name: "Alphabet", generalized in 2016.

and medical advice. In the United States, the ZocDoc pay site allows you to make appointments with healthcare professionals on the basis of a personalized selection; this site also takes patients' opinions into account by objectively measuring access to care, if accepted by public financial contributors. In this regard, the action of individuals, patients and associations could help to impose it[17]!

Public health: the right treatment at the right cost?

Today, some treatments are ineffective and even harmful because they do not sufficiently take the specific characteristics of each individual into account. To be able to reimburse treatments according to their effectiveness, would be a major change for both payers and patients! Whether to reimburse care or treatment, numerous performance-based reimbursement initiatives have been launched around the world, notably in the United States, United Kingdom and the Netherlands. In Germany, pharmaceutical companies now have one year to prove that a new drug provides more value than the existing drug, or else the new treatment is not reimbursed.

It is much cheaper to detect and prevent than to treat a disease when it is declared. The total cost of cardiovascular disease and strokes in the United States has been estimated at 500 billion USD. Reducing the bill by only 10% would therefore already have a huge economic impact. According to an American[18] report, connected devices could allow a saving of 500 billion USD per year worldwide, due to improved health and reduced costs of chronic diseases: increased compliance, decreased hospitalizations and post-hospital complications. However, no reimbursement policy based on the quality and effectiveness of treatment could be implemented without reliable digital data collected from patient records. In France, the shared medical record (DMP) project is currently a failure; but, as expected in Article 25 of the new Health Act, it was recently relaunched under the responsibility of CNAM[19]. Mr. Gagneux, president of ASIP, a government body, estimated that

---

17 Editor's note: it is a fairly advanced approach in America, by a process similar to the one that allowed the emergence of consumerism, of which the lawyer Ralph Nader was one of the main creators. Taking advantage of class actions, these collective legal proceedings, have only recently been instituted in France (Act 2014-344 of March 17, 2014 on consumption). As early as 1966, Mr. Nader exploited a federal rule of civil procedure enacted in 1938, little mentioned earlier, to engage the civil liability of a manufacturer (or distributor) in relation to a group of plaintiff consumers, and to have the damages caused to the defendant's expenses redressed. See Ndoubay D., *Mémoire de droit civil*, Faculté de Droit, Université de Nancy, 2011.

18 [MCK 15].

19 French National Health Insurance Fund (Caisse nationale d'assurance maladie)

15% of radiological and biological examinations prescribed in France were redundant. In addition, half of all patients with heart failure are rehabilitated within six months of surgery. Incidentally, it is estimated that out of a total of 1,750,000 hospital days per year, one third could be avoided. Compliance with prescribed drug treatments is also an important factor in monitoring.

The availability of data makes all the difference in this respect. The American group Kaiser Permanente (both an insurer and a hospital group) has a very old and rich integrated historical system, so much so that it is often cited as an example of care efficiency (Electronic Health Record). The TSN (digital healthcare pathway) project, launched in France in 2014 (2014–2017) by the Regional Health Agencies, particularly aims to simplify care pathways and communication between health professionals; the objective is also to develop services, speed up prevention and increase treatment monitoring.

In 2012, the United Kingdom's NHS launched an integrated care program and long-term risk stratification on fragile populations (seniors, diabetics) for five years. The initial program involved half a million patients, with the goal of reducing admissions to the ER. It reduced admission to the ER (-6.6% compared to +0.3% in the general population) and reduced costs by 24% over that period, in other words, 25 million GBP/year. The UK government is considering implementing the Care Data Initiative, which would not only provide access to the treatment data administered in the hospital, but also to the records of the treating physician and all patient data, in order to help understand why and how the treatment works and to have a comprehensive view of each patient.

Conclusion

The benefits of digital health will be practically unbelievable for some: who would have thought of detecting and treating a disease before its first symptoms? But there are many barriers to the potential exploitation of health data, including the following:

a) the limitation of access to health data, either because their collection is unorganized or because access is restricted by regulation; the issue of data ownership will be a key point, although interpretations are very different from one country to another[20];

---

20 One example is Iceland, which has sold the genetic data of its population to a private firm.

b) the uneven quality of data and models: some people tend to confuse correlation with causality[21]. In 2008, Google Flu Trends was supposed to detect the spread of influenza in real time through an analysis of queries made by Internet users; however, a later study showed that Google Flu Trends overestimated by half the figures of the epidemic during the last three years, in reference to those of the US Federal Agency for Disease Control and Prevention (CDC) during the same period[22];

c) lack of priority given to these issues and fragmentation of initiatives;

d) poor coordination between stakeholders and problems of interoperability between objects and data collected, as well as the lack of tools and certification, quality and safety bodies[23];

e) many human and social resistances, particularly from health professionals and institutions who fear that they are not prepared for change and/or the misuse of the data.

Recognizing these hesitations, traditional health institutions and stakeholders raise real social issues; new economic stakeholders are making major investments in eHealth[24]. A very precise vision of what deserves to be developed for health and for humanity inspires the transhumanist trend that is being carried out by the leaders of Google, among others. In order to make progress, it is necessary for stakeholders and patients to be involved, in order to prepare for collective decision-making, to reflect on what is good for individuals and society as a whole and what the law could prohibit: what about freedom and privacy for the patient? Which social choices: with or without individual selection? The mistake would be to disregard the subject and to rely on the massive investments made by digital stakeholders who, culturally, are concentrating on technological progress without the concern for the typical care from healthcare industries; or even to think that the solution lies in data protection, rather than in people!

Collaboration is essential between practitioners, pharmacies, laboratories, legislators, newcomers like social networks and Internet operators, all of are not very conducive in a cross-functional and collaborative approach and often not very used to trusting others. In this respect, the creation of the Healthcare Data Institute[25]

---

21 It's called the "stork effect"!

22 *Science*, vol. 343, p. 6, 176, 2010.

23 A comparison can be imposed here: 40% of the potential benefits of the Internet of Things would depend on this interoperability – see [MCK 15].

24 Google (already mentioned) and many other companies that invest in health and care like IBM did with Watson, Facebook in artificial intelligence, etc.

25 HDI site: http://healthcaredatainstitute.com/.

at the beginning of 2015, which brought together all of the health care stakeholders involved in the use of data (public and private stakeholders, patient associations, start-ups, large companies, etc.) would allow real cross-functional exchanges for a better understanding of the issues at stake and enable the development of concrete projects linked to the use of health data.

The capabilities of Big Data and artificial intelligence must not be left in the hands of a small number of specialists, but must absolutely be shared. We could well imagine, for example, that there will be a battle of algorithms in the future between different projects and methods. National competitiveness, strategic independence and individual and democratic freedoms could all be challenged in many ways! Initiatives such as Data for Good[26], MidataCoop[27] in Switzerland (health data cooperative project) as well as all open source projects which are accessible to all, have a pioneering role to play in this civic renewal.

Bibliography

[CUK 14] CUKIER K., MAUER-SCHÖNBERGER V., *Big data, la révolution des données est en marche*, Robert Laffont, Paris, 2014.

[GEO 62] GEORGOPOULOS B., MANN F., *The Community General Hospital*, Macmillan, New York, 1962.

[HDI 15] HDI, White Paper, http://healthcaredatainstitute.com/2015/11/25/white-paper-unlocking-the-full-potential-of-data-analytics-for-the-benefit-of-all/, 2015.

[MCK 15] MCKINSEY, *et al.*, Internet of Things, Report, June 2015.

[XER 11] XERRI J.G., *Le soin dans tous ses états*, DDB, Paris, 2011.

Internet references

BLOCKCHAIN, http://www.lehubsante.com/innovation, *Le hub santé*, 2016.

BLOG E-SANTÉ OBS, http://www.orange-business.com/fr/blogs/e-sante.

BUZZ E -SANTÉ, http://buzz-esante.fr/.

DIGITAL PHARMA BLOG, http://digitalblog.exlpharma.com/.

---

25 Non-profit organization that contributes its skills to social projects, such as the fight against unemployment, access to healthcare, etc.

26 Hafen E., "Freeing people from digital feudalism", *Technologist 06*, 2015, available at http://www.technologist.eu/freeing-people-from-digital-feudalism, 2015.

ECONOCOM, http://blog.econocom.com/blog/category/business/sante/.

EHEALTH NEWS, http://www.ehealthnews.eu/.

GENOMICS, http://massgenomics.org/2016/04/the-real-cost-of-sequencing.html, 2016.

HEALTH IT BUZZ, https://www.healthit.gov/buzz-blog/.

KEVIN MD, http://www.kevinmd.com/blog/.

L'ATELIER, http://www.atelier.net/trends/e-health.

LE MONDE, https://lemondedelaesante.wordpress.com/.

MHEALTH WATCH, http://mhealthwatch.com/.

MOBILE HEALTH NEWS, http://mobihealthnews.com/.

QUANTIFIED SELF, http://quantifiedself.com/.

8

Access to Health Data: Debates and Controversies in France

"Whatever I see or hear in the lives of my patients,
whether in connection with my professional practice or not,
which ought not to be spoken of outside,
I will keep secret, as considering all such things to be private"

Hippocratic Oath (5th Century BC).

The famous "Hippocratic Oath", foundation of the professional secrecy held by members of the medical profession since antiquity, is often used to deny third parties access to health-related databases. However, as the following text notes, the information collected in a large number of databases is not, strictly speaking, relevant to patient privacy.

The use of health data could improve public health and care, better describe the health status of the population, major endemics, prophylaxis and pathogenic behaviors. Such data should not only be accessible, but also freely available in order to strengthen research and promote practical implementations, a constant objective of open data!

In France, as in several other European countries, the debate over the use of such data is very lively, but rarely clear. In fact, health data is kept in a protective cocoon, as well as being fragmented over time and space, at the cost of a pricey and sterile redundancy; its access is difficult for anyone who is not of the inner circle.

Chapter written by Joumana BOUSTANY, Gabriella SALZANO and Christian BOURRET.

This chapter critically examines a large sample of situations: multiple data holdings are closed, there are only a few applications available to third parties. Data is not very interoperable. At the very least for the time being, access to health databases is as fragmented as it is limited. Yet, there are well-developed methods to make data anonymous and to give serious guarantees against the disclosure of indiscreet information[1].

---

1 See Chapters 3 and 4. The main acronyms can be viewed in the Appendix pp. 199–201.

Today, each country has its own approach to health data, based on different historical contexts and collective mentalities. Health data is very sensitive, with strong specificities, particularly relating to the privacy of patients and the confidentiality of diagnoses. On the one hand, improper manipulation of medical data can have extremely serious consequences. On the other, and as specified by the UK Health and Social Care Center, open data brings multiple benefits such as "increasing patient choice and improving their health, offering increased productivity, contributing to economic growth" [HSC 15]. This data accelerates scientific research and has a high economic value. According to the McKinsey Global Institute's estimate [MAN 13], "the use of open and proprietary data in health care could help generate a value of 300-450 billion USD per year in the United States. Most of this value would be in the form of cost savings for providers, payers and patients".

As the social security system has been in crisis, with a 2015 deficit of 3.9 billion in France [GOD 16], opening data could help to partially settle its accounts. This chapter, based on a literature and an analysis review of some major health information systems, examines the conditions of access to this form of public health data in France.

Methodology

To address this issue, we have adopted an empirical approach, appropriate for a rapidly expanding topic of study such as open and massive health data. Today, with connected devices, the Internet and social networks, the amount of collected data has multiplied to such an extent that "two days worth of produced data corresponds to what humanity has produced since its origins until 2003"[2]. In order to trace the progress of health data in France, we have explored the archives of French newspapers, official data platforms, government websites and the sites of the High Authority for Health (HAS). This method has allowed us to understand the views of various stakeholders on public policies relating to health and care information. For the analysis of databases, we have taken "operational" systems into account, with added value for research in different fields (public health, social sciences, etc.). We have excluded private databases such as the Longitudinal Patient database, recently acquired by imshealth.com or Xpr-SO, which includes "the real-time panel of 3,004 pharmacies, representative of the 22,458 pharmacies in mainland France"[3]. These databases as well as most of the massive data obtained via the connected devices are not accessible or are subject to a fee, so it is difficult to analyze them!

---

2 Eric Schmidt, Techcrunch, 2010, available online: https://techcrunch.com/2010/08/04/schmidt-data/.
3 https://www.xpr-so.net/pages/Public/Accueil.aspx.

In order to carry out this study, we used both quantitative and qualitative analyses. Qualitative data was obtained by analyzing several types of systems that were considered by experts to be fundamental to the measurement of health indicators, generating a large amount of data, but whose access is restricted or prohibited. It should be noted that few of these systems are open, with the exception of the most recent ones which have been designed to be accessible to all.

Literature review

Since 2007, a series of actions to open up health data have been undertaken at an international level. However, "France still lags far behind the countries of Northern Europe and North America in terms of cross-checking data sources (lack of a database providing information on the reasons for use and the main characteristics enabling the validity of a prescription to be judged) and above all, the partnership with the world of research" [BEG 13]. The widespread adoption of personal health records has accelerated the collection of sensitive and personal clinical data such as medical history, clinical and laboratory test results, reading and interpretation of medical imaging, etc. The re-use of this data is essential for research, because it generates new knowledge and supports strategic and operational decision-making.

Several authors have highlighted the benefits of sharing research data: "The practical and scientific arguments for data sharing include improving the accuracy of research, informing risk/benefit analysis of treatment options, strengthening collaborations, accelerating biomedical research, and restoring trust in the clinical research enterprise" [OLS 13]. Others also emphasize on the barriers to opening health data: differences between patients, data structured in different ways, privacy, data conversion, etc. Especially since each organization generally collects its information in different databases and for specific purposes. In addition, there are also major technical obstacles. They specifically address the heterogeneity of organizations, data and standards, which is one of the essential criteria for re-using data. Indeed, "parallel non-prescriptive parallel developments in multiple sectors lead to the substantial duplication of costs and human effort" [GEI 13].

The literature on health information systems in France reveals a system that needs substantial improvements: "The very large national databases present a major interest for the French health statistics system. However, the interest is currently limited because there are obstacles regarding their use for public health purposes" [GOL 12]. In reports commissioned by various French administrations, experts point to the abundance of public information that has no consistency in formats between them [PIC 12] and recommend improving the visibility of health information that is provided, by creating a single institutional portal [BRU 11]. They questioned the accessibility of health information in France by citizens. Health information systems offer highly dispersed information that is unintelligible for citizens. The report on the monitoring and promotion of the proper use of medication in France makes for a very worrying read on the French structures of monitored medicine consumption [BEG 13].

Many voices were raised in favor of opening up this data in France. In September 2013, a report on governance and the use of health data was submitted to Marisol Touraine, the then Minister of Social Affairs and Health. This report advocates opening up health data, but only when there is no risk of re-identification [BRA 12][4]. In October 2013, the Transparency Health Initiative, an association dissolved in October 2014, launched a petition for the opening of data. In November 2013, during the presentation of the national health strategy, the Minister reaffirmed her commitment, created the necessary conditions for open data with secure access to health data and launched a public debate on the subject[5]. This commitment has had little effect on the ground, given that three years on, renowned specialists are still demanding the opening of health data: Didier Sicard (professor of medicine, honorary president of the French National Consultative Ethics Committee) and Jean-Marie Spaeth (honorary president of the CNAMTS[6] and honorary president of the National Higher School of Social Security) who, in an article in *Le Monde* on September 27, 2016, wrote: "Our country has very accurate health data. Unfortunately, it is difficult to access it, despite what the state says. This has to change, and the democratic debate depends on it." One of the Senate reports on open data also pointed out that "the identification of the information sought often appears difficult; the information available is incomplete and its quality is uneven due, in particular, to the tardiness (sic) of updates, a certain methodological instability or its increasing technicality; and lastly, it does not necessarily meet the expectations of citizens" [BOU 14].

Years go by, writings and reports follow one another to apply the brakes on the opening of data. In its report from May 3, 2016 on personal health data, managed by the Health Insurance, the *Courdes Comptes* considered it a priority to secure the existing system, improve governance and ensure the fluidity of access using a rigorous and open approach, in order to encourage the use of health data for general interest purposes. This report [COU 16] regrets that, despite an extensive health database, France is lagging considerably behind when it comes to facilitating access, and recommends improving the quality of data with a view to building an open health database and simplifying procedures before the CNIL.

---

4 It is important to note that private life is notably protected in France by Act no. 78-17 from January 6, 1978, relating to information technology, files and freedoms.

5 The conditions applicable to the retention of "sensitive" and confidential data are also analyzed in Chapter 3 (p. 89 sq.).

6 For all acronyms, please refer to the glossary at the end of this chapter.

As this literature review shows, French political stakeholders are enthusiastic about the idea of opening up health data. The number of reports sponsored by the ministry attests to this, but results are slow to emerge. This observation is still valid in 2017. A strange step forward and two steps backwards seems to characterize the debate over open health data in France.

Information systems in France

Several health care regimes coexist in France. For example: the general social security regime, the agricultural regime, the RSI (Social Security Scheme for the Self-Employed), etc. As a result, there are several health information systems with different objectives and contents that make it difficult to cross-check data. The French Institute of Health Data (IDS) was created with the mission of: "ensuring the coherence and quality of information systems... under conditions guaranteeing anonymity set by decree in the Conseil d'Etat, following the advice of the National Commission for Information Technology and Liberties"[7]. In the meantime, the IDS has promoted several health and care collections of data[8]:

– medical data collected by a sample of general practitioners;

– hospital data transmitted by public and private establishments;

– disability data provided by the departmental homes for disabled persons (MDPH);

– data on dependency provided by nursing homes for dependent elderly persons (EHPAD);

– data on the causes of death sent by doctors and town councils;

– cohort data for research and health security;

– supplementary health insurance data;

– indicators from the decision support service, etc.

In April 2014, as part of the public debate on the opening of health data launched in November 2013, *Etalab*[9] published a mapping of databases listing and qualifying

---

7 http://www.institut-des-donnees-de-sante.fr/institut/la-loi/.

8 http://www.institut-des-donnees-de-sante.fr/connaissance/.

9 It is the Prime Minister's department, within the General Secretariat for Modernization of Public Action, that is in charge of the opening of public data.

the main health data and databases in France[10]. This mapping identifies 313 databases, surveys and publications related to public health and more specifically:

– consumption of care and expenditure (104 databases);

– public health and epidemiology (93 databases);

– offers of care (78 databases);

– performance and operations (38 databases).

To conduct this census, *Etalab* examined the main reports on health data in France, analyzed websites of different safety regimes and interviewed health data managers. This data can be divided into two levels: "the granular level (the most finely tuned level of data that can be obtained, according to the origin of the data and the collection system), and the aggregated level (data obtained by aggregating granular data according to one or more common characteristics)"[11]. That is to say, the same database can be found in both categories. In addition to its content, the importance of data also lies in the possibility of reusing it. The latter depends on:

– terms and conditions of access (free, restricted or reserved);

– the cost (paid or free);

– the format of the data (usable: ods, csv, json or not usable: in PDF or only available online);

– conditions of reuse (explicitly unrestricted, explicitly with restriction or not).

These criteria are taken into account in the mapping carried out by *Etalab*. Among the data sets surveyed, about one hundred are aggregated and freely accessible. For granular data sets, 70% have restricted access and 21% have open access, with the remaining data sets reserved for managers. The most finely granulated data involves individuals, institutions, companies and medicines; aggregated data is obtained by aggregating granular data, concerning for instance: people under 25 years of age or the number of beds available in the emergency rooms of public hospitals in France.

It is also interesting to understand data coverage. It can be heterogeneous or mixed, referring to a sample of patients, physicians, institutions, time periods or territories. Granular data is freely accessible. It relates to health care services and, more specifically, those relating to professionals, businesses and medicines. Approximately 50% of the databases surveyed are in a usable format. This data comes from health care institutions and systems such as the SNIIRAM (National

---

10 https://www.data.gouv.fr/fr/datasets/cartographie-des-bases-de-donnees-publiques-en-sante/.
11 Identical mapping of health databases.

Inter-Regional Health Insurance Information System) and the PMSI (Information Systems Medicalization Program). The number of databases with open access is very limited and the level of heterogeneity is very high. About one third of data is aggregated and freely accessible. More than two-thirds of the data is granular, 70% of which is restricted access and 8% closed access. Only 21% is open access. Open-licensed data is free to access. Given the large number of health information systems, presented below is a selection to illustrate our findings.

Restricted and controlled access systems

SNIIRAM

This database was created by the Social Security Financing Act in 1999. Article 2 of the Decree of July 19, 2013, amended on October 6, 2016 sets out its objectives: to improve the quality of care, to contribute to the better management of health insurance and health policies, and to provide healthcare providers with relevant information on their activity, revenues and, where appropriate, prescriptions. Patient information comes from health insurance schemes and hospital activity information comes from the French Agency for Information on Hospital Care (ATIH). Patient data includes: demographics, long-term conditions, health care use, consultations and visits with general practitioners, medical procedures, medication, analytical results and diagnoses, and medical devices. The care service includes prescriber specialties, implementers, implementing locations, geographical setup and contractual or legal status.

As this database is managed by the French National Health Insurance Agency for WageEarners (CNAMTS), its access is highly restricted and the use of data must be authorized by the National Commission for Computing and Liberties (CNIL). Article 4 of the above-mentioned decree lists the categories of people who may use SNIIRAM data. Although the data is anonymized and the anonymity number is established by irreversible computer coding (Article 5), researchers with access to this data may not simultaneously implement more than one of the four variables considered sensitive (common code, date of care, month and year of birth, date of death). The amendment from October 6, 2016 relaxed certain access rules. In particular, it has:

– extended the period of authorization to use data from three to six years;

– authorized the processing of information by research organizations, universities, schools and other research-related educational institutions. These authorizations are now subject to approval by the IDS office and the CNIL.

Despite this reform, the use of SNIIRAM data is highly regulated and we are far from the principles of open licensing and the reuse of data.

PMSI

When it was created in 1982, this program was presented as an epidemiological tool and as a system that fostered a better exchange between doctors, caregivers and administrators. It was generalized to public health institutions in 1994 and 1996 for the private sector. Since 2005, it has been a tool for describing and measuring the medical and economic aspects of hospital activity. It makes it possible to quantify and standardize the activity and resources of healthcare institutions and thus calculate the budget allocations for them. The data comes from different sources:

– PMSI MCO (Medicine, Surgery, Obstetrics and Dentistry) – Standardized Release Summary (RSS) for hospital care for short stays. These RSSs are automatically classified into diagnosis-related groups of patients;

– PMSI SSR (Residential Care and Rehabilitation): the identification of hospitalizations carried out in structures with an activity authorized in this field;

– PMSI HAD (Hospitalization at Home): collection of care methods classified as a homogeneous care group;

– RIM-P (Collection of Medical Information for Psychiatry): description of all the activity carried out for the benefit of patients by healthcare institutions, in full or partial hospitalization care (Sequence Summary) as well as ambulatory care (Ambulatory Activity Summary).

This database that is used to code, collect, analyze, return and disseminate hospital information in both the public and private sectors, is managed by the Technical Agency for Hospitalization Information (ATIH). While some summary data such as the mapping of establishments activity, the national cost reference system, perinatal health indicators, etc. are accessible on the *Scan santé*[12] website, access to detailed data and specific extractions are reserved for holders who have obtained the agreement of the CNIL, which is issued according to use.

What is the synthesis?

Access to and the use of these databases requires a great deal of expertise regarding the social security payment systems in France for providers, reimbursement laws (SNIIRAM) and the hospital payment system (PMSI). To facilitate the use of these

---

12 http://www.scansante.fr.

databases, training courses are set up. As the conditions of access are very strict and tightly controlled, potential users have to apply for access to different bodies from one database to another. For example, very reputable French research organizations, such as the National Institute of Health and Medical Research (INSERM), do not have direct access to the anonymized individual data of SNIIRAM. They can only ask the system manager to extract a sample of data from it. The average time to obtain this data is 17 months; sometimes it can exceed two years[13]. However, the information collected by these systems has added value for research. For example, to calculate the consumption of a medical treatment in France, in accordance to the beneficiary's profile and with the purpose of monitoring this consumption.

Cross-checking data

Despite the diversity of objectives and contents of these databases, some cross-checks are still possible:

1) in terms of patients, between SNIIRAM and PMSI: hospital activity and expenditure, ambulatory care requests, etc. Between SNIIRAM and the Health and Social Protection Survey (SAE): social determinants, healthcare needs and access issues, data on requests for care since 2012;

2) in terms of hospitals between PMSI and the Annual Health Facility Statistics (AHS) and hospital characteristics;

3) in terms of aggregated data: between all databases.

For example, the Ministry of Labor, Employment, Vocational Training and Social Dialogue has published information on distances to travel and access time to care in mainland France[14]. This data is accessible to all members of the public on the data.gouv.fr site. This represents spatial accessibility to healthcare in France, carried out on January 1, 2007 and in April 2011. The databases for analyzing access to care are numerous and concerns specific areas such as urban or hospital care. For ambulatory care, data is extracted from SNIIRAM. For hospital care, an innovative methodology for monitoring and the geolocation of specialized hospitals is mainly based on the PMSI, annual statistics and the National Register of Health and Social Institutions (FINESS). For heavy material equipment, annual statitistics and SNIIRAM data were used.

---

13 "Accès aux données de santé. Propositions du comité d'experts de l'Institut des données de santé (IDS) adoptées par la majorité de ses membres", *Institut des données de santé* (2013), available at: http://www.institut-des-donnees-de-sante.fr/site-download-process/56-d2cq8k.html.
14 This ministry has adopted a different name in 2017; but the above analysis is still a valid one.

Towards a unified open system?

Article 193 of the Health System Modernization Act of January 26, 2016 established the National Health Data System (SNDS). The decree establishing this institution was issued on December 28, 2016 and came into effect on April 1, 2017. The SNDS brings together data from the SNIIRAM, the PMSI, the Center for Epidemiology of Medical Causes of Death (CépiDC), medical and social data from the National Solidarity Fund for Autonomy (CNSA) and a representative sample of complementary reimbursement data. It will be managed by the CNAMTS and the Institute of Health Data (IDS) which will be replaced by the National Health Data Institute (INDS), which is expected to become the single window for data access. The SNDS data will be anonymized in an irreversible way and the National Institute of Health and Medical Research can, as the national coordinator of research infrastructures using health data, be responsible, within the framework of an agreement concluded with the French National Health Insurance Agency for Wage Earners, for ensuring the extraction and effective provision of data from the national health data system, for treatments used for research, study or evaluation purposes. The same decree defines the people who will have a right to access:

– CNAMTS personnel or service providers authorized and named by the Director General of CNAMTS due to their duties;

– INDS personnel or service providers and medical research whose duties justify it, authorized and named by its Chairman and Chief Executive Officer.

While the intentions to open up health data are put forward by the administrative authorities, in practice these intentions are accompanied by very restrictive access conditions and very complex procedures[15].

Restricted access systems

Ten-year health surveys

This survey is carried out by the National Institute for Statistics and Economic Studies (INSEE). The first survey was conducted in 1960–1961. The objective is to outline the health status of the population and to understand the annual consumption of healthcare and prevention, the reported morbidity and the perception of health. It covers fairly broad areas: living conditions, social protection, general state of health, disability, description of illnesses, use of doctors and hospitals, surgical history, disruption of activity for health reasons, dietary habits and prevention. The most

---

15 For the conditions of access, see discussion No. 2016-316 of October 13, 2016 giving notice on a draft decree in the Conseil d'Etat on the national health data system.

recent survey, conducted in 2002–2003 in accordance with the European Health Interview Survey (EHIS), generated three granular data sets for access by members of the Scientific Council and researchers.

Health barometer

Managed by the National Institute for Prevention and Health Education (INPES)[16], this barometer has been in existence since 1992. These surveys cover the behaviors and attitudes of French people (drug abuse, sexual behavior, etc.), occupational risks and prevention measures taken in primary care (detection, health education). The 2016 survey examined perceptions and practices related to infectious diseases. This barometer is a reliable source for public health studies, even if the questions are not the same from one survey to another. This health barometer generated granular data available free of charge to researchers after approval by the INPES. The data format is reusable, with some restrictions.

Open information systems

Thanks to the Internet, some health information has been made available online. Since 2013, several health information systems have been designed and developed for online release with an open data sharing policy under an open license. In addition to health facility statistics, we can also mention PDB and Scope santé, which are completely user-oriented.

Annual health facilities statistics

The first survey was conducted in 1995 to collect data from 1994. This is a compulsory administrative enquiry concerning all French public health establishments (about 1,000) and private establishments (about 2,500). It is carried out by the Directorate for Research, Studies, Evaluation and Statistics (DREES). This platform allows different types of queries and collection methods (tables, SQL, etc.). The topics covered are: types of rooms, capacity, equipment, personnel (employees, independent practitioners, pharmacists, etc.), activities (number of days in hospital, number of radiotherapy sessions, etc.). This statistic generates three sets of granular data, freely available to all in an exploitable (Excel) format.

---

16 On May 1, 2016, the National Institute for Health Prevention and Education (INPES), the Institute for Health Surveillance (InVS) and the Health Emergency Preparedness and Response Agency (EPRUS) were merged by Order No. 2016-462 and Decree 2016-523. These bodies now form the "Santé Publique France" agency.

Public drug database

Launched in October 2013, the public database of medicines provides the general public and health professionals with access to data and reference documents on marketed medicinal products or that have been marketed during the last three years in France. This administrative and scientific database on the treatment and use of health products is implemented by the National Agency for the Safety of Medicines and Health Products (ANSM), in conjunction with the High Authority for Health (HAS) and the National Union of Health Insurance Funds (UNCAM), under the aegis of the Ministry of Social Affairs and Health. In addition to the usual information on a medicine, each package leaflet gives two indicators of medical benefits: the Medical Service Rendered (SMR) and the Improvement of Medical Service Rendered (ASMR). These indicators help to answer two questions: is this medicine effective enough to be fully covered by social security? Is this medicine a real improvement over other treatments available? These indicators make it possible to determine the rate of coverage by UNCAM and to negotiate the sales price with pharmaceutical companies.

Scope santé

This database was launched in November 2013. It provides information on the quality level of hospitals and clinics in France, in other words about 4,000 health establishments. It is primarily intended for users, given that it can compare institutions according to different criteria; it provides official information evaluating the quality and indicators of activities, in addition to the quality and safety of care in healthcare institutions. Since 2009, public and private healthcare institutions have been obliged to report their results; this information was not available to the public until 2013. Scope santé presents unified and integrated data provided by qualified organizations and by: AHS, PMSI, HAS, the results of the Infection Control Committee (LIN balance sheet), and the National Register of Health and Social Facilities (FINESS).

The information in this database on institutions can be used according to different criteria: map search with geolocation functions, profile search (children and adolescents, pregnant women, elderly people, etc.), type of care (hospitalization at home, long-term care, etc.), medical specialties, available equipment (scanner, etc.), type of institution (public, private, private non-profit sector). Users can also use filters regarding the certification level (with or without recommendation, with reservations, not certified, certification in progress, etc.) and the performance level per indicator. This database illustrates the enormous task to be accomplished before the opening of the data, in particular to make it interoperable, to disseminate it and to be able to visualize it in different ways, to make its consultation adapted to the end user and the citizen. The transparency of such indicators has already been the subject of several controversies and this approach has often been debated. Philippe Leduc, Director of the Health Economics think tank, asks: "Is it normal that patients should decide on the future of a healthcare institution by avoiding going there where the score is shuddering? No, it certainly isn't."[17]

Going towards an opening of health data?

This review of French literature and health information systems demonstrates the complexity of the health data problem. The opening of data takes place in a fragmented context. Several executive agencies are involved; their areas of competence are telescopic. Systems that produce essential data to develop indicators and carry out studies are very difficult to access, even for researchers. Economists and researchers need to use this data and cross-check it in order to exploit its potential in a way that respects privacy. Indeed, "the CNAMTS alone does not have the means to make maximum use of this data"[18].

> "France has all the ingredients necessary to set up a national and reliable health information system. The main challenge is the absence of a real national health policy" [GOL 12]. Would political leadership be essential to improve the context and increase the transparency and effectiveness of health systems? Will the creation of the INDS with complex access conditions lead to the opening of data that many researchers have longed for? "Stakeholders – political and administrative leaders, decision-makers in social protection systems, health professionals, users, and organizations involved in public health studies and research – are confronted with issues that require a more comprehensive and shared knowledge of the health system." [IDS 13]

The efforts of the IDS (now INDS) can help public authorities to become aware of the difficulties of access and dispersal of information systems, to formalize problems and work to streamline interactions between multiple administrative bodies. The diversity and heterogeneity of this data constitutes a major obstacle to the interoperability between these systems; this is certainly unfavorable to the exploitation of this data. Moreover, the opening up of data often requires preliminary work, all the more important because the indicators are calculated from multiple sources, which are themselves heterogeneous and managed by different executive agencies!

---

17 Leduc P., "Scope santé exposes hospitals and clinics", *Les Echos*, December 4, 2013.
18 L'Hote Q., "L'open data et la santé en France", *Les Echos*, July 17, 2014.

The analysis summarized above shows that multiple resources using separate formats lead to high heterogeneity at different levels. Each system has a wide range of objectives. The opening of health data primarily involves consumption and health expenditure, public health, outpatient care and performance (financial, operational and qualitative) of the French health system. Open data is mainly aggregated from granular data. Much of the access to this granular data is restricted.

When information is unrestricted, it is usually free. Open granular patient data is always anonymized and access is restricted or closed. In 2013, granular databases (Scope santé and BDPM) were created under an open license. Since then, the administrative authorities have given rise to hopes for a better opening of data; but this hope is, for the time being, not effective on the field. Will the creation of the INDS be the sign of a real opening up of health data in France?

Conclusion

In this chapter we have presented positions, decisions and controversies concerning health data in France. We briefly described the state of open access to health data. This highlights the reluctance to open up and the poor recycling of health data in the short term. The process that could make the different systems interoperable will take time. Open data requires political support. It will proceed with the transformation of existing systems to render its data open and interoperable.

The barriers and boundaries between the different categories of data (personal or public, anonymous or identifiable, big data and open data) are not clear. On October 21, 2013, the European Parliament voted for a major revision of the 1995 directive to strengthen citizens' control over their personal data. On April 27, 2016, the European Parliament and the Union Council hence adopted a regulation on the protection of individuals with regard to the processing of personal data and for the free movement of such data[19]. This regulation (unlike a directive) is directly applicable to all member countries of the European Union (EU) starting from May 26, 2018. Point 35 defines health data; Article 9 prohibits "the processing of personal data revealing racial or ethnic origin, political opinions, religious or philosophical beliefs or trade union membership, as well as the processing of genetic data, biometric data for the purpose of uniquely identifying a natural person, data concerning health or data concerning the sexual life or sexual orientation of a natural person". Despite some exceptions (explicit consent, safeguarding the vital interests of the individual, etc.), access to data remains limited to categories of professionals. This regulation therefore does not facilitate the opening of health data!

---

19 This General Data Protection Regulation (GDRP) 2016 - 679 is applicable from May 25th 2018. See Chap. 3 note 17.

In a press release issued on July 9, 2014, the Minister of Health announced that she wanted to speed up the process of opening up health data. In particular, it would ensure that the results of investigations and research funded by public funds are made freely available. On July 4, 2016, at the presentation of the eHealth strategy, she recalled that the impetus for the controlled opening of health data must be sustainable. It would be necessary to create a health data administrator function in the ministry, one of whose missions would be to accelerate the opening of health data. Upon reflection on Big Data (or metadata), she launched a plan to go even further into the value of this data. Although actions have been carried out in the field, the results are not conclusive. This opening of data demanded by the research community is causing much controversy, as can be seen concerning the institutional and medicine data. What about open individual data, even if it is anonymous?

The minister's intentions were commendable; but did they take into account the extreme complexity of the often contradictory issues raised by the French health system, the interaction of stakeholders, their conflicting interests and the application of European regulations? Will any data be truly open? Within what timeframe? Many questions are still yet to be answered.

Bibliography

[BEG 13] BEGAUD B., COSTAGLIOLA D., Rapport sur la surveillance et la promotion du bon usage du médicament en France, French ministry of social affairs and health, Paris, 2013.

[BOU 14] BOUCHOUX C., Rapport d'information fait au nom de la mission commune d'information sur l'accès aux documents administratifs et aux données publiques, Sénat, Paris, 2014.

[BRA 13] BRAS P.L., Gouvernance et utilisation des données de santé, French ministry of social affairs and health, Paris, 2013.

[BRU 11] BRUN N., HIRSH E., KIVITS J. et al., Nouvelles attentes du citoyen, acteur de santé, French ministry of work, employment and health, Paris, 2011.

[COU 16] COUR DES COMPTES, Les données personnelles de santé gérées par l'assurance maladie, Paris, March 2016.

[GEI 13] GEISSBUHLER A., SAFRAN C., BUCHAN I. et al., "Trustworthy reuse of health data: a transnational perspective", International journal of medical informatics, vol. 82, no. 1, pp. 1–9, 2013.

[GOD 16] GODELUCK S., "Déficit de la sécurité sociale. L'effet de la crise de 2008 est presque effacé", Les Echos, 15 March 2016.

[GOL 12] GOLDBERG M., JOUGLA E., FASSA M. et al., "The French health information system", Statistical Journal of the IAOS, vol. 28, nos 1–2, pp. 31–41, 2012.

[HSC 15] HEALTH AND SOCIAL CARE INFORMATION CENTER, Supporting transparency and open data, HSCIC, 2015.

[IDS 13] IDS, Rapport au parlement 2013, Des avancées et des propositions raisonnées, 2013.

[MAN 13] MANYIKA J., CHUI M., GROVES P. et al., Open data. Unlocking innovation and performance with liquid information, McKinsey and Company, 2013.

[OLS 13] OLSON S., DOWNEY AUTUMN S., Sharing clinical research data, The National Academies Press, Washington, 2013.

[PIC 12] PICARD R., VIAL A., LAVAL D. et al., De l'information du patient à la démocratie sanitaire. Enjeux et conditions d'un usage efficient des technologies, Report, ministère de l'Economie et des finances, Paris, 2012.

Appendix. Main acronyms used in this chapter[20]

ANSM   *Agence nationale de sécurité du médicament* (National Agency for Medicines and Health Products Safety)

ASMR   *Amélioration du service medical rendu* (Improvement of Medical Services Rendered)

ATIH   *Agence technique d'information sur l'Hospitalisation* (Agency for Information on Hospital Care)

BDPM   *Base de données publiques des médicaments* (Public Drug Database)

CépiDC   *Centre d'épidémiologie sur les causes médicales de décès* (Epidemiology Center on the Medical Causes of Death)

CNAMTS   *Caisse nationale de l'assurance maladie des travailleurs salariés* (National Health Insurance Agency for Wage Earners)

CNIL   *Commission nationale pour l'informatique & les libertés* (National Commission for Informatics & Freedoms)

CNSA   *Caisse nationale de solidarité pour l'autonomie* (National Solidarity Fund for Autonomy)

---

20 To ease the reader's understanding of the many acronyms used in this chapter, their meanings are mostly developed here in the English language.

DREES   *Direction de la recherche, des études, de l'évaluation et des statistiques* (Directorate for Research, Analysis, Evaluation and Statistics)

EHPAD   *Etablissements d'hébergement pour personnes âgées dépendantes* (Accommodation Facility for Dependent Elderly)

EPRUS*   *Etablissement de préparation et de réponse aux urgences sanitaires* (Health Emergency Preparedeness and Response Agency)

ESPS   *Enquête santé et protection sociale* (Healthcare and Insurance Survey)

FINESS   *Fichier national des institutions sanitaires et sociales* (National Register of Health and Social Institutions)

GHM   *Groupe homogène de malades* (Homogeneous Healthcare Group)

HAS   *Haute autorité de santé* (High Health Authority)

IDS   *Institut (national) des données de santé* (National Institute on
(or INDS)   Health Information)

INPES*   *Institut national de prévention et d'éducation pour la santé* (National Institute of Prevention and Health Education)

INSERM   *Institut national de la santé et de la recherche médicale* (National Institute of Health and Medical Research)

InVS*   *Institut de veille sanitaire* (Institute for Public Health Surveillance)

LIN   *Luttes contre les infections nosocomiales* (Infection Control Committee)

MDPH   *Maisons départementales des personnes handicapées* (Departmental Home for Disabled Persons)

PMSI   *Programme de médicalisation des systèmes d'information* (Information Systems Medicalization Program)

PMSI HAD   *Programme de médicalisation des systèmes d'information hospitalisation à domicile* (Medicalization Program for Home Hospital Information Systems)

PMSI MCO *Programme de médicalisation des systèmes d'information médecine, chirurgie, obstétrique et odontologie* (Medicalization Program for Medical Information Systems in Medicine, Surgery, Obstetrics and Dentistry)

PMSI SSR *Programme de médicalisation des systèmes d'information soins de suite et de réadaptation* (Medicalization Program for Information Systems on Monitoring and Rehabilitation

RAA   *Résumé d'activité ambulatoire* (Ambulatory Activity Summary)

RIM-P   *Recueil d'informations médicalisé pour la psychiatrie* (Collection of Medical Information for Psychiatry)

RPS   *Résumé par séquence* (Sequence Summary)

RSI   *Régime social des indépendants* (Social Security Scheme for the Self-employed)

RSS   *Résumé de sortie standardisé* (Standardized Output Summary)

SAE   *Statistique annuelle des Etablissements de santé* (Annual Health Facilities Statistics)

SI   *Système d'information* (Information System)

SMR   *Service médical rendu* (Medical Service Rendered)

SNDS   *Système national des données de santé* (National Health Data System)

SNIIRAM   *Système national d'information inter-régime de l'assurance maladie* (National Inter-regional Health Insurance Information System)

UE - EU   *Union européenne* (European Union)

UNCAM   *Union nationale des caisses d'assurance maladie* (National Union of Health Insurance Funds)

---

* EPRUS, InVs and INPES merged in 2016, forming "Santé Publique France"; see footnote 16.

9

Artificial Intelligence: Utopia or Progress?

Does the very rapid growth in electronics since the 1960s justify the place that current affairs columns give to artificial intelligence? This paradoxical concept suggests that man and electronic machines have similar, sometimes interchangeable capacities. This has often been considered since the Industrial Revolution. Electronics and neurobiology have given rise to new questions since the 1980s: would mental activity, particularly in the cortex of higher animals and humans, be analogous to that of computers or electronic memories? Some discoveries in neurobiology have suggested bringing together, comparing and even simulating part of brain function with the help of electronic computers, an opportunity to bring Descartes' questioning up to date: "when a reasonable soul will integrate this machine, it will have its place in the brain"[1]!

Such approaches awaken the age-old debate between monism and dualism or between spiritualism and materialism, philosophical quarrels that have been going on for more than two millennia in the West. Queries aroused again by proselytes of singularity who predict the dawn of a bionic robot, autonomous from its programmer, and the addition of devices to mankind that would improve its performance; maintain its state of health and extend its abilities ad libitum, *well beyond normal biological life; even, ultimately, repel death[2]! Where would the line be drawn between credible technological foresight and the awakened dream? This is one of the themes in the following text.*

Chapter written by Jean-Pierre CHAMOUX.

1 In the "*Traité de l'homme*", Gallica reproduction, BNF, 1657; excerpt from "Sur la machine du corps", quoted by J. M. Tremblay at www/classiques.uqac.ca/classiques.

2 Themes of "transhumanism" and "singularity" for which Google (now called Alphabet) has founded a "university" with very appreciable means in terms of men and money: www.singularityu.org. Its Chancellor, Ray Kurzweil, who advocates for "the augmented man", says on this site: "Soon, we will literally become a hybrid of biological and non-biological thinking."

This chapter is based on a reflection by the late physicist Louis Leprince-Ringuet of the French Academy, written 10 years before his death in 2000: "the real problem of artificial intelligence: (is) what it brings to men, and what it puts at risk. Nothing is eluded (here) from the difficulties of science, the limits of technology, the exaggerations of the media, scientific illusions, idealistic terror [...] the moral difficulties [or] the responsibilities of the human being"[3].

For a long time, men have been tempted to consider machines as if they were working in their own way. "Artificial intelligence", which originated in the United States in the 1950s, suggests that there could be a merging of machine and man, or even a replacement of human intelligence by a digital system. This concept was forged during a seminar held at Dartmouth College around a group of scientists and technologists, who then scattered into numerous study and thought circles over the next thirty years[4]. It is somewhat of an oxymoron which paradoxically brings together an attribute that is difficult to define, but specifically human: intelligence, and the artificial qualifier, which is specific to objects designed by men to meet their needs, curiosity and pleasures: practical objects, tools, habitat, clothing, books, etc.

Before computers, there were robots

Mechanical robots preceded computers by at least two centuries. Vaucanson's marvelous robots were already programmed to "simulate man [...] Vaucanson never ceased to confront the question of the man-machine relationship in terms that haven't lost any of their relevance [...] For better or for worse, somewhere between new humanism and post-humanity"[5]. Vaucanson made mechanical dolls with watchmaking precision, faithfully reproducing the movements and postures of men and animals, as put in evidence by the historical texts and reproductions that have been passed down through the centuries.

---

3 Preface, in [MOC 90]. We have taken great advantage of the essays collected in this collection for the Frederik R. Bull Foundation; this book is still very topical, because its authors had remarkably grasped the meaning and scope of artificial intelligence at a time when technology was far from enabling the Internet and social networks. The assessments made around 1990 by enlightened minds remain largely valid in the present time.

4 A meeting organized in 1956 around several academics such as John McCarthy, Marvin Minsky, Alan Newell and Herbert Simon; the group's profession of faith affirmed, among other things, that: "every aspect [...] of learning can be described in a sufficiently precise way for a machine to simulate it", quoted by André Holley in [BLO 99].

5 Foreword by B. Roukhomovski in [SPI 10]. Published on the occasion of the 300th anniversary of his birth and the exhibitions organized in his honor in Grenoble, Paris, Lyon, etc. Such robots can still be found in the museums of Soulac, Neufchâtel in Switzerland, Arts et métiers in Paris, etc. The famous "digesting duck" built by Vaucanson disappeared in a fire in Russia in 1879.

The electric robots that have been regularly feeding the literary and film column since the 1940s are less elegant than mechanical robots; but, unlike the Vaucanson duck, they have sophisticated sensors that ensure a certain relationship between the robot and the outside world. They can feel, touch, see and act for those robots that have an operational function, such is the case in exploration devices at the heart of nuclear power plants, or those that can perform eye surgery and surgical experience, for example. The German flying bombs from the years 1943 to 1945, the V1 and V2, already included automation systems that helped to pilot their flight. Half a century later, cruise missiles like the American Tomahawk had a finer "terrain tracking" capability, a simulation of human piloting that makes them autonomous, especially since the programming of these missiles can be revised and updated remotely, during the mission!

In the civilian domain, electronic foxes and turtles have had a great success since the 1950s, which to some extent echoed Vaucanson's creations[6]. These electronic robots foreshadowed the many robots presented today in Japan and North America: all of them mimic either humans or animals; it seems that over time, we have become fascinated by familiar forms and are unable to imagine a robot that doesn't look like an animal[7] of some kind! This is a curious fact, because the design of a manufactured object generally answers only one practical concern: the schematic of a car, a refrigerator, a camera, a motor is guided by a functional analysis, that is to say the designer bends to utilitarian considerations. Robots designed since the time of the Enlightenment are a strange exception to this rule. Even today, novelists, filmmakers and even engineers still try to portray their robots as a charade of being alive, possibly deformed to make an impression, with legs, eyes, skins and a more or less canine or humanoid body. Why this lack of imagination? Why this attachment to a representation that maintains the idea of a man-machine?

Is the machine driving man away?

Bruno Bonnell, President of the Lyon Management School and leader of the French "robotics industry" at the time of writing, is just as surprised as we are[8]. He describes the robot as: "a knowledge machine" whose performance, although always improving, transforms and accelerates material processes and arouses, as

---

6 For example, the electronic fox from Albert Ducrocq (1953), who was a scientific columnist on radio Europe no.1 and at Le Figaro, and a great scientific popularizer in the aerospace sector until his death in 2001.

7 Except, of course, for weapons such as those just mentioned: their form is mainly dictated by operational considerations and the laws of physics and aerodynamics for flying objects.

8 Private communication, March 2016. Mr. Bonnel was elected in the French Parliament in 2017.

demonstrated by industrial history since the 17th Century, unfavorable and even violent instinctive reactions[9]. Robotics assists and sometimes replaces the subservient manufacturing tasks performed by workers (long-term slaves of iron, fire and other forces of nature); it has prompted strong reluctance however, since the revolt of Norman workers against the cotton spinning machine in the 18th Century, to that of the silk workers in Lyon who refused a drop in their wages, which was (wrongly) attributed to the use of a machine. The fantasy of replacing man by machine has a lasting influence on industrial history: at the beginning of the industrial renaissance of the "glorious thirty", after the war of 1939–45, a Parisian daily newspaper headlined, for example, in full page: "Will the conscious machine reduce man to slavery?"[10].

What does artificial intelligence cover?

Over time, the intelligence lent to machines has covered an increasingly wide range of fields: calculation, analysis, interpretation and translation of languages, piloting of factories and mobiles, musical composition, forecasting, etc. Since the development of the first electronic computers and their surprising ability to count, comparing and sorting figures have generated dreams: among all the speculative operations traditionally associated with human intelligence, those involving reasoning and memory (card or chess games, stock market speculation, for example) have naturally attracted the lust of designers of electronic machines. All hoped to do better with a computer than the best human players, to surpass man, to beat him in his own field, the field of his intelligence in play or intellectual speculation.

The context has changed, albeit at a slower pace than was hoped for by futurists of the 1960s. Limited by their memory and by the speed of electronic circuits, computers have taken 40 years to defeat man in chess and twenty more years to defeat him in the go game recently[11]. These were brilliant demonstrations indeed, but, in all rationality, of limited scope in view of the ambitions expressed by promoters of artificial intelligence of the past and today, because the success of the machine illustrates less a so-called "machine intelligence" than the ability of companies in question to conceive, script and finance the investments necessary to

---

9 For illustrative purposes, see [JAR 07].

10 *Paris-Presse-L'Intransigeant*, June 10, 1954, quoted by [MOC 90], p. 19.

11 Kasparov, an exceptional Russian champion, bowed down in front of the IBM Deep Blue machine in March 1996; AlphaGo, a Google-designed machine, defeated reigning world champion Lee Sedol of Korea in March 2016. It should be noted that these two operations, highly and skillfully publicized, are perfectly in line with the advertising expertise of the two American companies, which have obviously invested in the necessary means to succeed in a great promotional operation!

produce a computer designed for the circumstance, and whose performance is strictly limited to this use alone! No doubt, a completely different machine would have to be built and programmed to win other subtle games; the machines mobilized for these performances have little versatility, they are single-use demonstrators, like the Enigma machine that deciphered German codes during the Second World War. Which is why, to the question asked: "What is missing from AlphaGo to be human?", the French academic Jean-Gabriel Ganascia recently replied, in a nutshell: "Everything"[12]!

Impulse of video games

This point summarizes the progress of the ambitious project conceived in 1956 at the Dartmouth Colloquium: most of the significant advances in artificial intelligence date from the second half of the 20th Century, with the notable exception of the more recent developments related to video game production. These electronic entertainments, intended for the general public, demanded fast and powerful chips, adapted to the animated image processing and realistic simulations that characterize the latest generations of games. Their mass production is the result of the very strong commercial, profitable and international demand for these games, whose editors have improved realism and animation over the past 15 years: their characters move in precise and lively settings, which was impossible before the year 2000. A pragmatic approach to engineering, design and programming has made it possible, in just a few years, to offer players virtual reality that was unimaginable less than 20 years ago. This technical breakthrough benefits all animation: cinema, television, advertising and even military applications[13]. This technical progress is unquestionable. Imaging is spectacular. However, it is only a tool, designed by man to multiply his own abilities; like all tools, it extends his hand, improves his performance just as machines and even robots have been doing for a very long time.

Will man be overwhelmed by the machines he himself created? Does technical performance today, based on the progress of electronic computing, replace human skill or precision of great practitioners such as surgeons, accountants or airplane pilots? It is not the adventures of the rare individuals that emerge from dantean

12 Quoted from March 11, 2016 by www.lexpress.fr/actualites/sciences. The author of this aphorism contributed to the work of the Frederik Bull Foundation, see "Prophets et réalités" in [MOC 90]. Pr. Ganascia's most recent book also covers this topic: *Le Mythe de la Singularité. Faut-il craindre l'intelligence artificielle?*, Le Seuil, Paris, 2017.

13 On the progress of video games in the recent period, see our study [ISF 05]. Estimated at 60 billion EUR in 2016, this global market has more than doubled since 2001. See also *Digiworld Yearbook*, 2013, available at www.idate.org.

situations by the happy combination of fate, their physical resistance, their will and exceptional temperament that will deny law[14]: the computer (for calculation and evaluation), the robot (for the control of gestures) and the automation of radar and GPS (for the conduct of ships and aircraft) approach and surpass the safety and performance of ordinary men. Machines are more constant, more regular than the man who is subjected to the vagaries of his environment, his emotions and his passions. On the contrary, nothing of this kind seems to affect the machine, its program or its calculations. Will it last forever? It is doubtful, as Raymond Moch put it in 1990 in his introduction to the Frederik Bull Foundation's work, underlining Samuel Butler's prescience[15]: "I fear none of today's machines... what frightens me is the speed at which they are becoming different from what they are now." Under the California sun, are the Silicon Valley gurus preparing for what Butler envisioned? The prophetic, Paul Valéry declared: "There is a sort of pact between the machine and ourselves; the more useful the machine seems to us, the more useful it becomes, we become incapable of depriving ourselves of it!"[16]. Will Butler's fear materialize today? Does the attachment of our contemporaries to their iPhones, their tablets and their video games herald a dependency, a form of addiction that would confirm Valéry's intuition and Butler's imagination?

Ambitions of artificial intelligence

Raised yesterday by robots, today by computers and the Internet, all the preceding questions deserve to be studied and put into perspective, with the main applications of artificial intelligence, that are not easy to summarize. An extensive list would include at least the following domains, a sort of "catch-all" inventory:

– diagnostic assistance (medical, mechanical, aeronautical, etc.);

– allocation of resources or means (tactical, logistical, financial, etc.);

– entertainment and games (animation of the characters and a show);

– automated guidance and piloting (aircraft, machines, cars, trains);

---

14 We obviously think here of the mythical testimony of the air-post pilot, Henri Guillaumet, who fell in full gust into a snow-covered basin and became lost in the Andes, an adventure from which he left by his own means, declaring to his fellow squadron mate: "what I did, I swear to you, never any beast would have done it", in de St Exupéry A., *Terre des hommes*, Gallimard, Paris, 1939. (English translation: *Wind, Sand and Stars*, Reynal & Hitchcock, New York 1939.) St. Exupéry explicitly dedicated his novel to Guillaumet!

15 Cited in [MOC 90]. This anticipatory novel was published in 1872 in London. It is a little forgotten nowadays: *Erewhon, Over the Range,* Trübner & Ballantyne, 1872.

16 As cited by www.roseaupensant.fr.

- knowledge engineering;

- recognition of shapes, patterns and behaviors;

- simulations of: situations, flows, emergencies or disasters;

- translation of written and oral texts;

- natural language interpretation;

- search and inference engines, etc.

Such a list illustrates the variety of applications of artificial intelligence. It also underlines its instrumental character. The IT tool, which had long been limited to a purely deductive computational chain, can now address complex and multifaceted problems. The programming with which we grew up, consisting of a series of logical cascade operations, had to deal with less routine issues[17]. One of these novelties is the simultaneous (and interrelated) running of several interdependent processes that allow computers to address equivocal problems, evaluate and compare situations affected by probabilities. This parallel calculation makes it possible to study random or partially undetermined phenomena.

Simulating an analogical thought?

Taking advantage of this new method, the programmer tries to escape the determinism of pure computation. He has the ambition to approach new situations: to discern, for example, similarities of form between several objects, or to compare very diverse or heterogeneous[18] circumstances, measures or data. The program classifies this data according to similarities observed earlier, an approach that we have been able to assimilate with our analogical thinking, and is a very common mental approach that consists of associating one notion with another. The source of this analogy, which we use as a rhetorical reference is: "Such an approach is never innocent and [it is] very far from mathematical logic" and is underlined by Jean-Blaise Grize because "it is not included in the catalogue of logical-mathematical relations of order or equivalence". He concludes that "the possibility of machine simulation of some aspects of analogical thinking [...] is a mixture of inferences and deductions" [BLO 99], p. 240. This process is therefore similar to

---

17 Automated digital calculation in the 1960s was referred to in France as "*calcul de routine*" or, in short, "*routines*". The expression, which used to have meaning, has been lost. The methodical systematization of this form of programming applied to management, can be found in the book which was the bible of a generation of consulting engineers: Mallet R. A., *La méthode informatique*, Hermann, Paris, 1971.

18 See Chapters 2–4.

what could be described as an overall perception of the data collected by the machine.

This programming allows the machine to link shapes, words, sounds and movements, always by analogy or comparison with the standards written in its program. It also takes advantage of the context (e.g. a series of queries recorded by a search engine). Therefore, the robot can identify any element that is consistent with the context: for example, it can associate the high probability of a particular market behavior with the theme of an Internet query. In doing so, the computer (or rather, its "program") highlights significant data that its software distinguishes between scattered elements; the tool becomes one of connection: it highlights salient features from which it draws probable conclusions, by inference. This would be closer to the functioning of our own mind, which proceeds as much by association of ideas or by evocation as by deduction. The machine is not intelligent by itself; it only multiplies the programmer's intelligence, incorporated by him in his coding!

Deep learning and expert systems

A favorable branch of artificial intelligence only about 20 years ago, expert systems had their hour of glory before being slightly put aside, probably until better days. Their purpose was quite simple to summarize: to introduce into machines the knowledge that would be necessary for a living expert to carry out a delicate operation, such as the troubleshooting of a machine, a surgical operation, the optimization of an allocation of resources, etc. In an operational situation, the system would use a step-by-step approach, as would a consultant to methodically resolve a particular case. For the compilation of experience accumulated by specialists, such systems consisted mainly of two subsets:

– an expertise fund constituting its "knowledge base";

– a framework for dialogue with the expert (the plumber, surgeon, engineer, etc.), called the "inference engine".

At the end of a series of possibly numerous iterations, the machine's answers (its "acts", so to speak!) are a summary of the expertise integrated into its programs. Its intervention may surprise, or even suggest an autonomous "intelligence". But does it have any initiative? No, because it cannot get out of the framework imposed by its programmer; it has no degree of self-criticism.

Only imaginary conjecture can lead us to believe that such a tool could rebel against its programmer: a machine could, of course, escape control by drift, error of instruction or accident; it could also break down (very rarely!) as a car might. Here, we are very far from any intelligence, and even from instinct (as domesticated animals sometimes feel a coming earthquake) and, *a fortiori*, from an intention or a will because the machine does not "feel" or "know" (in the cognitive sense) the scope of what it observes and what it calculates. Data never makes sense to a computer! Its program runs mechanically, according to the routine that the programmer has planned. This is why, in real circumstances, the prodigies that expert systems have hoped for have rarely been achieved: such systems have encountered many difficulties, not least because of the fact that knowledge bases have perished over time, and also because the maintenance and updating of inference engines is a real headache in industrial reality. After having raised great hopes, the expert system is attracting much less interest than before: faced with the complexity of reality and the constant evolution of expertise, such systems have been a disappointment.

From machines to humanity

Computers, as we have already mentioned, perform calculations in accordance with the rules they have learned. Their program can also compare situations, calculate variance and even introduce laws, in other words regularities that go beyond the specific cases subject to experience. These are reasonable ambitions that we have just summarized. The artificial intelligence projects of the 1960s, however, were more ambitious, in that they sought to go beyond the instrumental applications we have just mentioned. They expressed, in particular, the hope of:

– deciphering the functioning of the human brain and deriving laws that would guide man's behavior, action and, if possible, thought;

– building electronic machines capable of approaching human abilities and reproducing the supposed functioning of the brain;

– finally, finding a technical answer to the question: just as we do (and think), would the machine be able to do (and think) by itself?

After 60 years of studies, tests and experiments, the results available are significant in terms of technology and practical knowledge; but their contribution to the founding objectives that we have just summarized is insufficient to affirm that the construction of an intelligent humanoid, in the full sense of the term, is within reach.

The first objective (decrypting brain functions) has proved to be unreachable by computer advances alone, at least for the time being: despite numerous efforts, powerful means and the mobilization of intellectual experts, attempts to describe brain mechanisms with electronic means have been disappointing; the brain knowledge on which we rely today essentially comes from neurophysiological experimentation, which is thereby inseparable from artificial intelligence projects. Admittedly, leading biologists and neurophysiologists have pointed out, for more than 50 years, the striking similarities between electronic machines and our brain mechanisms: analogies between brain physiology and electronic component networks[19], analogies between brain synapses and electronic circuitry connections that form the "core" of computers, tablets and iPhones[20], analogies between the potential differences observed between brain cells and those found in electronic components for performing binary calculations. The image has been taken up by brilliant minds and scholars who have helped to popularize these analogies and draw conclusions, some of which are controversial[21]. In this difficult area where there are daily deficiencies, let us try to distinguish what remains of the domain of conjecture from what is scientifically known.

Conjecture or knowledge?

First of all, it is conjectured that projections of the future or hypotheses claim that beyond what has been observed until now, electronic machines could manifest a "will" independent to that of their creators, escape their program and intentionally free themselves from the instructions written in their memories. For, in reality, the electronic machine acts only by following its program. It does not manifest or express any intention, it is not reflexive, it is "as indifferent to what it accomplishes as a log of wood"[22]. All other hypotheses are based on the romantic fantasy of the humanoid escaping its creator, a theme specific to science fiction, on which much of the audiovisual works that extend fantasy literature are based, such as *A Space Odyssey*, which admittedly founded a cinematic genre, but is still full of implausibility. These extreme extrapolations have purely promotional purposes: they are popularized by entertainment industries that understand the commercial impact on the general public; and by some concerned institutions that want to capture enough public attention to protect their budgets: *panem et circenses*! What do they really need to know? They are based on simple analogies such as the following:

---

19 For example, see [SOU 80], pp. 80–81 and 143. And, for a reflection including the physical, human and biological sciences, see [SIM 69], p. 80 ff.
20 The English word "core" stems from the same root as "coeur" (heart) in French. This custom emphasizes the anatomic analogy between computers and human beings. It reminds us of the similar metaphor used by French electrical engineers who qualify the "core" of a cable as its "soul" (*âme du câble*): why is the biological metaphor so successful in French?
21 In France, see in particular [JAC 70], [MON 70] and [CHA 83]. This latter work has aroused a plethora of comments and contradictions, such as Filloux J-C., "Le pédagogue et l'homme neuronal", *Rev. Fr. Pédagogie*, vol. 70, no. 1, pp. 51–57, 1985.
22 Expression due to Jean Moussé [MOC 90], p. 61.

– It is true that the finesse of sensors associated with a stand-alone device (for example, in space exploration) can create an illusion on the ordinary man: these electronic probes make it possible to "see", "touch", "grasp" soil samples or tools; but are these operations the manifestation of any "consciousness" and robot autonomy in relation to the remote operator of this object, its programmer and the creator of the machine? Of course not!

– The machine can sometimes help to reveal things or phenomena that were invisible until then. For example, by revealing a correlation between measurements or by detecting regularities that neither the human eye, nor human calculus had previously distinguished, the machine thus contributes to establishing facts, behaviors and resources that have escaped the wisdom of men; but would it have done so without the intention of its programmer in the past? Isn't it the *deus ex-machina*, the human programmer, who prepares the discovery by relying on a creative intuition that schedules machine calculations, as was often the case for many experimental discoveries?

On the other hand, the following points are scientifically correct and do not all contribute to validating the presumed analogy between digitalization and the brain. Rather, would reinforce this analogy:

– the fact that the nervous system is made up of a large number of neurons with computational capacity and some kind of communication with other neurons; this is why, for example, certain sensitive activities of a set of neurons have been described by algebraic formulae.

In the present state of our knowledge, other empirical elements would, however, contradict the analogy between the brain and the computer:

– the physiology of the brain appears to be very different from the current organization of a computer system[23]; despite numerous unsuccessful attempts, it has not been possible to locate a particular place or area in the brain that is assigned to preserve and record memories, or to keep track of previous perceptions. In electronic machines, on the other hand, all data has an explicit address;

– as we previously stated about expert systems, some electronic machines are able to assimilate new data and modify their in-service programs; their history (log) is stored in the software and memory so that past experience can be taken into account. Algorithms thereby adapt the mechanical response to external stimuli; but this "practical intelligence" is not that of the computer itself; it is imposed on it by

---

23 Sometimes known as the electronic brain, another metaphor of everyday language giving rise to fantasies.

the programmer who designed the machine. The latter therefore has no free will; nothing allows it to rebel against its programmer!

To sum it up in a few words: the project to build an artificial intelligence based on computers and respond to the hope of outperforming what men do, with a machine that would do as well and even better than them, encounters two major pitfalls: today's digital machines, even the fastest, seem powerless to produce a biologically plausible outline of brain function[24]; additionally, we have evidence that computational ability only explains a very small part of the brain's performance, which was already confirmed by physiologist André Holley in 1999: "Thus, the metaphor of the brain as a computer is now abandoned" [BLO 99][25], p.41.

Myths associated with artificial intelligence

Such elements therefore exclude, for now and probably for a long time to come, any hope of simulating, and, *a fortiori*, replacing the human brain with an electronic computer. The result of this is that the works of anticipation, (cinema, games and novels) which presuppose the manipulation of humanity by the machines we have built, are the product of a fantastic imagination rather than a credible extrapolation of technique and concrete knowledge. This persistent rupture between fiction and plausibility deserves a brief digression.

It is perfectly normal that imagination is detached from reality; it is even a traditional characteristic of the literary, poetic and artistic genre to escape from the constraints of the present to freely, metaphorically or ironically raise up subjects specific to the society in which one lives, in addition to locating the action in places or times that are out of step, around mythical and sometimes even improbable characters: Rabelais with "Pantagruel", Swift with "Gulliver", Voltaire with *Candide*, Jules Verne with "Captain Nemo", Huxley with *Brave New World*, Wells with *War of the Worlds*, Orwell with *1984* and Pierre Boulle with *Planet of the Apes* have left mythical works thanks to this process! What distinguishes their fictions from Hollywood blockbusters or video games of today is a socio-psychological distinction: the authors we have just mentioned created flesh and bone characters,

---

24 Paillard J., "*L'ordinateur et le cerveau*", in [MOC 90], p. 63.

25 While accepting some converging assumptions with the above, an essay released by Pr. Berry in October 2017 contains some views that partly deviate from the above, in particular about the usefulness of computational biology. He concludes: "It is not yet clear whether such an approach (computational biology) will help us understand our own memory or not, although nothing of the kind should be excluded, given such an open field". Berry G.: *L'hyper-puissance de l'informatique*, Odile Jacob, Paris, 2017 (see: pp. 247 *sq*.; quote from p. 262)

their behavior and psychological depth made them close to us and, above all, timeless. On the other hand, heroes from action films, television series and most contemporary video games are humanoid avatars with no personality or psychology; they move against a magical, imaginary and artificial backdrop and their stories are based on a caricatured representation of science and technology.

In short: the compendious behavior of the characters, the stereotype of fighting (often bestial cruelty), the absence of humor, detachment and subtle allusion to what touches us are striking. In this type of fiction, action is mostly reduced to blood clashes between raw forces and bionic puppets. Where then is the metaphor and allegory, the very credentials of fiction?

Does the reader, player or spectator learn from these stories in which man is overwhelmed or oppressed by his own mechanical creations? Are these shows, where only a primary force is deployed and is sometimes stupidly heartfelt, transposable in time and space? Such questions seem foreign to contemporary science fiction. By cultivating improbable dreams, it deviates from the plausible future; and the gap is constantly widening! One can then be tempted to apply, to contemporary anticipation, severe criticism that the German jurist Carl Schmitt used to make on romanticism: dragging his followers into artificial worlds, it "throws them frantically into the abyss of instinct"[26].

Rationalist temptation

Let us return, after this digression, to the links that have been continuously forged for more than half a century by artificial intelligence and the sciences of man and life, links that extend and develop the intuition of scientists of the classical era, such as Descartes and Leibnitz. Their essential question remains: could we reasonably pass, without discontinuity and without being captive of a new animism, from the biological dynamics of neurons, empirically demonstrated by experience, to the symbolic representation of reality and reflexive consciousness of a thinking subject? In trying to interpret the nature and effect of the genetic code, the philosopher Grégory Bénichou (he also acts as a biologist), makes the hypothesis that biological processes are: "determined historically and structured as language [...] physico-chemical analysis alone (hence) cannot reach the order of the signifier. The physical order does not cover the semantic order [...](which) is part of the cell, extends to the whole organism and[...] underlies the relationship of all organisms between them" [BEN 02], pp. 53–54. Therein follows more questions that we do not have to answer here: is the finished, limited and material man able to be cloned? If we admit to the vanity of dualism,

---

26 Schmitt C., *Political Romanticism*, translated by Guy Oakes, The MIT Press, 1986.

where and how lies the transition between Changeux's neuronal man, Kurzweil's augmented man and "the mind-brain (who) has shown itself to be so complex, that a general model cannot provide a satisfactory representation of it"[27]?

Mental phenomena do not seem ready to be reduced to pure digital mechanisms that would explain human behavior, psychology, feelings and aesthetic emotion! The fact that the psyche is based on anatomy, physiology and nervous circuits is not enough to give a complete account of it either: "The irreducibility of the brain and computer remains fundamental [...] there are wired circuits in the brain that it shares with other machines, (but) the brain also contains wet circuits of which there is no equivalent in artificial systems [...] this is one of the great challenges facing contemporary science"[28]. This opinion is confirmed by the reflections of Robert Sperry, Nobel Prize winner in medicine in 1981: "The laboratory tells us that science (current biology) marks a rupture with behaviorism and materialism"[29].

Assessing the intelligence of a machine?

Stressed already in two Turing[30] articles from 1947 and 1950, it is very difficult to assess the intelligence of an intelligent behavior. Using a theatrical subterfuge, this author devised a plot with three characters: a man, a woman and an investigator. Playing a game of disguise, the investigator interrogates the other two characters separately in order to discover, without seeing or hearing them, so as not to facilitate his discovery, who is the man and who is the woman. As for the respondents, between whom there is no exchange (as in the case of a judicial police investigation), they are free to lie and conceal who they are in order to deceive the investigator by their role-playing. This is followed by a dialogue in which the investigator strives to get out by revealing the true personality of each person. This scenario is disturbing, especially since the author's personal story reveals that he was himself capable of concealing his profound personality from those who employed him! In any case, the test devised by Turing (which was never, in fact, completed) would have consisted of entrusting the role of the man (respectively that of the woman) to a logical machine which would answer, out of the investigator's sight, the questions addressed to him with the same ability to lie or conceal the truth in order to confuse the leads. Turing was betting that if the machine in question tricked the investigator skillfully, it could be described as an intelligent one!

---

27 Paillard J., see footnote 24.
28 Holley A. in [BLO 99], p.41.
29 Thoughts collected in the aftermath of his Nobel Prize in *Science and Moral Priority*, Columbia University Press, New York, 1983.
30 Cited by Ganascia J.G., "Prophètes et réalités", in [MOC 90], pp. 65–69. See also Chapter 2.

However, this three-strip role-playing game is biased, so as not to answer the seminal question that has been raised for four centuries: "Can a machine think?". Turing's game is a procedural fallacy: he takes refuge behind a series of technological challenges that would have to be met in order to pass the test in front of skillful and twisted human subjects: many experts have indeed deemed that mastery of language by machines is a prerequisite for this experiment, so that the interviewees cannot guess who is questioning them: a machine or a man? The adaptability of the machine, its subtlety during the interrogation and during the script development are crucial; to make an inventory of these prerequisites is to write the project of artificial intelligence in an open framework, the development of which cannot be programmed!

Imagined almost 70 years ago, and despite technical advances, the test is still impossible to complete with today's machines; since the fifties, the best technical, economic and political authors have constantly underlined the speed of technical change and the increasing power of computers, illustrated by Moore's law, Moore being a scientist who has empirically observed a geometric progression in the power of electronic chips (memory and calculation)[31] since 1965. The record repeats, as expected, that this growth surpasses the wildest of hopes; however, still no machine has met the specifications designed by Turing between 1947 and 1950, testing the ability of a machine to reproduce (or to model?) human thought. Does this calm Promethean ambitions of rich Internet champions? It does not look like it yet!

Concluding reflections

The American delegates of the 1956 Dartmouth seminar were looking for cybernetic apparatus that could truly make an intelligent machine, in harmony with the mental mechanisms described and observed by experimental psychology and neurobiology. Had they previously dismantled the springs of intelligence and human memory? Not really! Let us dive further into this: if the dichotomy between weak artificial intelligence (that of engineers who build robots, without passion or anthropomorphism) and strong artificial intelligence (as far as imagining machines that are able to manipulate symbols and experience feelings, even dreams) is sustainable, is there continuity or rupture between these two options? The proponents of transhumanism seem to favor a semantic rupture, a mental revolution between the two branches of this dichotomy; their stated choice is in favor of disruption, the acceptable Anglicism which associates rupture and discontinuity.

---

31 The prophetic statement appeared in the American journal, *Electronics*, vol. 38, April 1965, available at https://en.wikipedia.org/wiki/moore%27s_law.

Beyond the "advertising coup" that constituted the success of a chess machine or go game against the greatest champions (illustrating a weak artificial intelligence), many Internet and computer entrepreneurs (essentially West Americans) are tempted to bet on a strong artificial intelligence; they are ready to mobilize means (intellectual, industrial and financial) even more important than those that allowed to beat a chess champion in the hope that the difference between the biological man, the one we are at present, and the bionic man, the one they present as their future goal[32], disappears. Could one then say, like the proselytes of the singularity, that all it would take is a functional and operative device in order to maintain life, to be free from aging, from the biological risks, even from random accidents that British insurers qualify by the pictorial expression "acts of God", as they are beyond our control?

Internet literacy is an obsession of very large companies that populate this network such as Amazon, Apple, Facebook, Google, IBM, Microsoft, Twitter, etc. Their somewhat passionate approach is quite surprising, because their international success proves that they are managed rationally: they respond to a very solvent demand and their services and products are appreciated throughout the world. Their expertise is unquestionable; the success of their services explains their near-universal presence[33]. Coming from an extremely competitive professional environment, marked by the quest for daily results and stimulated by the rapid pace of electronic innovation, the entrepreneurs who founded these huge companies (and who still partly manage them) invest heavily in the field of artificial intelligence: automated equipment linked to housing, commerce, transport, etc. In addition to electronic automated equipment, the very broad field of biology also seems to fascinate them. Their interest in these subjects, which at first glance falls outside the scope of their company's corporate purpose, deserves to be considered: is it consistent with their entrepreneurial approach?

---

32 www.singularityu.org; Ray Kurzweil sums up the objectives of Google's "university" in this way: "to educate, inspire and support leaders so that the major challenges of humanity are met by exponential growth techniques". Such a project cannot escape the criticism raised by other attempts to improve the human race: have we forgotten the lessons from a recent period that has so profoundly changed the modern world?

33 This success translates into high stock market capitalizations, sometimes considered excessive even by analysts accustomed to gauging multinationals! Investors believe otherwise, because they give a high price to these publicly traded businesses. Until the day when the odds may collapse, in other words when the public is disappointed (An example of this is Yahoo! for almost a decade and Tesla since the first quarter of 2016); or as a result of a cyclical crisis such as the one that led to the mismanagement of Internet values around the year 2000 (see Chapter 1 Appendix).

Among these companies, Alphabet (Google)[34] has a catch-all ambition. It is easy to understand the interest of such a company, in building a university-level training program, an objective asserted by Singularity University, its secular branch dedicated to the designers of digital applications, to the strategic marketing of computing and communication and all areas that extend Internet expertise. But the fact that this private educational institution also targets psychosociology, neurophysiology and social sciences such as linguistics, and that it sometimes uses rather naive rhetoric, in addition to deliberately directing its efforts towards public action[35], suggests that it relays a utopia which is reflected in the declarations of its leaders: "We will soon literally be a hybrid of biological and non-biological thinking", says Neil Jacobstein, Chair of Artificial Intelligence, echoing the aphorism of Kurzweil cited above[36]. This investment takes advantage of the wealth of the Alphabet group to promote positivist aims, similar to some of those of the 19th Century. What distinguishes it from the past is that it mobilizes the resources of a multinational company, established at the heart of the world's most promising market and that its ambition does not seem to merely be a response to an actual corporate project. Not being the product of dreamers, this university creation is therefore perplexing!

Artificial intelligence was presented for more than half a century as a technique intended to imitate a living being, to reproduce, with a mechanical tool, what we perceive in our thought. Then, to substitute a machine with the thinking subject. With what we have just mentioned, is it also moving towards an otherwise ambitious goal: to radically transform the condition of humankind. Laughing at the thought would be presumptuous; questioning only flows from simple reasoning. We will, therefore, wait for the experiment to produce its first effects.

At this stage, a reminder is in order: for information industries, stock market prices are more sensitive to future prospects than to the immediate performance of listed companies: net giants are no exception. For them too, as the Romans said: "The Tarpei rock is close to the Capitol", for every enterprise is mortal and it depends on the trust placed in it by its shareholders. A reversal of this trend can

---

34 Fifteen years before this change of brand, [BEN 02], p. 66 gave the key to understanding the ambition hidden behind this name: "how to read the (genetic) text in a coherent way?... this is not the real Alphabet given that, excluding the few lines where it explains, the rest of the message remains impenetrably obscure to me. The *true Alphabet* will be the one that gives full meaning to the letter of the genome" (emphasis by the author).

35 Governments, international agencies and non-governmental organizations are explicitly designated as a target of the training courses (free or paid) that this corporate university will provide.

36 Public Statement from July 28, 2016, available at singularityhub.com.

overturn the strongest positions, as many examples have shown, before and after the Internet crisis: companies like IBM were hit since the great era when informed commentators believed that "IBM dominance" was untouchable[37], just as Motorola's superiority seemed almost eternal and that of Nokia unbeatable! Another, older example: for years, Control Data pursued (beyond what was reasonable) very sympathetic ambitions in the field of education, but in just a few years, these Pharaonic projects led to its demise and it ended up disappearing! What about Google's academic projects in the event of a stock market storm? Only the future will tell, maybe. Wait and see, as the saying goes; we will do the same, based on a thought by the French philosopher Bergson that will give these lines some meaning:

"In the process of organic creation, we will undoubtedly discover an increasing number of physico-chemical phenomena. And that's what chemists and physicists will stick to. But it does not follow on from there that chemistry and physics must give us the key to life."[38]

What will happen to computer science and Internet platforms in the future? Would Bergson's statement remind the singularity animators of something?

Bibliography

[BEN 02] BENICHOU G., *Le Chiffre de la vie*, Le Seuil, Paris, 2002.

[BLO 99] BLOCH V. (ed.), *Cerveau et machines*, Hermès Sciences, Paris, 1999.

[CHA 83] CHANGEUX J.P., *L'homme neuronal*, Fayard, Paris, 1983.

[FIL 85] FILLOUX J.C., "Le pédagogue et l' homme neuronal", *Rev. Fr. Pédagogie*, vol. 70, no. 1, pp. 51–57, 1985.

[ISF 05] ISFE, *Interactive Electronic Games and European Privacy*, Brussels, July 2005.

[JAC 70] JACOB F., *La logique du vivant*, Gallimard, Paris, 1970.

[JAR 07] JARRIGE F., Au temps des assassineuses de bras: le bris de machines et la genèse de la société industrielle (1780–1860), Thesis, Université Paris I, 2007.

[MOC 90] MOCH R. (ed.), *Intelligence artificielle et bon sens*, Masson, Paris, 1990.

[MON 70] MONOD J., *Le hasard et la nécessité*, Le Seuil, Paris, 1970.

[NOR 81] NORA S., MINC A., *The Computerization of Society*, MIT Press, Cambridge, 1981.

---

37 A theme developed at length by [NOR 81], p. 64: "IBM is implanted with such a reserve of power that it cannot be sustained".
38 *L'évolution créatrice*, PUF, Paris, 1907.

[SIM 69] SIMON P.H., *Questions aux savants*, Le Seuil, Paris, 1969.

[SOU 80] SOURNIA A., *Dix milliards de neurones*, La pensée universelle, Paris, 1980.

[SPI 10] SPILLEMAECKER C. (ed.), *Vaucanson et l'homme artificiel, des automates aux robots*, PUG, Grenoble, 2010.

APPENDICES

Appendix 1

List of Figures

Appendix 2

List of Boxes

List of Authors

Christian BOURRET
DICEN – CNAM
Université Paris-Est
Marne-la-Vallée
France

Joumana BOUSTANY
DICEN – CNAM
Université Paris-Descartes – IUT
Paris
France

Jean-Pierre CHAMOUX
Laboratoire de psychologie
économique
Université Paris-Descartes – IUT
Paris
France

Jean DHOMBRES
CNRS – Centre A. Koyré
Ecole des Hautes Etudes – EHESS
Paris
France

Gérard DRÉAN
Expert-Consultant
Jouy en Josas
France

Isabelle HILALI
Centre de recherches
interdisciplinaires
CRI–Fondation Bettencourt
Paris
France

Gabriella SALZANO
DICEN – CNAM
Université Paris-Est
Marne-la-Vallée
France

Gilles SANTINI
VINTCO Conseils-Systèmes
Paris
France

Philippe TASSI
Médiamétrie SA
Levallois-Perret
France

Index of Names and Brands

Index of Notions

Other titles from

in

Information Systems, Web and Pervasive Computing

2018

ARDUIN Pierre-Emmanuel
Insider Threats
(Advances in Information Systems Set – Volume 10)

FABRE Renaud, BENSOUSSAN Alain
The Digital Factory for Knowledge: Production and Validation of Scientific Results

GAUDIN Thierry, LACROIX Dominique, MAUREL Marie-Christine, POMEROL Jean-Charles
Life Sciences, Information Sciences

IAFRATE Fernando
Artificial Intelligence and Big Data: The Birth of a New Intelligence
(Advances in Information Systems Set – Volume 8)

MANDRAN Nadine
Traceable Human Experiment Design Research: Theoretical Model and Practical Guide
(Advances in Information Systems Set – Volume 9)

2016

BEN CHOUIKHA Mona
Organizational Design for Knowledge Management

BERTOLO David
*Interactions on Digital Tablets in the Context of 3D Geometry Learning
(Human-Machine Interaction Set – Volume 2)*

BOUVARD Patricia, SUZANNE Hervé
Collective Intelligence Development in Business

EL FALLAH SEGHROUCHNI Amal, ISHIKAWA Fuyuki, HÉRAULT Laurent,
TOKUDA Hideyuki
Enablers for Smart Cities

FABRE Renaud, in collaboration with MESSERSCHMIDT-MARIET Quentin,
HOLVOET Margot
New Challenges for Knowledge

GAUDIELLO Ilaria, ZIBETTI Elisabetta
*Learning Robotics, with Robotics, by Robotics
(Human-Machine Interaction Set – Volume 3)*

HENROTIN Joseph
*The Art of War in the Network Age
(Intellectual Technologies Set – Volume 1)*

KITAJIMA Munéo
*Memory and Action Selection in Human–Machine Interaction
(Human–Machine Interaction Set – Volume 1)*

LAGRAÑA Fernando
*E-mail and Behavioral Changes: Uses and Misuses of Electronic
Communications*

LEIGNEL Jean-Louis, UNGARO Thierry, STAAR Adrien
*Digital Transformation
(Advances in Information Systems Set – Volume 6)*

NOYER Jean-Max
Transformation of Collective Intelligences
(Intellectual Technologies Set – Volume 2)

VENTRE Daniel
Information Warfare – 2nd edition

VITALIS André
The Uncertain Digital Revolution
(Computing and Connected Society Set – Volume 1)

2015

ARDUIN Pierre-Emmanuel, GRUNDSTEIN Michel, ROSENTHAL-SABROUX Camille
Information and Knowledge System
(Advances in Information Systems Set – Volume 2)

BÉRANGER Jérôme
Medical Information Systems Ethics

BRONNER Gérald
Belief and Misbelief Asymmetry on the Internet

IAFRATE Fernando
From Big Data to Smart Data
(Advances in Information Systems Set – Volume 1)

KRICHEN Saoussen, BEN JOUIDA Sihem
Supply Chain Management and its Applications in Computer Science

NEGRE Elsa
Information and Recommender Systems
(Advances in Information Systems Set – Volume 4)

POMEROL Jean-Charles, EPELBOIN Yves, THOURY Claire
MOOCs

2012

BUCHER Bénédicte, LE BER Florence
Innovative Software Development in GIS

GAUSSIER Eric, YVON François
Textual Information Access

STOCKINGER Peter
Audiovisual Archives: Digital Text and Discourse Analysis

VENTRE Daniel
Cyber Conflict

2011

BANOS Arnaud, THÉVENIN Thomas
Geographical Information and Urban Transport Systems

DAUPHINÉ André
Fractal Geography

LEMBERGER Pirmin, MOREL Mederic
Managing Complexity of Information Systems

STOCKINGER Peter
Introduction to Audiovisual Archives

STOCKINGER Peter
Digital Audiovisual Archives

VENTRE Daniel
Cyberwar and Information Warfare

2010

BONNET Pierre
Enterprise Data Governance

BRUNET Roger
Sustainable Geography

Printed and bound by CPI Group (UK) Ltd, Croydon, CR0 4YY

.